For Maree

# A Place on Earth

*An anthology of nature writing
from Australia and North America*

EDITED BY
Mark Tredinnick

**UNIVERSITY OF NEBRASKA PRESS**
Lincoln and London

 **UNIVERSITY OF NEW SOUTH WALES PRESS**
Sydney

**A UNSW Press book**

*Published in the United States of America, Canada and Europe by*
University of Nebraska Press
Lincoln, NE 68588-0255
www.nebraskapress.unl.edu

*Published in Australia, New Zealand and the rest of the world by*
University of New South Wales Press Ltd
University of New South Wales
Sydney NSW 2052
AUSTRALIA
www.unswpress.com.au

Library of Congress Control Number: 2003110878
ISBN: 0-8032-9457-3 (paper)

National Library of Australia
Cataloguing-in-Publication entry
A place on earth : an anthology of nature writing from
Australia and North America.
ISBN 0 86840 654 6.
1. Natural history literature – Australia.
2. Natural history literature – North America.
3. Australian essays.
4. American essays. I. Tredinnick, Mark.
814.008036

Book design  *Di Quick*
Cover photograph  *Getty Images*
Printer  *Griffin Press, Australia*

# Contents

# About the Contributors

**BARBARA BLACKMAN** is an essayist and the author of *Certain Chairs* and the memoir *Glass After Glass*. She grew up in Brisbane and wrote poems and essays from the very beginning. At seventeen she lost her sight. Barbara was married for many years to the painter Charles Blackman. She has travelled widely in Australia and Europe, and lived for a time in London. Barbara spent many years in the Kangaroo Valley, south of Sydney. She lives now in Canberra and is at work on a book of her correspondence with her friend, the poet Judith Wright.

**JOHN CAMERON**, once a geologist and for many years an environmental advocate with the Australian Conservation Foundation, now teaches in the Department of Social Ecology at the University of Western Sydney. All of his writing and research deals with the meaning and implications of a sense of place, and with ecological thought and practice. He lives with his partner, the painter Victoria King, at Faulconbridge in the lower Blue Mountains, west of Sydney.

**CHARMIAN CLIFT** was born in Kiama on the south coast of New South Wales. She is best remembered for her books *Mermaid Singing* and *Peel Me a Lotus*, which told of her life in the Greek Islands with her husband, George Johnston, and their family, and for the essays she wrote for *The Sydney Morning Herald* on her return to Australia in the 1960s. She died in 1969.

**JAMES GALVIN** has published five collections of poetry, including *Resurrection Update* and, most recently, *X*. He is also the author of *The Meadow*—from which his contribution to this anthology is abstracted—and a novel, *Fencing the Sky*. His honours include a Lila Wallace-Readers' Digest Foundation Award and a Lannan Literary Award; and fellowships from the Guggenheim Foundation, the Ingram-Merrill Foundation and the National Endowment for the Arts. He has a home and some horses outside of Tie Siding, Wyoming, and is on the permanent faculty of the University of Iowa Writers' Workshop.

**TOM GRIFFITHS** is a writer and an environmental historian. His books include *Ecology and Empire*, *Forests of Ash* and *Hunters and Collectors*, which won a number of prizes, including the Victorian Premier's Literary Award. He grew up in Melbourne and lives now in Canberra, where he is Visiting Fellow in the Research School of Social Sciences at the Australian National University.

**JOHN HAINES** was born in Virginia, and studied at the National Art Institute and the American University before setting out for Alaska, where he home-steaded for nearly twenty-five years. He is the author of ten collections of poetry, among them *The Owl in the Mask of the Dreamer* and, most recently, *Poems for the Century's End*. He has also written the essay collections *Living Off the Country* and *Fables and Distances*, and the memoir *The Stars, The Snow, The Fire*— from which his contribution to this collection is taken. Named as a Fellow by the Academy of American Poets in 1997, his honours include the Alaska Governor's Award for Excellence, two Guggenheim Fellowships, a National Endowment for the Arts Fellowship and a Lifetime Achievement Award from the Library of Congress. John Haines now lives in Missoula, Montana.

**ASHLEY HAY** is the author of two works of narrative nonfiction, *The Secret: Lies, Slander and the Strange Marriage of Annabella Milbanke & Lord Byron* and *Gum: The Story of Eucalypts and Their Champions*. Her short fiction has won awards in Australia and the United Kingdom, and she has worked as a journalist on *The Independent Monthly* and *The Bulletin*. She has also put in time at the University of London. Ashley was born in Bulli and raised in Austinmer near Wollongong on the south coast of New South Wales and now lives in Coogee. She studied at Charles Sturt University and the University of Technology, Sydney.

**PETE HAY** is a poet and essayist who works at the University of Tasmania and lives with his family in Hobart. Born at Wynyard on Tasmania's north coast, he returned to the State in 1985 to join the university's Centre for Environmental Studies after some years as a political adviser in Canberra and as an academic in other Australian cities. Pete's teaching and research concerns the linked fields of environmental thought, environmental politics, literature and the nature of place. He writes poems and essays when he can and lately is pondering much on islandness. His works of poetry include *The View from the Non-Members' Bar*; and his most recent books of prose are *Main Currents in Western Environmental Thought* and *Vandiemonian Essays*.

**LINDA HOGAN** is a Chickasaw poet, novelist and essayist. She was born in Denver, Colorado and travelled widely with her family during her childhood. She published her first volume of poetry, *Calling Myself Home*, in 1978. Her six books of poetry include *Book of Medicines*, which was a finalist in the National Book Critics Circle Award. She is the author of five novels, including *Mean Spirit*, a finalist for the Pulitzer Prize. Her collection of essays, *Dwellings*, from which her contribution to this anthology comes, appeared in 1995. Her honours include a grant from the National Endowment for the Humanities, a Guggenheim Fellowship and an award from the Lannan Foundation. She lives in Idledale, Colorado, and teaches at the University of Colorado at Boulder.

**WILLIAM KITTREDGE** grew up on the MC Ranch in southeastern Oregon and farmed until he was thirty-five, when he went to study at the University of Iowa's Writers' Workshop and became a writer. He taught creative writing at the University of Montana until his retirement in 1997. He writes fiction and essays, and his many books include *We Are Not in This Together*, *Who Owns the West*, *Hole in the Sky* and *The Nature of Generosity*. With Annick Smith he coedited *The Last Best Place: a Montana Anthology* and coproduced the film *A River Runs Through It*. He has received many awards, including election to the American Academy of Achievement in 1993 and the National Endowment for the Humanities prize for service to the humanities in 1994. He lives in Missoula, Montana.

**LAURIE KUTCHINS** was born in Wyoming and lives now in the Shenandoah Valley of Virginia with her husband and two children. She teaches creative writing at James Madison University and the Taos Summer Writers Conference. Her two books of poetry are *Between Towns* and *The Night Path*, which received the Isabella Gardner Prize and was nominated for the Pulitzer Prize. She is currently piecing together another book of poems and writing *Weather Quilt*, a mixed-genre work that explores the confluence of place, weather and narrative.

**WILLIAM J LINES** was born in Fremantle, Western Australia, and has spent much of his life as a vagabond. He once restored an old chapel in Wales and made it home. Later, in Vermont, he built himself another. He has worked at many jobs on several continents, most often as a carpenter. In his most recent book—a collection of essays, *Open Air*—Lines writes about the work, the places and the ideas that have made him the man and the writer he is. In 1990 he started writing about people and nature in Australia and has published five books since then, including *Taming the Great South Land* and *A Short Walk in the Australian Bush*. He is now writing a narrative history of the Green movement in Australia.

**BARRY LOPEZ** was born in New York and grew up in rural California. He has lived in the McKenzie River Valley in western Oregon for over thirty years. His six works of nonfiction include *Of Wolves and Men, Arctic Dreams*, which won the National Book Award, and *About This Life*. Among his eight works of fiction are *River Notes*, *Desert Notes* and *Light Action in the Caribbean*. His writing appears in *Harper's*, *DoubleTake*, *The Paris Review*, and *Orion*, and his many honours include an Award in Literature from the American Academy of Arts and Letters, a Guggenheim Fellowship, a Lannan Award and the Orion Society's John Hay Award.

**PETER MATTHIESSEN**'s travels to many parts of the world and his concern for the lives of endangered people and wild animals have produced thirty books of fiction and nonfiction, including the works of travel and exploration for which he is best known. Among these books are *The Tree Where Man Was Born*, which was nominated for the National Book Award, and *The Snow Leopard*, which won it, as well as *Wildlife in America*, *Indian Country* and *In the Spirit of Crazy Horse*. His novels include *At Play in the Fields of the Lord*, *Far Tortuga* and *Killing Mister Watson*. His most recent book is *The Birds of Heaven*. He is a member of the American Academy of Arts and Letters and the American Academy of Arts and Sciences. For his work as a writer and environmental advocate he was named the 1991 Laureate of the Global Honor Roll of the United Nations Environment Program and won the Heinz Award in Arts and Humanity. Since the 1950s he has made his home near Sagaponack on Long Island, New York.

**MICHAEL McCOY** is a passionate home-gardener, garden designer and writer. Michael was born to a musical family in Victoria but disappointed their musical ambitions for him and developed instead an obsession for gardening he has been pursuing ever since. In 1991, he lived and worked at Great Dixter in England with Christopher Lloyd, certainly the most controversial, and possibly the most prolific and influential garden writer of our time. Now, he runs a garden design business from his home (and garden) in Woodend, just north of Melbourne, Victoria, where he lives with his wife, Karen, and three children. He writes on garden and design matters for *The Age* and *Your Garden*. His book *Michael McCoy's Garden* was published in 2000.

RICHARD NELSON is a cultural anthropologist and nature writer. He spent many years living with the Iñupiaq people and the Gwich'in and Koyukon Athapaskan people of Arctic Alaska, learning about their relationship with the environment and their knowledge of the natural world. He has drawn on that wisdom in his many books, which include *Make Prayers to the Raven*; *Hunters of the Northern Ice*; and *Heart and Blood: Living with Deer in America*. He won the John Burroughs Medal for his book *The Island Within*, a personal exploration of nature, place and home, set among the waters and islands of Sitka in southeast Alaska, where he lives. Nelson is a keen naturalist, outdoorsman and conservation activist. He is, according to Annie Dillard, 'the nature writer the nature writers read.' He is a recipient of the Lannan Literary Award for creative nonfiction, and he was the 1999–2001 Writer Laureate of Alaska.

PATRICE NEWELL was for many years a model and a television researcher, then a newsreader and presenter of public affairs for the Special Broadcasting Service and commercial television. These days she raises beef and grows olives organically on a property near Scone in New South Wales and tries to keep the kangaroos out of her vegetable garden. She shares her life and the property with her partner, Phillip Adams, and their daughter. Patrice is the author of *The Olive Grove* and, with Phillip Adams, a series of bestselling Australian joke books. Her most recent book is *The River*.

DAVID QUAMMEN, a novelist and essayist, is the author of ten books, including *The Song of the Dodo*, *Wild Thoughts from Wild Places* and *Monster of God*. He writes about field science, conservation, landscape and history for *Harper's*, *National Geographic*, *Outside*, *The Atlantic Monthly* and other magazines, and has twice received the National Magazine Award for his essays and other work. He has lived in Montana for many years.

ERIC ROLLS, poet, nature writer, conservationist, was born in 1923 and brought up on a farm in western New South Wales. He began telling stories when he was five and has not stopped since. After serving overseas in the Second World War, he farmed his own land and kept on writing. His long career has produced many poems, books for children, books about the importance of the Chinese in Australia, memoirs of rural life, books of essays on environmental matters, books on food and wine and a memoir of the delights of the body, *A Celebration of the Senses*. The book for which he is most widely known, *A Million Wild Acres*, won *The Age* Book of the Year Award; it is a study of the natural and human history of the country where he lived and farmed for all those years. He now lives in Camden Head on the northern New South Wales coast, and fishes and writes. His recent books include *Australia: a biography*, *Celebration of Food and Wine* and *Visions of Australia*. Eric was awarded the Order of Australia in 1992 for services to literature and the environment.

SCOTT RUSSELL SANDERS is the author of eighteen books, including *Staying Put*, *Hunting for Hope* and *The Force of Spirit*. His writing has won the AWP Creative Nonfiction Award, the John Burroughs Award and the Lannan Literary Award. Scott is Distinguished Professor of English at Indiana University and a contributing editor for *Orion* magazine. He lives with his family in the hardwood hill country of the White River Valley, Indiana.

CAROLYN SERVID is the author of the essay collection *Of Landscape and Longing*, a personal reflection on land, home and community set in Sitka, Alaska, where she lives with her husband, Dorik Mechau. With Dorik she founded The Island Institute, an organisation dedicated to fostering collaborative, place-based thinking and action for social and natural justice. Carolyn edited the award-winning anthology *From the Island's Edge: a Sitka Reader*, and coedited *The Book of the Tongass* and *Arctic Refuge: a Circle of Testimony*.

GARY SNYDER is known as a poet, essayist, teacher, environmentalist, mountaineer and community worker. He lives in northern California in the watershed of the Yuba River with his wife, Carole Koda. His books include *The Practice of the Wild*, *A Place in Space*, *No Nature* and *The Gary Snyder Reader*. He teaches literature, writing and envrionment studies at the University of California, Davis.

JOHN TALLMADGE is Core Professor in Literature and Environmental Studies at the Union Institute in Cincinnati, Ohio. He is the author of *Meeting the Tree of Life* and the coeditor of a collection of essays in ecocriticism, *Reading Under the Sign of Nature*. He is writing a book about the urban wild, set in Cincinnati, where he lives with his family.

MARK TREDINNICK, a writer and teacher, grew up in Epping, New South

Wales, and lives now, with his wife and family, in the sandstone country near Katoomba, west of Sydney. His essays and reviews appear in *The Bulletin*, *Resurgence* and other newspapers and journals. Mark completed a doctoral thesis, *Writing the Wild*, on the literature of place in 2003. He is editing with Scott Slovic an anthology of Australian desert literature. And he is working on *The Blue Plateau*, a booklength lyric essay on the country in which he makes his home.

TERRY TEMPEST WILLIAMS was born, a fifth-generation Mormon, within sight of the Great Salt Lake in Salt Lake City, Utah. She lives now, with her husband, Brooke, near Moab, in the redrock desert of southern Utah. Formerly Naturalist-in-Residence at the Utah Museum of Natural History, Terry is best known for her book *Refuge: An Unnatural History of Family and Place*. Her other books include *An Unspoken Hunger*, *Leap* and *Red: Passion and Patience in the Desert*. For her work as a writer and her passionate activism for wilderness conservation and place-based democracy she was recently inducted into the Rachel Carson Honor Roll. Terry's writing has appeared in *The New Yorker*, *The New York Times*, *Audubon*, *Orion*, *The Iowa Review* and *Outside*, and has been translated into many languages. She is the recipient of both a Guggenheim Fellowship and a Lannan Literary Fellowship in creative nonfiction.

TIM WINTON lives, with his family, in Fremantle in Australia's southwest. An acclaimed novelist, his most recent book, *Dirt Music*, was shortlisted for the Booker Prize and won a number of literary prizes, including the Miles Franklin Award. His other books include *Shallows*, *Cloudstreet* and *The Riders*. He has written books for children and a collection of prose reflections (*Land's Edge*) on the coastal landscape where he has always been at home. Tim is increasingly engaged in projects of environmental activism, including especially the campaign to save the Ningaloo Reef off the coast of Western Australia.

# Acknowledgments

This book exists because of the work of the writers you'll find in it. I thank them, above all, and I offer them the book as a bow of respect.

I am especially grateful to those writers who sat down and composed fresh essays for this anthology. Those who did not write something new have let me choose some apt (and, I think, exemplary) pieces from their recent work, for which I thank them; and I thank their agents and publishers, too, who have permitted me to use this previously published work. Special thanks to Susan Bergholz, Caryn Burtt, Marianne Merola, Altie Karper and Chuck Verrill, who moved some mountains. And to Ben Barnhart, Saskia Cornes, Jenny Darling, Ruth Gilbert, Peter Matson and Clive Newman, for their grace and goodwill.

For putting the idea of a book of places into my head, I thank Peter Bishop. For their friendship and encouragement and for the example of their words and lives, I thank James Galvin, John Haines, Ashley Hay, Laurie Kutchins, Barry Lopez, Richard Nelson, Patrice Newell and Terry Tempest Williams. For his guidance and generosity, I thank John Cameron. For their early work on behalf of this book and for their hospitality, I thank George Thompson and Randall Jones at the Center for American Places. For believing in the collection, for making it a better thing than it otherwise would have been and for turning it into a book, I thank my agent Fran Bryson and her assistant Liz Kemp, my publisher Phillipa McGuinness, my editors Heather Jamieson and Angela Handley, along with Di Quick and the others at UNSW Press.

Carolyn Servid and Dorik Mechau of The Island Institute gave me a month's residency in Sitka, Alaska, in April 2002. My time in that place was a blessing to me and to this book. Thanks to them, to my hosts Galen Paine and Don Surgeon and to my friends in Sitka. And thanks to Elaine van Kempen and Eric Rolls, for their championship of this literature in Australia and for the shelter and nourishment they have given me at Camden Haven.

For helping me to know my place on earth, I thank the people who love me, especially my wife and children. This book is for them.

---

'The Centre' from *Charmian Clift Selected Essays* by Charmian Clift, copyright Jason Johnston, Roseanne Bonney and Rebecca O'Connor, is reprinted by permission of Barbara Mobbs, Sydney.

Excerpts from *The Meadow* by James Galvin, copyright 1992 by James Galvin, are reprinted by permission of Henry Holt and Company, LLC, New York.

A version of 'Cooper Dreaming' by Tom Griffiths, copyright 2001 by Tom Griffiths, appeared in *Inflows: The Channel Country* by Mandy Martin et al; and part of it was used in *Storykeepers*, edited by Marion Halligan and published by Duffy & Snellgrove, Sydney. It is used by permission of the author.

'Snow', 'Spring' and 'Other Days', copyright 1989 by John Haines, reprinted from *The Stars, the Snow, the Fire* with the permission of Graywolf Press, Saint Paul, Minnesota.

'The Red Steer at Rat Bay', copyright 2002 by Pete Hay, though written for this collection, appeared in *Van Diemonian Essays* by Pete Hay and is reprinted with the permission of the author and publisher, Walleah Press, Hobart.

'Creations' from *Dwellings: A Spiritual History of the Living World* by Linda Hogan, copyright 1995 by Linda Hogan, used by permission of W W Norton & Company, Inc, New York and Sanford J Greenburger Associates, New York.

Excerpt in Linda Hogan's essay 'Creations' from *Memory of Fire* by Eduardo Galeano, translated by Cedric Belfrage, translation copyright 1985 by Cedric Belfrage, reprinted by permission of Susan Bergholz Literary Services, New York and Pantheon Books, a division of Random House, Inc, New York.

# Editor's Note on Usage

Although we all speak English in this book, we do not all speak it alike. When we open our mouths to speak—I, from west of Sydney, for example, and Laurie Kutchins from Wyoming—you will know we come from different places on earth. You will know that the same language is spoken in those two places; and you will hear how that language resonates in each place with different inflections and rhythms, timbres and dynamics—qualities to do with the nature of the two landscapes in which that common language plays, with which it converses; and to do with the kind of relationship each of our cultures has made with the continent that houses and shapes it.

When we write, those differences diminish, and yet they persist in small ways. Two continents and their English-speaking settlers have evolved some different rules for spelling, punctuation and usage, and you will find them in this book. Because this is a book about the beauty of difference and the necessity of listening; because it is an essay in diversity; because it opens up a conversation between these places, I have let each author's essay carry the markings of the place and culture from which it comes. The differences are subtle. But they matter.

Though it is conventional for each of our publishing cultures to change a 'foreign' author's spellings and comma-placements (to comply with local style) when we publish his or her works, I have let such differences stand in this book. In Australian entries, Australian usage runs; in American essays, American usage runs. If this causes confusion, I apologise—or is it 'apologize'?

Whatever I have written—this note, the acknowledgments, the notes on contributors, the introduction and my own essay—I have composed in conformity with my own local style, since the jurisdiction of Australian usage runs through Lavender Bay and Katoomba, where I write. And so you will find me writing about the 'honours' various American writers have received, even though those writers would have called them 'honors'. They are the same honours, however we spell them.

Many of the contributors to this collection would never once in their lives have thought and spoken the word 'honour,' as though it had that 'u' in its second syllable; and others will never have used it without that 'u' (as 'honor'). The same is true of 'labor' and 'labour'; of 'traveling' and 'travelling' and so on. I don't think it is either respectful or necessary to insist that a writer from another place spell or punctuate the way that I do. Such small differences in our prose habits can sometimes express and sustain what is unique about a place and the way a people relates with it. We must learn to let each other speak and write out of our local ground, out of our vernacular rhythms, in our own voices. We must not listen as though our own ways of speech were superior. We should try to keep our local differences alive in our conversations.

I believe in places much more than I do in nations. But nations tend to define and defend such matters as spelling, usage and style. So it is, on the whole, such *national* differences you will find preserved here. Understand, though, that my true respect extends deeper than national differences to the particularity of each author's voice, each writer's place, the song they share. Something of those inflections is preserved, I think, inside the differences of word use, of spelling and punctuation that the Australian *Style Manual* and the *Chicago Manual of Style* insist upon; something particular certainly would be lost if we did not let those differences stand. So they stand in this book.

What are these differences? I can't be complete here—anyway, it would be dull. But here are a few things. Several words are spelled differently between us. I noted 'honour/honor' and 'labour/labor' above. In Australia, one would write 'harbour', 'favourite' and 'aeroplane'; in America, 'harbor', 'favorite' and 'airplane'. (One would also, in America, put those commas and that full stop *inside* the quote marks in that last clause, as I will explain.) In North America, it is conventional to put a comma before 'and' when it occurs between the penultimate and ultimate word in a list, as in '... spelling, usage, and style.' In Australia, a writer would drop that final comma: '... spelling, usage and style'. In Australia, a full stop (such as that at the end of my last sentence) normally goes outside the closing quotation mark, unless it is also part of the quoted words; in America, the stop (or 'period') normally resides inside the closing quotation mark. In Australia, 'practice' is a noun and 'practise' is a verb. In North America 'practice' is generally used for both parts of speech. In Australia, you 'license' me to pull water from a river, but you grant me a water 'licence'.

Many of our words for land and landform are common, although the kinds (and therefore the names) of plants and trees, of course, are not. We all have 'mountain', 'plateau', 'river', 'plain', 'desert' and 'meadow'. We share 'habitat', 'ecosystem', 'ridge', 'valley' and so on. On both continents we speak of 'rangelands'. But some of our words for landuse do not travel well. No one in Australia 'homesteads' or 'ranches', though we do 'settle' or 'pioneer' new country, and we 'run' or 'raise' livestock on 'stations' or 'properties'. Australia has no 'prairie'; and North America, as far as I can make out, has no 'outback' or 'outside country'. (On the other hand, in Australia, I might have a shed or some bushland 'out the back', not 'out back', of my house.) '[T]he bush', in Australia, is an expression that encompasses all land that is not in the city, not merely the forests, wild or tame. A 'footpath' or a 'pavement' in Australia might be a 'sidewalk' in the USA. A 'trail' in the US would nearly always be a 'track' in Australia.

And then there is 'watershed'. In Australia, the word 'watershed' designates the high ground that separates two areas of drainage. In Australia, 'watershed' means 'divide', and 'catchment' is the name we use for the drainage basins. In North America, it's different: 'watershed' refers not to the divide between catchments but to the catchment itself. Confused? It would be better, as ever, to be having this conversation outside and watching the streams fall either side of a ridge. But words will have to do for now; and if we use them differently here and there, we will just have to be patient with each other. It is what the ground itself says that counts. Listen mostly for that—earth and falling water came before all the words we have for them.

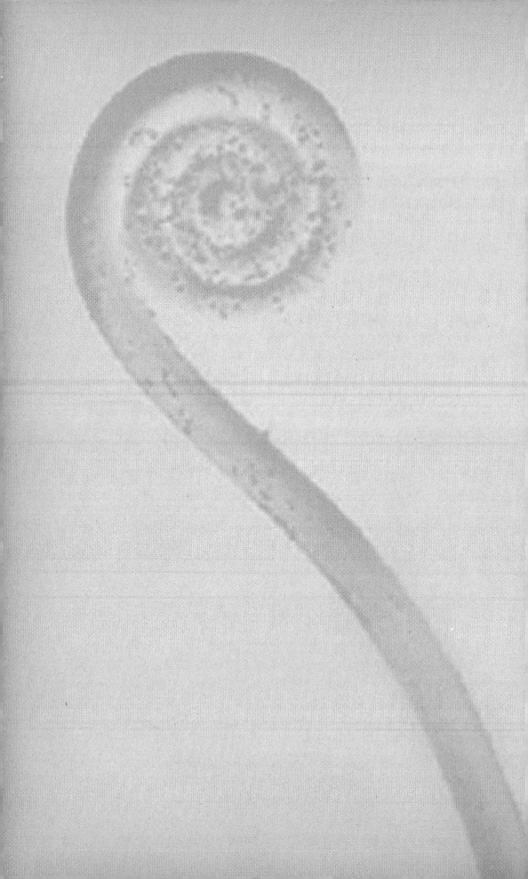

# MARK
# TREDINNICK

## Belonging to Here: An Introduction

### I

Beside my desk in the highlands where I live stands a four-drawer filing cabinet made of wood. It holds my work, my failed ideas, my paid bills, my stashed receipts and bank statements, the children's artwork, things I can't forget and others I need to remember. On top of the cabinet, among a selection of my favourite books, upon a pile of magazines, a photograph rests. In the photograph I lean, with a book in one hand, into the weather. It is a winter afternoon, the sea breeze is soft, and the sky is clean of cloud. The book I hold is a book of poems. I look out, over the words, to the sea that breaks beneath me, down the smooth shoulders of the land's edge. Behind me a thin road runs. Elegant spans of concrete carry it over gullies where the sea presses inland and the coast falls back, where the heath-clad granite has surrendered to the work of streams and the persistent surf. The coastline runs away, beyond me, spur after spur of the coastal range, to the last promontory south that eyesight and camera frame will hold. The sea pushes in against dark congregations of basalt, gathered just off-shore, and surges white over them to the sands. And salt-haze softens the distance.

The ocean washing in on this calm day of late December is the Pacific. It pushes itself against the flanks of granite that compose this shore, near Big

Sur, below Carmel, on the west coast of North America. Around my boots stand sagebrush and lizardtail, black sage and asters, though my Australian eye is not good enough to know one from the other yet.

I am reading Robinson Jeffers and standing where he often stood, before the road came, before it carried all this traffic from the city, brought folks like me in SUVs to this spare and quiet coast. I am looking out, as Jeffers did, for vultures who might ensky me. Jeffers lived near here, walked and wrote this coastline in lines composed of granite and saltwater swells. He loved this place, mourned its settlement, but knew that it would—these cliffs, this sea, these gullies and attendant skies—outlive everything men did to it. I stand here reading what Jeffers made of home. I am reading his poem 'Tor House'. There, Jeffers writes that, if you came looking for his ghost, as I was looking for it, and for the place that was home to him, you would find them (ghost and place) not in whatever remained of the house he built himself here, but in the 'wild sea fragrance of wind', in basalt tongue and granite outcrop, river and ocean and tree and gull. Even after ten-thousand years, he says, he would be there in those things.

As I write, though, I sit in a cottage high in a country of sandstone plateaus. Take an atlas. Find Australia and on its southeastern shore, Sydney Harbour. Look inland from the coast there, and you will come upon the Blue Mountains. (They are not really mountains, despite their name, though that may not be apparent from the map. We speak of them loosely and, doing so, hide their true character in a borrowed word. This is a wide, rent and weathered plateau, dissected by time and water, crazed with deep and sudden valleys.) Look in that plateau country for Katoomba. Find the Kedumba River and its valley to Katoomba's south. And picture me high on this undulant ridge above it. This is my home. I am here in the rocks, as Jeffers is in his.

If you had come to me at Big Sur and asked me where I was from, about the place where I live, I would have spoken to you about escarpments and the wooded valleys they ring, about the windy country of the sky above, the voices and trajectories of birds that describe the great valleys the plateau contains; and then I would have spoken of a small timber cottage I share here with a woman I love—the woman who took this photograph—and where I write, from which I wander into sclerophyll woodlands hoping for weather to report, for birdsong to hear, for silences to join and depths to plumb. And I would have spoken of a valley called Kanimbla where I ride horses with my children and my wife, guided by a man called Jim, whose family has lived there for three generations, raising sheep and cattle and horses on its pastures, cutting and milling and husbanding its timbers, and in whose blood that valley's story and all its weathers run. I would talk of the Wolgin Valley, Kanangra Deeps, the blue flash of the sacred kingfisher, the song of the lyrebird, the glow of the sandstone cliffs at dusk. I might describe the cottage, yes; this room where I sit now; but most of all I would speak of eucalypts (Jeffers' 'dark-leaved Australians') and a garden-full of green-leaved Europeans; of eroded valleys, the rivers that make them—on and on—the blue air the trees breathe into them, the temperate air, the pining call of black cockatoos.

If you came to find my home, you would find it here, in Katoomba, in the Kedumba Valley and the Kanimbla, and in all the sandstone country of the plateau; in all the patterns and forms, in the natural history, of this place on earth. I have a feeling that the patterns articulated here, that the music embodied in this geography, may teach me how best to live the life that has been given to me; that I need to let it school me; that any work I do that is ever any good will be some kind of transcription—no more than that—into language, into acts of love or parenting or husbandry, of principles this place expresses in lives at play here—lives as slow as sandstone, as fast as wren, as eternal as weather, as good as those of many men and women whose home this was or is. I want to witness it well. I suppose I want also to belong very deeply here, and I know I never will—being too hasty and busy and human, like most of us—and I know that that matters less than the attempt to belong, which is an attempt, as Barry Lopez puts it, to grow intimate.

I sense that human beings live best when they remember that they live inside a natural order, that the land includes us and all our schemes and creations, and that when we begin to imagine our lines of kinship and our bonds of responsibility extending out, beyond ourselves and our human families and our nations to the many forms of life and intelligence that comprise our home place, then it is that we will learn how to behave well, not only at home, not only in human society, but as inhabitants of the earth.

I am a fool, as you see, for landscape, particularly for this one. I believe in natural histories. You cannot know me until you know the weather and the country that surround me, the trees and rocks and animals, as well as the people, that keep me company—it would help to look at my bookshelf too, and my music collection and my memberships. None of us is finished at the fingertips or toes. Our identities are formed and constantly reformed in relationship with everything else in our experience that is not merely ourselves. We are made and remade by engagement with creation; and since we cannot engage with all creation, we tend to be shaped by that part of it we can know, above all the material pieces that compose what we might call a place, our home place. To know me you must know the things in relationship with which I live. And I would expect the same to be true of you. I would ask you where you live and what you love there. I would piece you together from what you tell me of home.

And if I tried to spell home for you, I would spell it out as I have done; I would, if I could, sing it as Jeffers did—in metered lines of lovely lugubrious length. I would spell out home in letters, shaping words, that make the note of the country that houses me, this place, its stone, its breath, the trees and grasses and flowers it speaks, the birds that speak of it.

*Gnunungulla.* That is a word in the tongue of the people—dark-skinned Australians—who lived first where I now live. It is their word for the idea of 'belonging to here'. They are called, this place's first people, Gundungurra, and their descendants live here still. This is still their place, as it is also the place of the silver top ash and the red mountain devil, of the Antechinus, the lyrebird, the sandstone and the waters that cut it, and me. I can claim it only in my imagination—in the way I practise being present here. I listen, I walk, I notice, I love; I picture its old stories, feel its patterns on my skin, breathe its air, write its names—and so it claims me.

If you shape their name, the name of these people, and roll their word for this practice of belonging in your mouth, you will sound out something of the music of this place; you will loose the hard round music congealed, embodied, in this sandstone country.

## II

This is a book of places, such as the world is made of. It is a collection of small essays of place drawn from two continents—Australia and North America. Each essay articulates the nature of a place, in most cases a home place, but in any event a geography—large or small, as vast as a landmass, as modest as a drainage—to which each writer feels attached. Each essay describes a place on earth, special to one writer, a large or small part of his or her natural history. Most often, as I say, this is the place where that writer lives (so it is with James Galvin, Ashley Hay, Barry Lopez, Peter Matthiessen, Michael McCoy, Richard Nelson, Patrice Newell, David Quammen, Carolyn Servid, Gary Snyder, John Tallmadge, myself, and Terry Tempest Williams). Sometimes (as with Eric Rolls and Barbara Blackman) it is the many places they have lived. Sometimes it is the place where their heart resides, though they do not (this is so with John Haines and Laurie Kutchins). Bill Kittredge writes in his essay about the place of his childhood and younger days as a rancher. John Cameron recalls the Canberra of his childhood and his adult years and finds in what he loved there, in its rocks, a metaphor for his own life's course. Pete Hay writes of his second home, his shack in Rat Bay. I write of two places I move between. Scott Sanders writes also of the place where he grew up and the place to which he returns, a much altered place, to recall why places need our love. Linda Hogan writes of a place she goes in search of her own indigenous origins, in search of new beginnings for us all. Others write of visited places, other people's places that ignited imagination (Charmian Clift, Tom Griffiths, and William J Lines). Tim Winton writes of the continent in which he lives, seen from the air, and encourages us all to come down to earth.

I have gathered pieces, I have collected places, from North America and Australia—from those two places for some particular reasons. In the one place this literature is lively; in the other it is hardly known. I wanted a book that honoured and included many of the great contemporary writers in this field, most of whom are writing in America. I wanted to put their work alongside that of Australian writers for whom the genre, the very idea of a place-based essay, was something new..

I am eager to encourage a place-based literature, an antipodean nature writing, in my own homeland, and I saw the book as an opportunity to foster just such writing, at least from a few writers, and to offer it to a readership in Australia and America. These Australian writers are familiar to Australian readers, although this genre and many of the American writers are not; on the other hand, the genre (and the North American contributors) will be familiar to many North American readers, although the Australian writers and their landscapes are not. Here are some new authors, some new ways of thinking about place, and some new kinds of landscape for American readers and students of this literature; and here, for Australian readers unfamiliar with this literature, is place writing at its best. In addition, I had in mind students in courses dedicated, in both places, to the study and writing of such literature; courses in literature and place, the sense of place, responses to landscape, social ecology and so on. For such readers the book will combine the familiar and the unfamiliar—in terrain, in authorship, in modes of witness and ways of thinking about land, about nature and culture.

I might have commissioned essays, I suppose, from all parts of the world. The idea occurred to me. Where to stop was then the question. That is another project all together, much more encyclopedic: I may make that my next project. Having dreamed of a book of places, of other people's home landscapes, I chose in the end what I know and what I love. I know and admire the American literature of place, and in the course of my own studies have met many of its finest contemporary practitioners, and most of the contributors here. I sought essays from the best writers I knew. I have travelled in many of the American places written of here, and have formed deep attachments to them from those travels, as well as through the writing that celebrates them—Wyoming, Oregon, Southeast Alaska, the Colorado Plateau, the Great Plains, the Rockies and Long Island. So you will find these places here. And I chose Australian writers whom I know, with whom I had talked about literature and landscape, whose love of place I knew about, and whose writing I admired. I chose them too, to some degree, for the country they would write about—the Channel Country, the east coast of Tasmania, the Pilliga, the Hunter, Sydney Harbour, the Kangaroo Valley, the mountains of Canberra, the deserts of the red centre, the southwest and the Great Australian Bight. And so I made, in the end, a book of my favourite places and my favourite writers, a book written by people I know and admire about places they love.

More largely, I wanted also to see how some places on the two continents—which have a similar mass and share the same language and a superficially similar history, but little else—might sound together. More simply, I hope the book takes its readers on paths they will emerge from changed, through some shapely sentences and some memorable country.

You will find here desert and plateau, river and ice, city and farm, garden and desert, forest and grassland, man and woman, horse and bear, coyote and salmon, lyrebird and eagle, stone-curlew and junco, wind and rain, outback and seashore, sandstone and granite, sheoak and cottonwood, highland and lowland, harbour and wetland, hanging swamp and mountain meadow, snow and wind, fire and flood, petroglyph and cartograph, ancient and modern, earth and sky, birth and death, and many of the compass points, the contour lines, the latitudes and longitudes of home.

Specifically, this anthology of place writing arose from a journey I took across North America to chart the geography of the American literature of place; and from an idea that grew out of conversations I had at a gathering of nature writers at Harvard University in late 2000. But its roots go down deeper, to a conversation I had here in my home plateaus, with Peter Bishop, a man who runs a writers' retreat on whose board I serve. The place is called Varuna. It sits near the edge of the same valley my house does, a little west and north of me, where the escarpment bends around. It is now a decade since its house and garden, tall with oaks and pines and scribbly-barks, were gifted to the community of writers by the man who inherited it. Mick Dark is the son of Eleanor and Eric Dark, a writer and a doctor, thinkers and activists both, for social justice and the wild places they loved. Mick grew up here and still helps tend the garden and keep the old place in repair. But he and his wife Jill chose to make it a place where writers might come to shape and shelter books, as he had watched his mother do for long years. Obliquely and without ceremony, then, this book of places, of written places, celebrates that writers' place and Mick's gift to us all.

I offer this book, then, as conversation about belonging on earth; a complex essay in bioregionalism; a study in ecological imagination; a cycle of the stories these places have to tell; a journey through the homelands of others. Some of these pieces are new, commissioned and written specially for this book. Some have appeared before. But each of these I have chosen because it speaks so well to the idea of this collection and because it is such a fine piece of writing. Each of them is alive, though, with one place on earth. And these places, these voices, these many natural histories, call each of us who reads them home—home to these many places not our own, and to those to which we truly belong. They remind us how wild and lively and vulnerable the world is; how full it is of places whose nature we will never in a lifetime fathom, but which will school us in so many crafts and truths we need to conduct that lifetime wisely and well.

Each of the essays in this book expresses—it sings the life of—a place that is sustaining, sacred, special to a writer who lives in it or remembers it well: a place where deep attachments rest, a storied place. Each is a natural history, a sacred geography of a place on earth.

### III

North America has been home, since Thoreau, to a rich literature dedicated to bringing places—landscapes and the people and other beings who inhabit them—to a second life in the imagination of readers. This writing is sometimes, and inadequately, called nature writing. It is really a literature of place. Places—particular pieces of country—have, it seems, called forth much of the most thoughtful, shapely and enduring prose of our time, particularly in nonfiction. In addition to Thoreau, himself, I think of Mary Austin, Aldo Leopold, Rachel Carson, John Muir, John Burroughs, Henry Beston, Joseph Woods Krutch, Wendell Berry, John Haines, James Galvin, Peter Matthiessen, Edward Abbey, Annie Dillard, Norman Maclean, Barry Lopez, Simon Ortiz, Linda Hogan, Ted Hoagland, Mary Oliver, Scott Russell Sanders, David Quammen,

Gary Snyder, John Hay, Terry Tempest Williams, Bill Kittredge and Wallace Stegner.

In recent years this literature has flourished. It has not, of course, entered the mainstream of writing or of readership, but more books and essays appear each year, new writers emerge, and the writing has growing standing among critics and departments of literature. Scholars like Larry Buell, John Tallmadge, John Elder, Scott Slovic and Cheryl Glotfelty are forging a new genre of literary analysis, ecocriticism, one of whose concerns is to study this literature and, more broadly, to read all literature as though nature really counted.

At its best, this literature listens to the land and to those people intimate with its places. It puts words and their music, it puts imagination, to work in service of that larger order—the land, natural history—in which we humans live; on which we depend for air and ground and water and for lessons in grace and endurance, beauty and necessity. Emily Dickinson observed once that places speak, and the poet learns to listen. Perhaps the work of literature attuned to place is, finally, a listening. It tries to discern the soul of, the music of, a place on earth; and in the work, if it has listened well, we hear the place, or hear it as it manifests itself through the memory and nature and gift of the writer. The poem or the piece of prose, at its best, is a choreography in words of an act of careful listening; and through that listening we may hear the place express itself. We may catch the lyric of the country. Or we may not. But we will catch the world of a place somewhere; we will feel that it is alive to the writer, and, through her text, becomes alive to us. Thomas J Lyon, a scholar of nature writing, begins his essay, 'The Nature Essay in the West', in *A Literary History of the American West*, with these words, which pick up Dickinson's thought: 'The function of the nature essayist, as Henry Beston pointed out some forty years ago, is like that of the poet. Both attempt to reforge a fundamental continuity between inner and outer, so that for the reader the world is alive again, seen precisely for what it is, and the mind is alive to it.'

The nature writer listens to the world, then—to some of, or to one of, its lively, articulate places, divining their nature, looking for words to shape the stories embedded in them—stories of those places, including stories of the people who have participated in them, been claimed by them and whose lives seem to articulate the country somehow. Through the art of words, their music and form, she or he, this nature writer, tries to return places to life for us—for most of us have grown used to abstracting and attenuating the rest of nature, beyond the human. We are perhaps not only less at home, because of that civilised habit, in the weather and the wild: we are less fully human.

So nature writing tries to waken the world again for us; and waken us to it—not some romantic image of it, but to the wild world just as it is, for its own sake. This literature, which is, at its best, part science and part poetry, passes on lessons—from the more-than-human world, and from those who live intimately with it—about living with dignity, with restraint and wisdom, with intelligence and grace, within the places on earth; and about the nature of the real world. It looks more and more to indigenous peoples, where they survive, for those lessons, and explores new ways of belonging together in a landscape already damaged by our occupation of them.

One way or another, this literature witnesses places. The reality of a place, a piece of country, is what it tries to give us, transcribed through language, its currents of connection and disjunction transposed into the kind of music words, articulated thoughts and observations, make. Mostly this literature of nature is framed by the author's own experience of a geography. Without a personal presence nothing may be witnessed. But when the writing is good, the work, you feel, is not really *about* the author. It is about a place—and its meaning for one writer. (Conversely, when this writing fails, it fails because you feel that the writer has not transcended their merely personal concerns and reactions; you feel they are writing all about themself, and that the place has become a means of elaborating that alone.)

In the literature of nature, places are not stages, as they are in most literature, for merely human dramas; they are not backdrops to stories—they *are* the stories, to paraphrase Barry Lopez's neat encapsulation. Human nature contemplated outside biology, outside ecology, abstracted from the rest of nature, will not be properly understood. This literature asks us, as Jeffers put it, to uncentre ourselves from ourselves; it sings the songs of creation as they manifest somewhere. It sings the songs of places, often as those places are manifest in the lives of local men and women. Sometimes (as is the case here with James Galvin's piece 'The Real World') this literature gives us the lives of landscape-steeped people, not the writer himself. The lives and dramas of human folk may be seen more fully, known more deeply, this literature contends, when they are seen in relationship with more-than-merely-human things. Usually, though, the local person in question is the essayist him or herself. Most nature writing, most of the literature of place, writes the natural history of its author—for that natural history's own sake, rather than because the author regards her own life as particularly important and therefore the natural history worth telling by way of explaining it; and because of a belief that the life of the writer will make sense, and is significant, only seen in conversation with his or her ecology.

I think the nature writer, the writer of this literature of place, tries to imagine their place as though they were not merely one man or woman within it, but as though they were, in a sense, the whole place, as though they saw, for a moment here and there, what it sees, as though they felt the complex history, the concatenation of forces, the dance of atoms and cells at play within it. They try to imagine events from multiple points of view, in geological time, in tree-time and animal-time and human-time—in all the frames and scales and tones, at all the paces and from all the viewpoints that run in a place, that may even *be* a place or ecosystem. They try to see through nature's eyes, to hear with its ears; they try to write from the point of view of the land, that complicated set of relationships, *here*. The personal, and the human, will be set in that kind of frame, imagined in that kind of ecological context. The place is where the centre of such writing lies—it is ecocentric, place-centred, not anthropocentric. Nature writing is an attempt, and has been at least since Henry David Thoreau, at ecological imagination.

Mankind, said Jeffers, in another poem, may be nature, dreaming. I take him to mean we are the part of the living world (and perhaps there are many others too) that dreams, thinks, reflects, sings, makes poems of the rest. And, if this is so, then it may be that the kind of singing of place a nature writer attempts is nature, writing—is places, singing. The writer, in other words, is the part of the place that imagines (imagines its whole ecology); he or she is the part of nature, here, that writes. Indeed, we might begin to remember the extent to which the text that any writer turns out is not merely the work of that author, but the work also of that part of nature in which they live and breathe; it is the articulation, the manifestation, the emanation of place—and of that dreamer, that writer, within it.

Or perhaps it is—as my friend George Seddon wrote to me in an email when I was speaking with him about this collection—that places do not speak at all, not even in the way that I mean here. Perhaps it is, as Annie Dillard once wrote, that nature's silence is its one remark. I am inclined to think it is a matter of how—and how subtly—one understands the word 'speak'. In the end it may not matter. It may just be, as George Seddon concedes, that some writers simply have the gift for writing about places more movingly, powerfully, eloquently than others. George Seddon is certainly one of them. And there are many such writers, with a fabulous gift for place, on show in this collection.

Seddon's remark reminds us that not every writer understands their business the same way; and that the enterprise of place writing includes much more than what John Burroughs (speaking of Whitman) called 'spiritual auricular analogy'—that is, an attempt to make the words sound like the spirit of the place. Most of the time a writer, with this gift for place, just describes places with care and allows himself or herself to be led into lines of thought and memory, into hope or despair, into polemics or riffs of delight. Most of the time they just write, following the words through places to which they are drawn. They attempt, on the page, nothing but writing; as places themselves attempt nothing but life. And so you will see in the essays that follow a wide diversity of styles and approaches to place: some are personal; some detached; some autobiographical; some political; some quick with anger; some gentle with love; some like poems; some like papers. We need such diversity.

This literature is various and rich (and some of it, as in any genre, is bad). Thomas Lyon, in an introductory chapter to his anthology of nature writing, *This Incomparable Land*, offers a 'taxonomy of nature writing', which gives a sense of the variety of approaches embraced by what we might see as this single literature, attempting what I have described as this place-oriented, eco-centric enterprise. Lyon suggests that 'the literature of nature' has about it 'three main dimensions': 'natural history information, personal responses to nature, and philosophical interpretations of nature' (Lyon, 2001, p 20). This is helpful, as far as it goes. From the weight that each of these elements receives in a work of nature writing, and the play between them in that work, Lyon distinguishes seven categories of nature writing . He cautions that these categories overlap and 'intergrade'. '[N]ature writing is not in truth a neat and orderly field,' he says (Lyon, 2001, p 20). Lyon's categories are these: *field guides*, which mostly aim simply to inform; *natural history essays*, which offer 'expository descriptions of nature' or places; *rambles*, which bring more of the author's personal response to places into the text; *nature experience essays*, where the element of personal experience 'frames the narrative', with three subcategories—solitude, travel and adventure, and farm life; and finally *man's role in nature*, philosophical and political essays on the state of relations between culture and nature.

More useful than these categories and subcategories may be Lyon's three dimensions. You can see how much variation of approach those elements of informing, responding and philosophising might allow in such a literature. Elements of each run through all the essays in this collection, for instance, and each essay differs from the others partly to the degree it does more of one than the other. Just to pick two, notice how Linda Hogan and David Quammen compose their pieces out of personal story, philosophical reflection on ecology and creation, and natural history observation, making through the force of their intelligences essays that escape any category really, but belong clearly in this literature. And notice how different each of these two essays is from the other.

But there is a dimension missing from Lyon's analysis, without which the best of this writing cannot be properly understood. My sense is that Lyon overlooks the element of much of this prose—what you might call its poetic or lyric aspect or its literary dimension—that makes it worth reading, and through which it attempts the hardest of its work, which is its listening, its singing with, its witnessing of places. What Barbara Blackman, James Galvin, Ashley Hay and Laurie Kutchins—and perhaps John Haines and Terry Tempest Williams too—are attempting, for instance, in their essays for this collection would fall outside any of Lyon's categories, I think, for mostly they are not informing, responding personally and philosophising about places. They are listening and speaking as a poet does, and that work depends upon a musical, a lyric, sensibility and voice. They are giving lyric witness. They are writing what might be called lyric essays of place, prose poems perhaps. They do not tell their stories straight—they don't really tell stories at all. Nor do they inform or report or preach. They do not exactly expound or argue or explain. They do not write all their sentences plain. It is the musicality of their prose to a very large extent that carries the burden of their purpose, which is to wander and discover, to let the country do the talking, to move us with it and its wisdoms.

This lyric element runs strongly also through a number of the other essays here—essays that would not be seen as lyric essays, that may be claimed more readily by one of Lyon's categories. It is this quality that makes them readable, memorable, capable of expressing the places they engage with and the principles that arise from them. This is true of Tom Griffiths, Barry Lopez, Eric Rolls and Linda Hogan, for example, and many of the others here. By contrast, Gary Snyder, both a poet and a philosopher, is writing pretty plainly in 'Kitkitdizze', relying very little on anything but the clearest description and exposition.

All of this is a way of saying that you can expect a wide variety of approaches here, though each of these essays, looked at one way, attempts the same task, in its own particular place. None of these writers has attempted anything so dull as to write a piece that fits or does not fit one of Lyon's modes. Each of them writes the way their nature and their country suggests. Like a healthy ecosystem, this collection—and the whole literature it represents—is rich with diversity, not only of country and personality, but of approach to the enterprise of waking the places to our minds and our minds to the places of the earth.

Though this literature may be said to be flourishing in North America, we hardly know what it is in Australia. It matters less that we have not heard of it by name than that our writers have not often attempted the hard and important work it demands. It serves the land, this literature; it helps us to remember our places and to know the country that sustains us. It even models a way of living with ecological awareness, of framing a sense of ecological self. So it would be a good thing to attempt. And we haven't done much of it yet. I mean specifically that we have had few essayists—lyric or prosaic—who have turned their attention to natural history, to the larger order, that is, that contains the merely social and personal order of our human lives. Specifically what we still do not have is a land-oriented literature of fact, an Australian nature writing turned to the nature of these antipodean places and drenched with them.

I should say something then about why the essay is so well made for witness (the witness, specifically of places); about why such essays may have flourished in North America while not yet flourishing in Australia. And I should say first of all that the Australian essays in this collection show that an Australian literature of fact, an Australian literature of place, is now upon us.

These are large matters. I engage with them apprehensively, for any conclusions about them are difficult to sustain and will always remain contentious. It is presumptuous, of course, to enter into a succinct summary of the nature of the American engagement with wild new country; of the nature of Australian settlement and our imaginative possession of this land. It is presumptuous to source the differences between our literary traditions, at least so far as essay writing and engagement with place are concerned, in the differences between the landscapes of the two places and the way we have engaged with them. Still, one of the reasons for bringing this collection together was to invite thinking about those matters. So here I go.

IV

Why should this literature have flourished in North America, when it has not done so yet in a land and culture—Australia—that is similar in many ways to America? Part of the answer lies in the triumph of the essay in America, the ongoing renewal and liveliness of her literature of fact. For essays, engaging as they do with the nature of what is actual, have usually and quite naturally turned their attention to land and to the natural history and ecology of human society or of one human life. Among the things an essayist will turn to is the nature of the place in which that essayist lives. Witness Seneca, Cicero and Montaigne, for example; or E B White and Gilbert White. If you are witnessing—I mean if you choose as a writer to set your imagination the task of knowing the actual things and setting their nature down, transcribed into linguistic forms—surely the nature of one's place would be one of the things you would witness.

But why has the essay, why has that particular enterprise, done so well in North America, and why so often turned to landscape? For the essay—as an instrument of what Goethe called 'exact sensate imagination', written in the engaging and deeply personal voice of reflection—has declined in England and given rise to the more formal essay of criticism or polemic; and the essay has never really got off the ground in Australia. Nor has the essay in Europe or Australia turned so often and so powerfully to the land, to the personality of places, to natural history, as it has in North America.

In his essay 'Landscapes of the alternate self', the essayist and critic Franklin Burroughs observes that the personal essay 'offers the same tempting amorphousness, autonomy, and freedom from traditional entailments that the unclaimed continent offered Euro-Americans' (Burroughs, 1994, p 2). This idea links the flowering of the essay in North America since Emerson to the nature of the land itself—its generosity, its diversity, its wildness, its invitation to adventure and inhabitation; and it links the American essay to a disposition toward discovery and possession that characterised the western expansion and settlement of North America. It suggests the rich idea that the land itself demanded, or at least encouraged, a literature of personal essay, such as has prospered there since the 1850s. Burroughs has the landscape-oriented essay particularly in mind, essays such as he writes himself, such as Thoreau wrote, such as James Galvin—whose book *The Meadow* Burroughs reviews in 'Landscapes of the alternate self'—writes. The essay is well made for witnessing such a land—in all its elusive, vast, various and dramatic reality. And the same set of landscapes that suggested the essay as an American form, suggested *themselves*, quite naturally, as its subject matter.

I wonder what it is about this land of mine, then, that has failed to inspire much essaying into it with words as stirring and sound as Thoreau's or Leopold's, Austin's or Galvin's, Lopez's or Williams'. Australia has not produced many essayists, fewer nature essayists and fewer still in whose writing the land itself seems to speak. Is it, perhaps, that our writers have gone into the landscapes of a big and arid island armed with too much of the literature of a small lush island (the United Kingdom, I mean, the motherland); too uncritically adopting the diction and sentimental imagination of English romantic poets (completely out of keeping with the place itself)? Have we gone with too little of the wonder and excitement, the openness to new kinds of country, that the American frontier awoke (admittedly after a couple of hundred years of settlement); too little of the autonomy and inventiveness of literary expression American writers demonstrated from Emerson and Whitman, Dickinson and Thoreau on?

Is it that the land itself here largely defeated what stirrings of originality arose, what temptations to wander with freshness into unfamiliar territory, to open one's eyes and witness without prejudice? For the land defied notions of the sublime—born in European landscapes, carried in European images, spoken in European (in Australia's case, English, of course, and a little German) languages—with which many writers went to it; it disappointed pastoral visions of rolling grassland, mighty river or gentle rill, towering mountain range, and delivered instead landscapes of impossible spareness and difficulty, ground of low relief, landforms restrained in their gestures, sclerophyll trees and heath and grasses, saltpans, dryness, weirdness of form. So far at odds, aesthetically and formally, was all this from the essentially urban, pastoral vision—with its conventions of diction, voice and style—of the English prose tradition in which our literature was so steeped, that the dissonance silenced for a long time the kind of intimate, mindful, musical literary engagement with landscapes that gave rise to the American nature writing tradition. It also seems to have discouraged much personal essay writing, much lyric nonfictional engagement with place, of the kind that Franklin Burroughs celebrates in the United States. Perhaps the land conquered in spirit those who went to conquer it. Its (apparent) silences silenced the essayists, anyway.

In any event, Australia does not have a strong tradition of essay writing in the Emersonian, the Montaignian, the Baconian, in any tradition. We have and have long had historians, journalists, polemicists, intellectuals, ratbags, apologists, pamphleteers, some of whom have written memorably—Bob Ellis, Germaine Greer, Robert Hughes, Don Watson, Manning Clarke, Geoffrey Blainey, Valerie Lawson, Robert Dessaix, Judith Wright. But we have had few essayists. One thinks of Walter Murdoch and Charmian Clift, Douglas Stewart and Marjorie Barnard, Jill Ker Conway, Helen Garner and David Malouf, one or two others. The list is too short to make a tradition, though it seems to be growing of late.

Perhaps the land suggested that reality here had no poetry in it; that the world of fact could only be engaged with practically; and that a literature of fact, likewise, could have no music or wonder in it. Much of what passes here for essay is oddly stiff and formal, utilitarian, didactic, rarely engaging, rarely even attempting to hold that ground where the essay lives—the middle-voiced, the reflective, the lyric, the wondering. And it is partly because we have not had essays—at least not the kind of lyric nonfiction that true essays are meant to be—that we have not had much place writing either.

If the land has defied and defeated the essay here so far, I can't believe it is forever. I think it is more likely we are only just now finding ways to witness this land, to know it and let it speak. We Europeans are only recently coming to sense the music in the earth here. So perhaps a literature of witness, of essay and other forms of literary nonfiction, may emerge with more force and character. And perhaps more of it will engage with the land—this is already happening.

Let us say, then, that the landscape of North America has itself begotten this literature of place—encouraging wonder and lyric, nurturing contemplation of the actual world, the solid earth by virtue of its demonstrable wildness, its generous scope and diversity, its great scale, its high drama and grandeur, its fecundity and pastoral plenitude in the east, and its spareness and toughness in the west. 'The first and greatest influence on nature writing, of course, is the land itself,' writes Thomas Lyon (Lyon, 2001, p 26). He means the American land, all its rich landscapes, in particular. '[T]he setting,' Lyon goes on, 'that F. Scott Fitzgerald described so memorably as "the fresh green breast of the new world" continues in mythic potency to generate profound allegiance and durable affirmation' (Lyon, 2001, p 35). After a time, a way of writing, if it is widely enough practised and read, sustains itself, like a healthy habitat. And so the literature, once begun, has gone on in America. After Thoreau came Muir and Burroughs, then Austin, then Leopold, then Abbey and Snyder and all the rest. But why did it take hold in the first place? Why were conditions right for its propagation and spread? Is there something about American culture, itself shaped, of course, by the encounter with American landscapes, that helped give rise to Thoreau and all his progeny? And, if so, what was so different about the natural and cultural history of Australian settlement that has so far stunted a literature of nature?

For all of the superficial similarities between the settlement of North America and Australia—the vast scale and essential wildness of both landmasses compared to the settled old world out of which the settlers came; the prior occupation by indigenous peoples; the extension of frontiers from east to west, led by pastoral and mining interests; the taming of wild lands in a spirit of capitalist enterprise—four factors make the two stories fundamentally different.

First is the matter of time. European settlement of North America began over two centuries before the British settlement of Australia—its roots reach back to premodern times, to an age of idealism before the Enlightenment. Britain colonised Australia from 1788. European life in this land has a history that does not run back past the Enlightenment. This has endowed Australian cultural life, particularly the apprehension of the land, with a much less romantic, a much more sceptical disposition. Matter had already been rendered unmysterious in settlers' imaginations before they ever beheld this place.

Second, there is this matter of cultural disposition or national temperament. North America was settled in a very different spirit than Australia. The one was settled in idealism; the other unwillingly and utterly pragmatically. America was an enterprise of conviction, an attempt at a new Jerusalem, from the puritan beginning; and American thought and governance have carried a spiritual note, oriented toward and fed by the new land, from the start. America was also a statement of idealistic nonconformity—it was, after all, puritans who founded her, turning their backs on all that England and the old world meant. It was founded in, imagined in, faith. Australia, by contrast, was always utterly a secular idea in the minds of its newcomers. Australia was a convict colony, founded in pragmatism and without any hope or ambition that a new kind of life, a new nation, might rise here. Australia was never the promised land, as America was. Australia was never a new beginning. It was not, until very late in the day, an idea that sang in anyone's imagination. It was just a gaol to which no one came by choice; a gaol that gave rise to a nation.

Australia was not the child of nonconforming faith, nor of rebellion. It was an enactment of Britain, an attempt by that power to rid herself of people it wished gone. It began as a place of exile and became an unchosen home for many who could not leave. Australia is an accidental nation, which spread herself, out of need (of food and water), out of a secular, imperial spirit, out of adventurism and toughminded entrepreneurialism, out of creeping national ambition, over a landmass that could not have been less in keeping with the aesthetic of those who built that nation and those who reflected upon its building.

That is the third, telling, difference: at settlement, there was not a plant or animal native to the new country—Australia, as it came to be called—that had any place in the European imagination, memory and culture with which Australia was settled. America had some strange things, it's true, but it had wolf and deer, elk and bear, squirrel and acorn, oak and chestnut, snow and ice, four differentiated seasons; it was in the same hemisphere, so Christmas fell in winter, Easter in spring. Australia spoke to its settlers in a bafflingly foreign language—kangaroo and wombat; emu and platypus; cockatoo and kookaburra; eucalypt and waratah; aridity and sclerophylly; restrained seasonal variation; and being south of the equator, Christmas fell in summer. It is impossible to overestimate the sheer otherness of this place. This part of the New World—it is in fact, geologically and anthropologically, the Old World, of course—offered no 'fresh green breast' to succour the newcomers. Australia, the land, greeted the scepticism, the pragmatism, the resentment and opportunism of its white settlers with a landscape of bewildering and unrelenting foreignness, of scratchiness, hardness and aridity. This was the antipodes, the underland, the diametric opposite of the known world. A hard place to love—unless, like the indigenous peoples (whose existence here, in spite of all their battles with them, the new settlers officially denied) your culture had grown from that antipodean earth. This was a land of denial, of irreconcilable oppositions.

There is a fourth thing that distinguishes the Australian experience from the American. For among these antipodean oppositions, from the very beginning, was that between the city and the bush. Australia, unlike America, or at least to a much greater degree, was urban from the start, more than it was agricultural. Its geography did not encourage or sustain a network of large inland agricultural communities; it bred a few large cities at its edges, centres of culture and commerce, connected as much to the European world over the seas as to the great land at their backs. An overwhelming preponderance of Australia's people has always lived in the urbs and suburbs, rather than on the land. One of the things that this has meant is that culture, including literature, has been identified with and coloured overwhelmingly by an urban sensibility. Literature has belonged much more to the city than to the country; urban and then suburban life shaped Australian literary diction to a large degree. And Australian cities were already large and sophisticated—provincial cities within a proud British Empire, as David Malouf reminds us in *A Spirit of Play*—before much of the country was very well known. City and bush have been, as I say, divorced from the beginning.

The literature of landscape we have made, therefore, has tended to take as its models for literary engagement with landscape the works of other citified cultures—it has written about landscape as Rome's writers did, as London's have. We have written pastoral, as George Seddon argues in his essay 'Farewell to Arcady' Seddon, 2003). A pastoral engagement with land is sentimental and escapist rather than realist and vernacular. In it, nature is a foreign place to which one escapes, when one can, the stress and grime and world-weariness of the city. Pastoral does not witness; it idealises or demonises; and it sounds, even at its best, unrooted in the soil of the places it evokes. The place escapes it. It is an idyll of landscape made in the city. This is the nature of the greater part of our writing about place. Until now.

In 1961, Judith Wright still saw a gulf yawning between the voices of the country and the words our writers had found for it. In her essay 'The Upside-Down Hut', Wright wrote:

> Australia is still, for us, not a country, but a state—or states—of mind. We do not speak from within her, but from outside: from the state of mind that describes, rather than expresses, its surroundings, or from a state of mind that imposes itself upon, rather than lives through, landscape ...

IN MULLIGAN AND HILL, 2001, P 96)

We have so little writing yet to make us fall in love with where we are, writing in which you feel the force of the character of these places themselves. European Australians have not, until recently, found an authentic language apt for this land. It is coming now. The land has, as Judith Wright once suggested, withheld itself from us. We have not earned its love yet. Its geographies are cryptic, weathered, sclerophyllous, laconic. They are old and evasive. You have to stay with them.

Australians have not—in literature anyway, particularly in the literature of fact—come home to these geographies. In Australian culture, home has continued, until only the last generation, to lie elsewhere than this soil: it has been in England, in Empire. We have stood here, farmed and cleared and built things here, but we have not grown native to the place. Our heads and hearts have been in the Northern Hemisphere. We took our models, looked for approval, found the syntax of our thoughts, the shape of our sentences, the grammar of our belonging, in England. This has been so in literature more than in any other artform. How do you find the words to render these places when the literature you value, most of the books you learn to read with, arise out of green fields, fens, canals and country lanes; out of Northern European weather and landscapes shaped by western civilisation for centuries? The time has come now, as it came in America with Dickinson, Whitman and Thoreau, for an authentic language to arise from these, our own, places; to name them, serve them, sing them as hundreds of indigenous languages and songs did for those long ages before English ever arrived. You may find it in some of the Australian pieces gathered here. Perhaps the land is withholding itself less now that we are learning, as that generation of North American writers did, to love her just as she is.

We have not been completely bereft in our literature, of course. Most of the work Judith Wright had in mind—the expression of country in literature—has been left to the poets. Australia has a rich poetic tradition, truly local in sound and spirit, and much of it turned to the land. We have had poets who have sung Australian places—Judith Wright, Douglas Stewart, David Campbell, Les Murray, Robert Gray among them.

And we have novelists in whose work the vernacular of Australian places speaks out authentically. This process is now in full swing in the work of Tim Winton, Thea Astley, Richard Flanagan and others. Australia began to sound out in our novels from about the 1930s. Frank Dalby Davison's *Man-Shy* (1931), the story of a red heifer running wild in the ranges of southern Queensland, is an outstanding example of a novel in which the country seems alive, its nature authentically expressed. It is a rare example of an Australian novel successfully imagined ecologically—it is written from the heifer's point of view, even from the point of view of the ranges and waterholes. (It may be no accident that Davison spent some time in his youth in North America, where he began his writing career.) In other novels, from 1930 onward, literature turns to landscape and increasingly sounds with its note, smells of its earth, notwithstanding an abiding pastoral note: Katharine Susannah Prichard's *Coonardoo* (1929); the stories, poems and essays of Mary Gilmore; the detective fiction and essays of Arthur Upfield; Xavier Herbert's novels of the Northern Territory, *Capricornia* (1938) and *Poor Fellow My Country* (1975); Miles Franklin's *All That Swagger* (1936); Kylie Tennant's novels of slum and country and her account of Diamond Head, *The Man on the Headland* (1971); Eleanor Dark's *The Timeless Land* trilogy (1941–1953); Patrick White's *Voss* (1957); Randolph Stow's *To The Islands* (1958); Donald Stuart's *The Driven* (1961); David Foster's *The Pure Land* (1974); David Malouf's *Johnno* (1975) and *The Conversations at Curlow Creek* (1997); Richard Flanagan's *The Death of a River Guide* (1994); Delia Falconer's *The Service of Clouds* (1997); Michael

Meehan's *The Salt of Broken Tears* (1999); Julia Leigh's *The Hunter* (1999); Alex Miller's *Journey to the Stone Country* (2002); strikingly in the novels of indigenous Australians Alexis Wright (*Plains of Promise*, 1997) and Kim Scott (*Benang*, 1999); and the novels of Murray Bail, Thea Astley and Tim Winton, particularly *Dirt Music* (2001), which is itself an exploration of the music of landscape.

And in nonfiction, which has a special role to play in witnessing place, the last ten years have seen a dawning of land-oriented writing—almost enough to suggest that our literature is opening to the Australian geographies, their cities and wilds. I am thinking of books by Peter Timms (*Making Nature*), Peter Read *(Returning to Nothing* and *Belonging)*, Ashley Hay (*Gum*), Roger McDonald (*The Tree in Changing Light*), Mark McKenna (*Looking for Blackfellas' Point*), Patrice Newell (*The Olive Grove*), Barry Hill (*The Rock*), Tim Flannery (his many books of natural history and exploration), George Seddon (his ongoing work on landscape, gardens, sense of place and literature, especially *Searching for the Snowy*), Tom Griffiths (*Forests of Ash*), Bill Lines (*Open Air*), Deborah Bird Rose (*Nourishing Terrains*), Paul Sinclair (*The Murray*), Kim Mahood (*Craft for a Dry Lake*), and Eric Rolls (his ongoing work). There is almost enough here to convince me that the long drought is over, that Australian landscapes have found their witnesses, have found expression in a literature of fact, in essay, that form so apt—in its rude and democratic, vernacular music—for country. Maybe Australia is getting itself a literary geography. I hope this collection shows that this is so; I hope it helps make it so; I hope it demonstrates that we are beginning these days to write the lyric essays of place that we need, that the Australian places need, more than anything.

V

Late in October 2000 a symposium of nature writers at Harvard University was drawing to a close. The first snow of the winter came down among the oak and maple of the garden as I finished telling a story of home. I told it, I suppose, to suggest an answer, learned from the place where I make my home, far from Harvard Yard, to the question we had been turning over for four days: 'What good is a literature of place, no matter how lovely, in the face of global ecological crisis?' What is the use, in other words, of nature writing?

The valleys I live by compose a landscape of loss. They bear witness to the slow work of rivers. For small rivers, with the pattern and persistence of prayer itself, have shaped the landscape of my home against all probability, working their way down through deep time in the places where this hard and ancient geology gives a little, changing its face through gentle work that now and then causes an entire cliff-face to tumble.

Grace comes like that, against all hope, a gift in return for prayerful work. It falls like snow, like cliff walls.

The writing I do is an act of love for a piece of ground. I am called to it, I'm sure, and am quite unable not to attempt it. By themselves the words I assemble will save nothing. They will not cool a warming earth, feed the hungry, unsalt the rivers, halt our gross consumption. They may do little even to save the places I love. I write without expectation. The writing is a practice in faith and hope and, mostly, love. My work is my prayer. It witnesses the gifts I live within and makes an offering in return.

Being present on the ground—in the way my writing requires—never fails to restore me to a state of wonder and wholeness, though; and it is that I mean to embody in my work; it is that I most want to arise in anyone who reads. I think that the things we will all need to do to defend the places of this earth must grow from love, first of all. Anger and grief should be bedded in places intimately known; and they should be schooled by the stories of endurance and eternal re-creation that go on there, daily. For this reason I want to come to know my place; and I want to give it voice. I want to persist in that work as the streams persist, hoping only to keep alive a love of earth and shape my country in the minds of a few readers. There is no saying what may then happen.

This collection, which arose as an idea out of that Harvard gathering, contains twenty-six places and hopes to shape them in the imaginations of its readers. While I think that many of the writers might share my hope for the work that such writing can effect, I must not impute my motives to anyone else. You must take them as you find them. Their source will lie in the places they describe; they have no other meaning than the resonance they leave you with. And you may go to them again and again, as you might to a place you hold close to your heart, and if you keep your eyes and ears open, your body alert, you will never find the terrain of the text the same twice.

There may be as many purposes at work here as there are voices, as many understandings of language and land as there are places. I hope that is so. I offer them all just because they are beautiful, truthful things. Each should differ as much from the other as each of its writers, and each of these places, differs. Life and creativity depend on diversity and, to some degree on discord, after all.

## VI

The day I gathered up these pieces and wrote the last words of introduction to them, a cold wind pressed down hard on the ridge, coming out of the southwest, and let slip a light snow upon us. The ground was too warm, after months of mild weather, and the winds too fierce for the snow to stay long. It comes four or five times a winter to this high country and its valleys. It comes on the skirts of cold fronts that sweep from west to east across this continent across the skies of July, August and September. West wind, arid cold air, the quieting of birds, the blueness of sky, the softness of light through windows, and the unsteady falling of snow: these are among the gestures of winter in this place on earth.

## REFERENCES

F Burroughs (1994) 'Landscapes of the Alternate Self', *Southern Review*, Winter 1994, vol. 50, issue 1, p 143.

T Lyon (2001) *This Incomparable Land*, Milkweed Editions, Minneapolis.

M Mulligan and S Hill (2001) *Ecological Pioneers*, Cambridge University Press, Melbourne.

G Seddon (2003) 'Farewell to Arcady: or Getting Off the Sheep's Back', in Dale (ed), *Terra Recognition: New Essays in Australian Studies*, University of Queensland Press, St Lucia.

# BARBARA BLACKMAN

## Symptoms of Place

I love weather: winter sunshine poured out like an oil slick on an ocean of chill air with the suspended odours of simmering bushes and basking rocks; fierce winds that rock the trees, combing the twigs and old nests out of their tresses, tug-o-warring with earth for their roots. And rain. 'You blind people,' said an indoor wife, 'you are all rain addicts.' And we are. Her husband has built himself a little rain house, roofed with a patchwork of iron, thatch and plastic, a percussive theme and variations. The blanketing of rain on sleep. The walling in of rainforest in heavy deluge like Noah tight in his tent lest his sons see him in liquor. The door of the earth held open by rain emitting odours pungent as from a bakery—parched earth hiccuping in the waters, desiccated turds moistening into sod. The first few staccato drops of rain, an almost inaudible petit point, then the celebration of its myriads of separate soundings, until the last shake of it, last leap spill and gutter leak of it. The tropic rain incessant, ever forever increasing in density, becoming mantra, can drown the imagination until only dreams surface from a submerging of senses like sleep. Yes, we are all addicts.

For the first twenty or thirty years I could see, somewhat. After that I have been on automatic. I 'went blind' not by a sudden dropping of a curtain but by slow osmosis, a gradual substitution of what is remembered for what is seen, a seeing with the inner eye rather than the outer, finding it difficult, or unnecessary, to distinguish between the two, juxtaposing memory and image. For me, place, decomposed of visual substance, is left fallow to fructify again with intimations from all other senses, some not easily imagined by those whose perceptions depend so much on sight: as in translation of poetry, the original words divest their attaching atmospheres to be released into the different atmospheres of another language.

Kenneth Clarke, writing about imaging, landscape into art, observes that painters did not see the landscape as having any significance until well into the eighteenth century. Mountains threatened, land evoked cultivation, the rest was backdrop rock. As soon as mountains were climbed, pyranee by pyranee, and passes found, alp by alp, landscape became visible and in that sense man-made with meaning, painted as picturesque: a familiarizing of both wild and formal gardens.

It is much the same for growing children. They look outside the door to see if father is coming or if they will need a rain coat, not to be filled with the beauty of the hills or the light on wet grass. Colette, in a vignette 'Look,' tells how she tried to show a two-year-old child a beautiful garden, the 'pretty flower' and the 'colorful butterfly'. But the child had new shoes and could see nothing but the shoes. Miracle by miracle, footstep by footstep, she was looking at her shoes.

In adult life it is the familiar—things seen so often that they are not seen at all—that resides in the inner eye, images of place that become the unconscious carriers of sentiment, evoking vaster memory. The inner eye inflates recall with all that is more than inventory, with anecdotes of feeling, so the childhood home revisited is deceptively smaller as is the corpse of a loved one in the coffin.

It is a dreamtime pleasure of mine to visit the houses in which I have lived, enter like a ghost and ramble upstairs and down, through rooms, doorways now walled up, inhale the odours of my own era in that house, feel my younger self visited by the sweetness of scenes recaptured, darkened by forebodings that the future has revealed. My losses and longings: angel presences carry that load—not 'anger' but 'angel.' This ghost self retraces the places of unknowing with the grace of now-knowing. I pull out the drawer in the cupboard beside the stove, feel its exact weight, smell its well-used cutlery, hear inherent a child's 'Mummy' close at hand question. I lie awake again in the bed of a friend's house, listening for her morning movements in the kitchen to gauge my time of appearance, prick ears again to that house's particular celebration of sleepless nights, its stitch-scratch of clock and creak-sigh of stair, its cedar ether odour. I enter the large dining room of my teen years. My body estimates exactly the number of paces to far table, the weight of chair pulled out, the creamy smoothness of starched tablecloth, the measured unrolling of serviette from silver ring.

Thus comes the recollection of some holiday afternoons when I sat with the chain-smoking landlady at her table outside the kitchen, rubbing on the metal-breathed misty polish and buffing softly with old rags of sheeting the battalion of forks and spoons, seeing that mysterious shrunken face of mine in the bowl of every well shone spoon.

That particular house of adolescent years, that house of happy self, recurs often in my dreams, the metaphor of starting out afresh. Once recently, enjoying a reverie upon it, I realized with a certain alarm that I could no longer remember whether the stove in the kitchen in that high-at-the-back wooden house was a woodfire stove. I could not picture any woodstack below, hear any chopping. I was appalled, like those who already feel one month after a mother's death that they can no longer see her face or hear her voice. I telephoned a friend left from my youth of that time. He assured me that it was a woodfire stove, that, as I had not been the one to carry in the wood, I had no memory of it to recall. I only remembered seeing the baked dinners coming out from the oven and our relay stirring of the Christmas pudding. His assurance mended the breach in my wall: security restored.

Actual displacement is not in itself discomforting. In my travels I have slept up to fourteen nights in a row in fourteen different beds, fourteen awakenings to blankness, each place slowly reconstructed out of last night's memory. When the awakening precedes the act of reconstruction, there is a delicious moment of self-uncertainty, a question and answer of one's whereabouts; the mis en page of oneself to be dredged up from the refraction of deep sea sleep. The unexpected touch of a leftside wall, a spurt of certain half-remembered unfamiliar smell, the fingering of bed cover; down and across clues gathered. Then, with the joy of a child finding a lost treasure, one finds oneself properly in place after all.

I imagine my surroundings like any set designer his stage from the script he reads. My visible memories are flexible. Like the rock backdrops in the early paintings, something symbolic will do. I have as good a Heathcliff, as good an Antarctic as any other reader. Colours, shapes, textures, perspectives are my deck of cards shuffled soft, and I am dexterous at card tricks. But without any kind of camera in my eye I am often myself tricked.

'I think of her,' says a friend of my adult life, 'as someone living anchored offshore.' The land has different dimensions than the sea; is sure-footed, firm under step, stays still, keeps space. The sea is full of change and misdirection, uncertain depths and latitudes of landfall and horizon that give clues and hide conclusions. Those who live sure-footed on a swaying deck lubber about conspicuous on the solid earth, conspicuous and suspect, drinkers of strange libations.

Sometimes, offshore, I am no more than an island the size of my feet, seas of space around me, drowns of unknowing. On what perilous edge does Gloucester stand? In which direction is the nearest stepping stone, the flutter of a nearby voice, touchstone of a recognizable solid, to give me bearings. Generally I proceed one hand for mapping, one for carrying. One time, daring to use both hands for carrying plate and cup out to where friends were sitting around the verandah table, I got disorientated. 'Lost table, lost chair,' I proclaimed. 'But found floor—' said the friend who steered me on. We are all comic characters in one another's scenarios. How they course when the lights go out, when the Circe of darkness turns them all to staggering swine, hands to cloven searching. Then, in the dark, I can cook their dinner for them, put out the rubbish and feed the cat as well. Things for their part have stayed in place, their touch and texture, bulk and balance, the same as when they could be seen. 'God gave us all these other senses,' I say. 'But you lot didn't pick up the users' guide.'

These other senses that befriend can also betray. Sometimes, up North, finding crocless streams flowing between and over rocks, we would horizontalize and, and still wearing shoes and clothes, swim leisurely as a walk, for quite some distance, often leaving mouth open to take in, fish-like, the sweet clear fresh water, then alight and lay ourselves out to dry. But bathing just a little beyond the breakers, I have lost the nearness of horizon, slope towards beach, have rotated out of depth, floundering until sign was found, the voices of children in shallow water.

I am at home with gravity on earth or buoyancy in waters, but the above and below of them dispossess me. Depths and heights dismay and dislocate. The first time, at nine, climbing the highest mango tree in the back yard, I felt stricken, seized by terror, terror of a fear, a desire, to fall, so that the tree was too insubstantial to hold me. I cried. I hollered. Help came. Schoolgirl friends threw my hat down into the struts of a bridge and dared me to climb down after it. I died a little. Climbing round the inside of the dome of the Duomo, I broke out in fever. Cajoled into spiralling up the outside steps of the Tower of Pisa, I had to cling with coward's dread and descend on all fours. At Coober Pedy, invited to tour down into the underground, I was so seduced by the sweet soporific aroma that I felt my limbs dissolve, as one drugged for a live burial. People, seeing how white I had gone, ushered me above. I was gripped and followed by my younger Aboriginal friend, feeling she had gone white herself. Surfaced on ground under safe sky, we found ourselves close to a sweet shop selling licorice. We blackened up with that.

Sometimes the land itself uplifted into mountain becomes a sacred place, an eternity in time, so that climbing it becomes a pilgrimage: Delphi for instance. A few years ago in early summer I went up Gulluga, understood by its Aboriginal tribespeople, welcoming to those who come now. A part-Aboriginal woman, well known and loved by many, had died a fortnight before and some sixty of us had come to weep for her. A straggle of women, Aborigines and whities wearing red head bands, set out from a siding behind the village store. First a dirt road, then ascending on gravel, then sharper stones, pasture left behind. Strata of birdsong. Road meandering in bigger rock forms. Trees dwindled. Slowing, sweating in the heat of the day. Occasional small pools in which we splashed our faces. Overshirts removed and tied around waists. Stride steady, longer, more deliberate, path steepening. Single track. It took about two hours to reach the flat patch before the steeper path to the summit. Here we stopped, sat quiet on the logs dragged up beside a plank table, from this platform we scrambled down and down over elephants of rock and sliding shale to where certain massive rock forms thrust up before a cleft of escarpment. Standing stones, Woman stones. We each stood leaning into the stones, feeling the heat-held vigour of them, the ancient patience beyond human sorrow. Space, sky, silence.

Rattling sound of stones giving way to ascending speechless figures. As afternoon cooled we began the slow descent, a long and tranquil coming down. The wonder of it was that none of us felt tired, strained, had any thirst. Spirits had lifted us up and carried us down; lingered with us. Round the camp fire that evening there was quiet song but no one felt hungry. We went to such oceanic sleep in our tents beside the sea.

In the late years of my life I have preferred to take my place in the country. Alone on my home ground, stick in hand, I walk my dirt road of known footfall, over the creek and up the hill, finding my self in the landscape. I am swept up into the scent of a flowering tree, grounded by the squelch and stench of cow pad clods, described in the arc of bird flight, distance by the grizzle and groan of chain saw paddocks away. I play about in the landscape, interrogating fallen branch and mossy rock, snapping sticks for kindling, sitting in earshot of creek running under culvert, its monotony changing undertone to keep pace with my thoughts.

When the little girl lived here, I would often go up the hill to meet her from the school bus, making a certain hoot-owl-hoot cry. When she came within earshot she began to run towards me. 'Here come the ponies,' I would call and catch her in my arms. Together we would find crystals in the gravel, funny animal figures in twigs, sometimes a bone man to start a story with. We looked for things beginning with 'g' one day, 'p' another. At the creek she would take off school bag and hat, set them on a flat stone, while she bent to splash her face and hands—'to be nice and fresh for coming home to Mum and Dad.'

There are times I have sat sodden with sadness beside the waterfall until it righted me and I heard it throb like Bach; times I have sat indolent among friends at midnight with all the infinite activities of the bush under moonlight, alive with the cumulous secret sounds of preying, slithering, seeding, scuffling, subsiding earth and cracking twig. I tried to sleep on a verandah bench alone in the beauty of one March night, in the ecstasy of the ginger lilies' brief flowering. But the cacophony of these discordant minute busy nocturnal happenings kept me awake. I crept upstairs to my usual place and there in lavendered sheets beside the sandalwood drawer I descended into sleep as happy in my dreams as any little creature with its prey.

# JOHN CAMERON

# Beneath Capital Hill:
# The Unconformities of Place and Self

The word place is best applied to those fragments of human environments where meanings, activities and a specific landscape are all implicated and enfolded by each other.

EDWARD RELPH

I remember my delight as a teenage rockhound growing up in Canberra when a new roadcut was established for State Circle, exposing the Capital Hill unconformity. The local geological society organised a visit to the site to celebrate the occasion, and I stood trying to understand that I was looking at a line that represented a gap in geological time, that divided rocks that dipped at such different angles from each other. The unconformity was formed when a layer of mud was deposited under the sea and compacted and heated to form the State Circle Slate around 440 million years ago. It was then raised up above the surface of the sea and eroded. About ten million years later, it sank down again below the surface of the sea and a layer of sand was deposited on top of it, but not parallel with, not on the same inclination or surface as the original sediments. These were later compacted to form the Camp Hill Sandstone (Abell, 1991). It's called an unconformity because the sandstone does not rest conformably on the slate.

The Capital Hill unconformity interests me physically and metaphorically. Looking at the unconformity in the roadcut you cannot tell that there is a gap of 10 million years between the time that the State Circle Slate was formed and the Camp Hill Sandstone directly above it was formed. You are looking at a line that records a hiatus in what appears to be a continuous sequence of rocks. You can see the unconformity because the angle of repose of the two formations of sediments is quite dramatically different. When I look back on the time I first witnessed it, I not only see the exposure of the unconformity as marking a period in my life, I also see it as metaphorical of the many layers underlying the place called Canberra; some of these layers do not rest in conformity with the others. The same can be said for the layers within my psyche.

My experience of growing up in Canberra in the 1950s and 1960s was a tale of two hills. Capital Hill was then the site of an old hostel that served as the living quarters for single men working on the many building projects around Canberra in those boom years. My best friend Alan and I were fascinated by the Hill as a place of danger. The inhabitants were dangerous, particularly on Friday and Saturday nights—drunken men from strange countries behaving unpredictably. Poking around the back of the hostels during the weekends we'd find bottles of strange substances, strange-looking magazines, strange photographs of women in them. It seemed to be everything that the rest of Canberra was not—exotic, risky, a hint of the foreign that was so different from the sanitised foreignness of the embassies that dotted the neighbourhood.

It was also a place where we could give vent to our destructive impulses. We fashioned our own hand-made catapults from the forks of small trees cut for the purpose on Capital Hill. Constructed with aeroplane rubber and a leather pouch, they were capable of launching a pebble at a fearsome velocity. We set up some of those exotic bottles on rocks for target practice and (I'm now ashamed to say) we progressed to anything that moved as a target, although we were seldom successful in bringing down the small birds and lizards that caught our attention. We also cut down several large trees each year for the centre-pole and supports for a huge bonfire around which the entire neighbourhood's garden rubbish was collected. The highlight of November was Bonfire Night when all of the families gathered around the immense blaze that quickly consumed the straw Guy Fawkes set up on the centre-pole. Then the fireworks started—we had spent our year's savings on Double Rockets, Double Bungers, strings of Tom Thumbs, Mount Vesuvius's and all the other now illegal boyhood delights.

The second hill of my childhood was Red Hill, which I usually visited with my younger brother and sister. Although I must have gone to Capital Hill hundreds of times with Alan, I don't ever recall his accompanying us to Red Hill. Up there, we usually headed for our favourite haunt, which we called Lunchtime Log. Mum would make us sandwiches and we'd hike up to the log, which was a long way for short legs, but in reality was probably no more than a kilometre from where we lived. We'd sit up on the fallen log and watch the ants burrowing their way below it, and enter into an imaginary world. The creatures that lived in the fascinating and scary holes around the log became a strange fusion of what we knew about the native fauna and the magical creatures that we read about from the fantasy fiction that my sister and I were devouring at the time, such as the Magic Faraway Tree and the *Tales of Narnia*.

During our semi-regular visits, the place became infused with a combination of quiet observation of the real animals that lived there and imaginative invention of the fantasy creatures that might also dwell there. I wouldn't have dreamed of chopping down a tree on Red Hill, and I never took my catapult along. My recollection of those expeditions to Lunchtime Log stand in very stark contrast with the rampages that Alan and I got up to on Capital Hill, occurring as they did over the same five year period. Two sets of childhood experiences, repeated many, many times, in the years before adolescence, two ways of being, that just sit there within my psyche, resting unconformably, one on top of the other, coexisting in a strange way.

I have always been fascinated by the natural sciences. One of my first childhood memories is of pressing my nose up against the window on a cold spring morning watching the bees that had arrived for Spring. I was amazed at their dance backwards and forwards to the wisteria that fringed the window—neither direct nor random but wonderfully elaborate. That delight in the natural world extended to the rocks. On our family picnics to what was then called Rock Valley in Tidbinbilla, we were sometimes accompanied by a retired professor of the natural sciences. Prof Baas-Becking would point out to us the life on the rocks, the lichen, and the life within the rocks, the insects that lived in the crevices. He also taught us to look at the granite outcrops themselves, to appreciate their form as shapes as well as to think about why they were shaped into domed tors. When I took geology in high school, we went on field trips including a return visit to the celebrated Capital Hill unconformity. Out in the field I had two contrasting responses to the rocks that stayed with me in my training and work as a field geologist. One response was a growing understanding of the science of geology, what it was that I was actually looking at in geomorphological and geochemical terms. There was a great intellectual challenge in attempting to deduce hundreds of millions of years of the geological history of a place from the weathered and patchy outcrops of rocks on the surface. The other response was pleasure in being with the rocks themselves, a sensed appreciation of the form and feel of them in their pure physicality, regardless of how old they were or how they were formed.

These two ways of appreciating the rocks of the world sat easily with each other at first, but rested increasingly unconformably with each other as the years progressed. Ten years after graduating as a geologist (and gathering a PhD in applied economics along the way) I found myself in charge of a geological exploration site in an isolated part of the Rocky Mountains in Montana. On a day I'll never forget, I drove my pickup truck behind a bulldozer that was gouging its way up a narrow old track, felling the fir and aspen trees that crowded the sides. I had spent the summer prospecting for gold and silver in this high country, filling cloth sample bags with soil and rock chips gathered from months of geological fieldwork. After months of poor assay results, I had been amazed to receive news of enough precious metal values to justify exploration drilling, and had arranged for a bulldozer to cut the track up to the drill site.

Towards the top, the 'dozer carved into a small grassy hillock. It happened to be the place where I had sat and eaten my lunch in the expansive mountain setting dozens of times in the past months. From that spot I had gazed up to the higher bluffs, and down to the plains; an in-between place of silence punctuated only by the wind sighing through the conifers and by the squeak of the marmot. Now it was reduced to a roadside marker, painfully signifying to me what had been there, and what I had wrought.

I drove back to my cabin that night feeling like a criminal. The damage done by the 'dozer in widening and extending the track was insignificant compared with what would happen if the drilling were successful and an open-pit mine were developed on site. I was distraught, feeling that I had betrayed the mountain country that I had come to know so intimately. I recognised that I could no longer hold contain two discordant impulses within myself—tremendous intellectual excitement of the quest for gold and silver, and love of the Rocky Mountains the way they were. The resulting decision to leave a career in geology and turn towards environmental studies is still echoing through my life today.

Meanwhile, back in Canberra, they were remaking Capital Hill. All the hostels were removed, the entire vegetation and soil beneath it was removed.

Perhaps some of the bush still bore the scars of my previous activities. A reconstituted Capital Hill was put back on top of a huge building, the new Parliament House. These days, when I drive towards Capital Hill from the south, and see an immaculate curved green hill topped with a massive flagpole, I recall the scruffy and dangerous Capital Hill that I used to know. I do appreciate the intention of the designers that the new Parliament House not dominate the landscape and that it appears to be part of the hill. That is a symbolically significant gesture that the centre of our political culture appear to be held within the contours of the land rather than rising dominantly above it.

Of course, it's not the original Capital Hill that Parliament House is part of, it's a manufactured Capital Hill. All that lawn on the top leading up to the flagpole is part of a new Capital Hill that rests unconformably on the earlier Capital Hill that still exists within my memory. I still feel the ghosts of the former Capital Hill, the inhabitants of the hostel, the bushland bearing the scars of my activities there, who I was then, with my catapult and axe. That in turn carries the reminder of my Red Hill self, with a head full of fantasies from Olde England and an eye for the local fauna.

Interestingly, the construction for the new building uncovered an even greater degree of unconformity than is revealed in the State Circle roadcut: 'Locally, there was considerable uplift and erosion. An angle of discordance of about 60 degrees was exposed in the excavations for the new Parliament House' (Abell, 1991). The heart of Capital Hill itself apparently contains the greatest degree of discordance in any known exposure of the unconformity, which is of geological curiosity as well as metaphorical significance.

In the late 1980s I returned to Capital Hill in a new guise, having made my life change to environmental work. After consulting for a US conservation organisation I decided to return to Australia and commenced work with the Australian Conservation Foundation (ACF). Since their need was for an applied economist to consider alternative strategies to the current policy of clear-felling all the native forests, I commenced a study of forestry and eucalypt plantations that led to the publication of a major report in 1988. Because the report was released at a time when green electoral power at the Federal level was at its height, there was enormous government interest in the report. I found myself involved in months of intensive lobbying and meetings at Parliament House with Ministers and their staff, as well as in departmental offices and public forums elsewhere in Canberra. It culminated in my making a presentation to Federal Cabinet on the economic and conservation significance of the ACF's proposed policies. Deep in the heart of Capital Hill, I was in an entirely different world than I had ever experienced before. The sense of power was palpable. It was dizzying to find myself in the Cabinet Room presenting my analyses to the Bob Hawke and his gathered Ministers. I did understand that it was not the appeal of my ideas themselves, but the perceived electoral appeal of embracing forestry conservation that was engaging the government leaders. Nonetheless, I emerged from the Cabinet Room and subsequent press conference in a dazed and intoxicated state.

As the tumult subsided, I still made occasional visits to Parliament House from my base in the Sydney offices of the ACF to follow up the forestry proposals. I found myself spending quite a bit of time waiting outside of offices, eating in the cafeteria and taking in my surroundings. I was fortunate to have some conversations with parliamentarians who were observing the phenomenon of daily life in Parliament House with some detachment. Ted Mack, the independent MP from North Sydney, commented that the House was like a self-contained city. The committee structure and administrative arrangements, even for an Independent, could be all consuming. He found the place distressingly cut off from the rest of Canberra, let alone from the rest of Australia. I left Parliament House on some of those days wondering about the relationship between the intense political activity and the lives of ordinary Canberrans, ordinary Australians. I also wondered about the context of what was occurring in the bowels of Capital Hill and any larger sense of the place.

I learned that there were groups of workers and some parliamentarians who were holding regular meditation sessions in one of the thousands of meeting rooms in the building. There were people actively working to 'raise the energy' of the place, there were visitors such as Tibetan monks who came for several days to do sand paintings in the central foyer. Slowly, as the drug of being in the governmental and media spotlight wore off, I began to see that there was a sub-current of a different form of power manifesting itself in Parliament House. I don't know if these meditation and consciousness-raising sessions are continuing, but I wonder how those two forms of power can coexist. I suspect that they are resting quite unconformably on each other in the heart of Capital Hill.

Other stories of Capital Hill are emerging. I was fascinated by the recent article in the *Canberra Times* that refers to the way in which the stars of the Southern Cross constellation map onto the main features of Canberra as identified in the original plans of Walter Burley Griffin and Marion Mahony. Griffin and Mahony identified a number of central topographic features of

Canberra as places representing certain elements of Canberra, the new capital city, which would be focal points for the architectural design. It is noteworthy how closely a scaled-up overlay of the Southern Cross matches the features of Mahony and Griffin's plan, and of course, Capital Hill is one of these places. The overlap can be interpreted in many ways; from intriguing coincidence to an indication of the intuitive depth of Mahony and Griffin's understanding of power configurations in Canberra, to the recurrence of archetypal patterns of significance at all levels of material reality. Whatever the interpretation, it is another view of the power that is manifesting itself in Capital Hill.

When I was growing up I was completely unaware of the existence of the Ngunnawal people in the Canberra region. The prevailing view was that Aboriginal people lived elsewhere, lived outback, somewhere back of Bourke or in Central Australia. I regret that the people of Canberra in the 1950s and 1960s were largely unaware that there were descendants of the original indigenous inhabitants living in the region who had valuable things to say about Canberra and the way in which a life in the place might be pursued. I now know that Ngunnawal people are a presence in Canberra and always have been. At least they are now acknowledged a little more openly than when I was a boy but not being a resident of Canberra I can't say how full this acknowledgment is.

Doubtless there is a Ngunnawal Dreaming story that includes Capital Hill. I don't know what that story is, and I don't know whether it is still being sung. If it is now missing, as so sadly many of the place stories and myths of the indigenous people in eastern Australia are, then it is another major unconformity underlying Capital Hill. That gap, the missing tens of thousands of years that are no longer represented, is essential to a full understanding of what Capital Hill, the place is and was. No doubt it had, or has, a Ngunnawal name that is more resonant than 'Capital Hill'. Even if parts of the story are still known, much material has been eroded away in the 200 years since the first European settlers came to the Monaro Plains. It may still be possible to follow the course of that erosion to find some of the missing stories and ways of being, and to re-imagine our way collectively into another way of being in Canberra in which the many cultures of Canberra can rest more conformably with each other. I can only hope that the impressive mosaic in front of the main entrance and the abundant works of Aboriginal art throughout Parliament House are being accompanied by an increasing presence of local Aboriginal people there.

Capital Hill is many places, Canberra is many places, and the layers of those places often rest in unconformity with each other. Equally, there are many places within myself lying unconformably, such as my 'Capital Hill self' and my 'Red Hill self'. In terms of the quotation from Edward Relph that begins this essay, these two Canberran hills, the activities I engaged in, and the meanings I gave to them, then and now, are all implicated and enfolded by each other.

The process of moving towards a place responsive society, as I have written elsewhere (Cameron 2001), is a very significant intercultural project for contemporary Australians of all backgrounds to embark upon. The potential is for the love of place to bring about a more heartfelt revolution in the way in which we treat our ravaged natural environment. Love of place can motivate a care for country that expresses itself in a lighter ecological footprint than the one at the moment that is stripping bare our soils and despoiling our rivers. Love of place can be the basis of real dialogue between the first peoples of these countries and the many settler cultures that have come after. It could provide a practical expression of reconciliation, in deed as well as word. However, the many layers within ourselves, within our cultures, within our places, do not rest easy with each other.

There are many unconformities to be acknowledged, many barriers to the potential for the place responsive society, and recognition of these has to occur at all levels. I acknowledge and am still coming to terms with the destructive, uncaring, Capital Hill part of myself. I now recognise and value the boy who was drawn to the wildness of the Hill and the strangeness of its inhabitants in a bland city that at the time was almost entirely populated by middle-class Whites. At the same time, I am concerned that I could behave in a callous and brutal way towards the bird and animal life in one place, yet with sensitivity and awareness in another without any apparent connection between the two ways of being. I divided off compartments of myself with no dialogue between them so that I could more comfortably embark upon the adventure of life without dealing with the inner contradictions. It took the destruction of a place that I had come to love in the Rocky Mountains to bring me to my senses.

At the collective level there are many structures in society that keep us divided off from each other, economically, socially and politically. We are a divided country and this shows up no more strongly than in the relationship between Aboriginal and other Australians. Until we deal with the compartmentalisation in society that turns different minority cultures into the 'Other' that is to be marginalised, discriminated against or romanticised, the walls of the compartments will remain intact and the layers of our society will continue to rest unconformably against each other. A divided society of divided individuals cannot hope to lead sustainable lives and to treat each other, our fellow species and the land itself in a just and respectful fashion. It is not a matter of doing away with difference, but allowing the different parts to enter into real dialogue.

There are many layers to Capital Hill, the place that exists in my psyche in as complex a fashion as it exists in a particular part of Canberra. It has been made over into a grass-covered model of its original, rough, scrubby and dangerous self. Much personal and political work needs to be done in order to bring the different parts of Capital Hill to life so that the political manoeuvring in Parliament House can exist congruently alongside a Ngunnawal Dreaming story of the place and the echoes of its non-Aboriginal history. Beginnings have been made but the unconformities need to be brought to the surface within ourselves, between the cultures and in the land itself. Only then can the place-making, in Relph's sense of mutually enfolded meanings, actions and land, truly occur in Canberra.

## REFERENCES

R Abell (1991) *The Geology of Canberra*, Bureau of Mineral Resources Bulletin 233. AGPS, Canberra.

J Cameron (2001) 'Place, Belonging and Ecopolitics: The Debate over the Place-Responsive Society', *Ecopolitics: Thought and Action*, vol. 2, pp. 18-34.

E Relph (1992) 'Modernity and the Reclamation of Place' in D Seamon, ed, *Dwelling, Seeing and Designing*, SUNY Press, New York, pp. 25-40.

# CHARMIAN
# CLIFT

## The Centre

If you come to the Centre, as I did, by air from Adelaide, the surprise of it is infinitely more surprising than you are prepared for, even though you have prepared yourself by much industrious homework on the geology of the place, its flora and fauna, climate, characters, myths, legends, yarns and tall tales.

You get there already visually bruised and aching, tender in the sensibilities with the effort of belief in the awful innocence of your country so exposed to your inspection, drinking cold beer and eating more airline chicken and advancing your watch a half-hour. You are a little ashamed and uneasy, as though you have taken an unfair advantage, and you think of the explorers crawling like maddened lice across that vast wrinkled anatomy, crazed by thirst and dreams and the radiantly tender pink blush on beckoning hills. From twenty thousand feet the hills are like fat squishy tumours, or dried-out scabby ones. Benign compared with the incurable acid-wound of Lake Eyre, steaming corrosive white and vitriolic after placid Torrens, where, all unknowing, Swift set the longitude and latitude of Lilliput. Gulliver sprawls defenceless for your microscopic examination. Pitted sores. Dried-out capillaries of watercourses. Culture slides of viridian clotting thick creamy yellow. Wind ridges raised like old scars, and beyond them the even, arid serrations of the Simpson Desert, dead tissue, beyond regeneration.

And yet, the tenderness of the pinks, the soft glow of the reds, the dulcet beige, and violet seeping in. The landscape, after all, is alluring beyond reason. Voluptuous, even. You could abandon yourself to it and die in a dream, like those savages of whom Kafka speaks, who have so great a longing for death that they do not even abandon themselves, but fall in the sand and never get up again. Such unearthly beauty, one knows—and still yearns—is fatal. It is a landscape for saints and mystics and madmen.

And after that the vibrant shock of being terrestrial again, bucketing in toward the Alice in a Landrover with the air singing clear and thin and sweet and your lap filled with the strange flat-podded pink flowers that are clumped beside the road and under the ghost gums and the wattle. You could not have foreseen that, nor, with all your homework on the history and geology of the MacDonnell Ranges, could you have foreseen the lilac beyond the red and the gold, floating in a boundless clarity where perspective is meaningless. You accept that the mountains are as old as the convulsions of the earth. They had suffered a sea-change before life crawled on the land. They were old, very old already, when life was new. They were worn down and weathered before such as we were even heralded by creeping things. To see them is to know that they could not possibly be less ancient than that. A thousand million years at least it takes to make something so rich and strange, so profound, so unbearably potent with dreams.

It takes less time to make an Alice. Contemporary Alice, that is. They say it was different before the tourist boom. Old hands mourn, bitterly. It was nearly evening when we reached it, and the mountains were moving in close about hotels and motels and gem shops and rock shops, banks, garages, milk bars, tourist agencies, boutiques, galleries and the Old Timers' Home. Is it Persian lilac that lines the main street? The scent in the evening air is enough to bowl you over. Fronded trees sparking delicately with little starry clusters, and between them a desecration of imbecile Op lighting, great lozenges of red and blue and green and yellow clownishly colouring the tourists stepping eager for bargains, souvenirs, and drinks before dinner. And through the tourists, the lilac-scented air, the hectic funfair illumination, the slow lurching drift and black shadow-weave of the disinherited, stripped of ancient dignity, degraded, subservient, aimlessly drunk on a Friday night.

A lady inheritor, sensible in drip-dry, shoulder-bag bulging—rocks? gems? berry necklaces? mission grass-weaving? bad bark paintings—postcards poised ready for the slot, pounces on a tall black trio teetering in the most curiously graceful progression. Cheap boomerangs, she wants. The real thing.

Not the junk in the tourist shops. She is loud and articulate. Imperious. (I think of the last Afghan and the last camel train, also imperious, stepping out slow slow from the Alice and disappearing into the vast distance.) The black trio, thus accosted, are soft, slurred, incomprehensible and perhaps uncomprehending. They sway away and back again, surprisingly regrouped under the ghastly green of the street light, awaiting the lady's exasperated dismissal. Two barefooted women scuttle under the Persian lilac and across the street to their men on the opposite corner. They are high in the haunches, long in the heels. Their legs are like thin crumpled brown ribbons flying, their hair pale straw. Drysdale has drawn them often and compassionately, by tin huts and shanties, patient on the street corner, movement arrested, patiently waiting as if waiting was an end in itself.

But the hotel bar is air-conditioned, clean, contemporary, anonymous. Around the small plastic-topped tables there are tourists in holiday gear and every degree of age and sunburn. The girls behind the bar—and this is to be true of most hotels, motels and restaurants in the Centre—are European or from the south. Girls on a working holiday. Transient population. But there is to be a cattle sale the next day, and among the clean white shirts ranked against the bar there are some of the men who brought the cattle in, so authentically themselves in jeans and battered drovers' hats, so weathered, leathered, creased and sun-cured, so thirsty, exuberant, excited and vocal that you can't quite believe in them, not even when one of them takes a guitar that is leaning against the bar and they all begin to sing. Cattle songs. Outback songs. Melancholy or ironic. They are probably film extras, togged up for another cheap outback drama. And the black one, confidently harmonising, must be in make-up, because he cannot possibly be of the same race as the frieze moving on the other side of the plate glass, although the frieze is also costumed in jeans and slouch hats, but out of step and coordination, somehow terribly vulnerable. Occasionally a figure detaches and pastes itself against the plate glass, looking in.

'The Aryans,' one of my companions says. 'Looking at the Huns and wondering whatever happened.'

So this is the Alice. And the Alice is thriving and putting on sophistication, although a little uneasily, like finery to which it is not yet accustomed. Selfishly, I am glad of the comfort of the new motel where our working party makes base. Glad of the good bed, the air-conditioning, the hot water, the private shower, the swimming pool, the excellent food and wine and service in the restaurant. It is good enough to satisfy the most fastidious traveller. In the days ahead we are going to see many exciting places, talk with many unique people. There will be much discussion and instruction on the Question. The Problem. Let them die out. Assimilate them. Put them on reserves. Forget them. Wait. Keep out the do-gooders. And in all our comings and goings, reeling, all of us, with the revelation of wonders, I will be haunted by that daily frieze impasted on banks and tourist agencies and galleries and gem shops and rock shops. Patient. Waiting. Moving, if at all, from one side of the street to the other. The women and girls squatting in ripply black silk circles around groomed trees in a groomed park. Looking on.

I want to say, 'I'm sorry.' Apologise. Absolve myself. I want to tell them that I was not one of those maddened lice of explorers crawling to the discovery of their magic tribal place. I did not personally dispossess them of the ranges and the gorges and the waterholes and the caves where the Huns leave beer cans now, and crumpled paper tissues, and dubious identities chipped into the ancient rock. I did not personally disinherit them of the most sophisticated, ethereal concept of origin that ever a people dreamed. Their blood, for all I know, might be bluer than our heaven.

But here in the thriving Alice the guilt hurts intolerably. What are the dreaming people dreaming now?

# JAMES
# GALVIN

## The Real World

The real world goes like this: The Neversummer Mountains like a jumble of broken glass. Snowfields weep slowly down. Chambers Lake, ringed by trees, gratefully catches the drip in its tin cup, and gives the mountains their own reflection in return. This is the real world, indifferent, unburdened.

Two rivers flow from opposite ends of Chambers Lake, like two ends of yarn being pulled off a spool at the same time. The Laramie River flows through its own valley, through its own town, then into the North Platte. From the opposing end of the lake the Cache la Poudre gouges into a steep canyon down to the South Platte River. At North Platte, Nebraska, the two forks of the Platte conjoin and the separate, long-traveled waters of Chambers Lake remarry.

The real world goes like this: Coming down from the high lake, timbered ridges in slow green waves suddenly stop and bunch up like patiently disappointed refugees, waiting for permission to start walking out across the open prairie toward Nebraska, where the waters come together and form an enormous inland island, large parts of three states surrounded by water. The island never heard of states; the real world is the island.

There is an island on the island which is a meadow, offered up among the ridges, wearing a necklace of waterways, concentrically nested inside the darker green of pines, and then the gray-green of sage and the yellow-green of prairie grass.

The story of the meadow is a litany of loosely patterned weather, a chronicle of circular succession. Indians hunted here in summer, but they never wintered here, as far as we can tell, not on purpose. It's the highest cultivated ground in this spur of the Medicine Bow, no other level terrain in sight. There have been four names on the deed to it, starting just a hundred years back.

The history of the meadow goes like this: No one owns it, no one ever will. The people, all ghosts now, were ghosts even then; they drifted through, drifted away, thinking they were not moving. They learned the recitations of the seasons and the repetitive work that seasons require.

Only one of them succeeded in making a life here, for almost fifty years. He weathered. Before a backdrop of natural beauty, he lived a life from which everything was taken but a place. He lived so close to the real world it almost let him in.

By the end he had nothing, as if loss were a fire in which he was purified again and again, until he wasn't a ghost anymore.

———

The way people watch television while they eat—looking up to the TV and down to take a bite and back up—that's how Lyle watches the meadow out the south window while he eats his breakfast. He's hooked on the plot, doesn't want to miss anything. He looks out over the rim of his cup as he sips.

The meadow is under two feet of snow, which looks gray but not dirty in this light. Leafless willow branches make an orange streak down the middle. Each year the snow tries to memorize, blindly, the landscape, as if it were the landscape that was going to melt in spring.

The wind has cleared a couple of knobs above the meadow, and the silver-gray sage throbs out. Above that stands the front line of timber, where the trees begin, or end, depending, still dead black though the sky has brightened behind it, a willing blue. Nothing is moving across the meadow this morning.

Yesterday sixteen elk streaked across the hillside above the meadow. Lyle could easily imagine what they had done to the fence where it runs under deep drifts on the east side. They walked through it, not even feeling the barbs through their winter coats. They dragged broken wire through the woods, strewing it like tinsel. He'd find the pieces in the spring like tendrils of steel briar growing along the ground. It doesn't make him angry anymore, as it did in the early years. He figures the elk have been crossing that section of timber to forage on the north side of Bull Mountain for a lot longer than there has been anyone here to build fence and get pissed off every time the elk tear it up. Now he splices the fence with baling wire, which is lighter, so it will break easier and always in the same place and not get dragged so much or pull out posts.

The first light hits the meadow and the kitchen window, and it's like Christmas lights going on. The trees go from black to loden green. The snow turns a mild electric blue and sparks.

A white crown sparrow lights on a small juniper branch that bends down and springs back up. Lyle says, 'What kept you?' The sparrow hops onto the windowsill as a chickadee lights and begins bouncing up and down on the juniper branch just left by the other. 'And you, you cheerful little sonofabitch, you don't waste no time either, do you?'

Lyle slowly straightens his stiff joints as he gets out of the chair and shuffles (his shoes are still untied) over to the wood stove. He picks up the plate with the extra pancake, carries it back to the table, and sits down. He cranks the window open about an inch—not enough for the birds to come in and kill themselves trying to get out—pinches off some warm pancake and crumbles it onto the outside sill. 'Little beggars.'

When the day's first visitors have finished their crumbs and flown, Lyle picks up a two-month-old newspaper Ed Wilkes brought and begins to read, but he is soon interrupted by a tiny beak tapping on the glass. This one is a junco, and then the chickadee is back, bouncing from branch to branch chirping. Lyle gives them some crumbs. Addressing the chickadee, 'I don't know what you're so goddamn happy about all the time.'

There's a racket of chirps and squawks by the front door. Lyle unbends out of the chair again, takes another pinch of flapjack to the door, and steps outside on the stoop. The screeching squawk is a Stellar's jay, who flees the wire he's perched on as soon as the door opens. He's had enough stones and snowballs pitched at him to know. To the little row of sparrows that has returned to the perch Lyle says, 'That hatchet-head won't bother you now.' All at once they fly down and light on his uplifted palm. They peck off pieces of cake and flee back to the wire like greedy children waiting another turn. When the pancake is gone Lyle goes back inside to wash the dishes.

Once, coming back from town, I saw Lyle's truck parked at the Wooden Shoe. I stopped to say hello. Lyle was building a new garden fence, and as I approached, he held up his hand, a signal not to come closer. Then he leaned his shovel against the post he was setting and walked slowly across the garden to where a barn swallow was perched on a rail. Lyle took off his glove, and with the back of his huge index finger, touched the swallow gently under its throat, then ran his finger down once, gently, over its breast. Then he put his glove back on and walked away, and the bird took to the air again.

Lyle said, 'Up close them swallows are the funniest damned looking things you ever saw. They fly like angels and then up close they look like little clowns. The damndest thing.'

———

White as death and twice as cold, mathematical, it offers itself as a symbol of all stillness, all isolation when it reaches the windowsill and no one is going anywhere for awhile, or when, by March, the drifts loom higher than the roofs of houses. The snow is deepest up on Deadman, where all our streams begin, where timber combs the snow out of the wind.

Sometimes in summer the air is so dry the rain evaporates before it reaches the ground. When it rains hard the soil can't take it in. It washes out the roads and pours off the surface of the pasture. Here what living things depend on is the snow that melts off mountain faces and high timber, swelling our springs and streams, filling the reservoir, infusing miles of irrigation ditches, making the meadow green.

———

Lyle is down mowing. From up here by the cattleguard on the hill, the Farmall looks like a river barge, low in the water, pulling upstream as it makes its first swath through the deep timothy that borders the streak of willows along the creek. The tractor moves forward but Lyle is looking back as he goes, watching the scissoring blades of the sickle bar take down the tall grass. Going forward looking back, spiraling toward the middle of the field.

There's a coyote following the tractor, just about ten feet behind it. Every so often he pops into the air like he's been stung and pounces. He's catching field mice the mower turns up. Lyle isn't paying any attention to him.

A lot of people would shoot a coyote if they got that close to it, which is why a lot of people never get that close. This one isn't Lyle's pet; coyotes can't be tamed, even if you start with a pup. It's as close to a pet as Lyle has, though. He won't have a dog or a cat for fear of becoming too attached.

Lyle admires coyotes for more or less the same reasons others hate them.

To begin with, the average coyote is smarter than the average human. That is why it's so difficult to trap them, and why they haven't gone the way of wolves. Then there's their toughness and uncompromising independence: if by some lapse in attention one is caught in a trap, off comes the offending limb and he's on his way.

As the price of defiance they have to work harder than most animals just to stay alive. They live mostly on mice and insects. When they are lucky or clever enough to come up with something bigger they are overcome with joy and love for one another. They rhapsodize their loneliness and sorrow and they don't care who likes it.

Lyle says for coyotes, 'They sure never pity themselves.'

When he gets done mowing he will climb down, choke the tractor, and walk around where that coyote is sitting down just looking at him. He'll chuck a stone or a block of wood at the critter and say, 'Don't you know better than to come that close to people?' The coyote, trotting casually away, watching Lyle over his shoulder as he goes, of course, does know better. He knows the difference between this man who lives in the meadow alone, summer and winter, and the ones who set the traps and poisons and poke the muzzles of .30-.30s out the windows of their pickups. This human has somehow raised his consciousness almost up to coyote level.

———

Sometimes the winter sun is so hot coming through the south-facing kitchen window, Lyle has to scoot his chair over and draw the curtain. But this morning the cold air hangs still down in the meadow, and there is enough haze in the air to filter the sunlight so Lyle can lean on his elbows over a cup of steaming instant and smoke a Prince Albert and gaze out the picture window he now spends most of his life perched in like a hunched up old raven. The air, so heavy-cold and striated with strangely floating frost, is like cotton candy. Hoarfrost builds and grows on the fenceposts and pickets like tropical ferns, but white. White.

He looks out across the meadow filled with snow, across the leafless, oddly orange willow branches along the stream and on over to the wind-bared hill that heaves itself toward the evergreen ridges of the National Forest. The woodcutting trail climbs the bald hill: two parallel lines like railroad tracks, but where the hill steepens, the road curves around the worst part of the grade so that the foreshortened trail looks like a question mark hovering over the meadow.

'I've been staring at that confounded meadow and those idiot hills and lodgepole stands for over forty years now. I'm done for and I'm still not sure I've ever *seen* any of it. All I know is I'm damned tired of looking at the sonofabitch.'

He thinks about how completely the meadow changes with respective seasons, how much it can change under light and clouds between two times he raises his eyes from his book and looks over the top of his half-lens reading glasses.

———

Lyle flicks the long ash from his cigarette. He watches from the kitchen window as his dead sister and his younger self glide elegantly and happily around their own private skating rink in that meadow tucked back in the mountains, where no one else could ever know or see, with all the happiness they ever held inside themselves at one time, when the family was far too poor to be fooling around with exotic sports. But Lyle was twenty and Clara was alive, and poverty seemed the least of burdens a man could hold in his heart.

Now Lyle catches sight of the young coyote angling back up the bare hill toward the edge of the evergreens where the ridge begins. The coyote is drenched and his usually apparent bushiness has collapsed around the reality of his impossibly skinny frame. He is carrying something in his mouth, even more drenched and limp-looking than he is, something that he carefully drops in the snow long enough to look back over his shoulder at the house, where smoke rises from the chimney into the sky without a twist or curl, so straight it looks solid.

He licks his left forepaw, probably cut on the ice. Lyle wonders if the coyote can actually see him, the only other animal around, where he sits in the kitchen window. Lyle often wonders how well different animals hear or see or smell, and what, for instance, it would be like to see what the red tail sees, to be behind his eyes, or to smell mice under the snow asleep, the way coyotes do. To *see* with your sense of smell would be to see things narratively, to know not only where things are but where they have been, and how long they have been gone, as if everything seen had a gently diminishing streak behind it like a comet, showing where it came from and how fast it had traveled. To hear what an owl hears, a mouse rustling dry leaves a hundred feet down in the timber, in a tangle of roots and undergrowth.

Lyle knows that coyote isn't much concerned about being followed or hunted, since he's passed by here so often before. Lyle thinks it's more a matter of showing off, showing Lyle, who had doubted the wisdom of hunting the creek bottom on a day as cold as today, that it had indeed paid off, and that he didn't mind being soaked to the skin in ten below. So he turns and fixes his gaze on the kitchen window in a superior kind of way, then picks up the brown lump that is now rolled in snow like a drumstick in flour, and haughtily trots toward the cover of the timber.

Lyle stubs his smoke and says, 'Better keep movin', you little bastard. It's cold and your ass is soaked. You fell through the ice and got drenched just to catch some goddamn disgusting muskrat that you are going to eat raw while you shiver yourself dry, and you think that's something to be proud of. Well here's to you, you puffed up little bastard. You can have it. You're a fool to survive if that's all your life is for. But I'll say one thing for you. You're tougher than a pine knot, by God. There's no denying you are one tough little hombre.'

———

Full, the reservoir looks all right: a mirror Sheep Creek dies in, timber straight and still along the edge, and sky swimming through its face.

Drained of water, the reservoir that used to be a hayfield is a barren gravel pit with the dead creek laid out in the bottom of it.

Just below the outlet Sheep Creek resurrects itself in an instant. It leaps from the outlet into boulders, tangled willows, and tall grasses. Below the gunsight rock outcrops that pinch the valley into a waist, Lyle's haymeadow opens like a proper afterlife.

In spring the new grass grows in standing water. At sunset the white mirror-light shines through the grass. That's when the beaver ponds light up, too, and the rising trout make bull's eyes on the surface.

A doe that has been drinking lifts her head to listen. Done irrigating, Lyle heads home across the shining field. He has a shovel on his shoulder that looks like a single wing.

———

The water we count on is the runoff from high snows gone underground. Some years the rain we get wouldn't fill a thimble. All our streams and springs come from melted snow. After a mild winter the streams are weak by August, so you need a bad winter to have a good year.

A contour map of America shows a heart-shaped basin covering several western states, from southeast Oregon and Idaho down through Nevada and Utah, the real heart of America, where cold air sinks in and falls, like a reservoir of air, until it rises to the spillway and pours through Divide Basin and South Pass like water through a pitcher spout. Only it isn't water, it's all the wind in Wyoming. Snow that settles in open country soon rises into the wind and falls again into the deep timber of mountain ridges where it will be safe. The prairie is often scoured when there's ten feet of snow in the woods.

Ditches they built in the twenties and thirties with dynamite, slips, and mules gather several streams up on Deadman and divert them into the reservoir. Someone has to go up there in the spring and shovel snow out of the ditches to get them running and keep them from washing out. Water is saved behind the dam till they run it out to irrigate the Colorado Plateau. The snow that was saved in the timber is saved again in the reservoir. They sell the water.

In Lyle's meadow a system of ditches girdles the hillside, delineating hay from sagebrush hills. Ditches fork like nerves to reach every part of the meadow. A wooden flume vaults the creek, water crossing water, to irrigate hay on the far bank. Lyle made hay over forty years. It snowed and flooded the meadow. He cut the water off and cut the hay. He saved the hay in the barn. It started to snow again.

———

*Virga* is when rain falls and fails to reach the earth, beautiful and useless as the vista it elaborates. Most angels aren't allowed to touch the ground. We pray for real rain to save the pasture; when it doesn't come we pray for rain to keep the timber from burning. Dry lightning pokes at the timber's green dress. Almost every summer there's a major forest fire somewhere near. Every year we don't disappear in fire we pray our thanks. The summer Lyle died, fires in Yellowstone four hundred miles away smoked us in so we couldn't see the barn from the house. The sun was gone for weeks. It never did rain, though all summer long flotillas of sheepish clouds sailed in and tried to look like rain. They turned dark and sexual. They let down their hair, like brushstrokes on the air, like feathers of water, like the principle it was named for, sublime indifference in its gesture, its lovely signature over us.

————

Lyle told me he could hear different tones emitted by different stars on the stillest, coldest winter nights. He said he could tell which notes came from which stars. He couldn't hear them all the time, just winter nights, and then, when he was about sixty, he admitted sadly that he couldn't hear them anymore. Age, I guess. When he said he heard the stars, though, he wasn't exaggerating. In fact, he was worried I'd think he was nuts, even though he knew I had never in thirty-five years heard him say anything but the absolute truth as far as he knew it. If Lyle said he heard stars he heard stars. The only reason he mentioned it was because it was curious to him, the idea of the music of the spheres and all.

Another time, while sorting through a fruitcake tin filled with old buttons, he told me how once in winter he was walking in deep timber with his axe. He heard a wind coming up, firing the treetops. He heard it getting closer. It reached the trees directly overhead. As it rushed into them Lyle felt the wind blow through him, blowing right through him as if he wasn't there.

————

The sky was not blue all summer, nor did it rain. Sunsets were bloody without clouds. Half the west was on fire and no way to stop it in the driest summer in recorded history. The timber not already ablaze was sunsoaked to the point, it seemed, of spontaneous ignition. You couldn't see the mountains for smoke. Four thousand acres of timber burned not eight miles from us, and smoke from the Yellowstone fire four thousand miles away covered out state. There was a grass fire that barely sidled by us.

At the same time the land was being brutalized by fire and drought, we saw more wildlife than ever before: bear, puma, snowy egrets.

Waiting for winter to stop the fires, we started feeling better when the meadow wore a slip of frost through the morning. There was something reassuring about the meadow under snow, but then I thought of Lyle's empty kitchen up there some midwinter night: no light, no fire, rooms colder than the outside air, cold moonlight on the cold iron of the Majesty kitchen stove—no one looking out the window at the meadow, luminous in her snowy bed, a sleeping princess who doesn't care for waking.

————

People who didn't know Lyle well considered him moody. Ed Wilkes wouldn't sit down when he first came in, until he'd tested Lyle's mood. If Lyle's mood was good, Ed'd sit and visit. If not, he'd just leave. No sense in getting chewed on by some pissed hermit. Those of us who'd known Lyle longer knew he didn't have moods, he had weather. Not some inner weather that could have been a mood—Lyle had *the* weather. Inside him he had going on exactly what was going on in the sky, or some combination of recent weather and what was likely to develop. Old friends were perfectly happy to sit down and get snowed on for a couple of hours over coffee, though anyone would have preferred the happy emanations of cloudless sky and sun, even if the sun was shining on a snowdrift ten feet deep.

That high in the mountains a man lives less on the land than in the sky. After forty years the weather had all the bearing. It's like the drive train in a car, going through the differential and turning the wheels.

Oh, I know everyone's moods are affected by weather, but with no one around to put him in a mood, and his own actions honed down to rightness, Lyle just had straight weather inside and out.

It takes a lot of weather to make a winter bad, whereas a couple of weeks in summer, with the east wind dug in, cold vapor shifting in the meadow, the garden's fenceposts and the timbered ridges hard to make out except for dreamy glimpses, could generate as much gloom as being snowed in for a month. A week of wind could make him edgy as a civet cat. A piddle of useless thundershower on cut hay could make him almost cynical. But when the sun shone and the air was mild, a cheerfulness that had no source in his circumstance or prognosis emanated from his soul. A January thaw made him transcendently cheerful, though tobacco smoke had opened its black cloak inside him and he knew it. He could be happy snowed in and dying alone, if only the sun kept shining.

We say the meadow is in clouds when really clouds are in the meadow. We say steam rises out of the creek like it's turning its soul loose inside out and it is. Dew has neglected not a single leaf or blade of grass of all the millions. The fenceposts past the garden disappear again. We can't start haying till the sky returns. Lyle sits in the kitchen by the window not smoking, not reading, not drinking coffee. This morning he woke up without the heart even to go out to the shop and get after some useless project, like those earrings. He is concentrating hard on just sitting, trying to shoo his mind away from the regions of memory and despair. He is waiting for the weather to change and it won't and he is waiting.

Who wouldn't want to die in good weather, instead of some mood?

———

Lyle's last winter was too mean to die in, though it would have been easier to die then. Five months he couldn't get to town. Bert hauled oxygen tanks by snowmobile; Ed and Toya brought groceries in the company's new Trackster. The gasoline power plant quit and Lyle didn't have the strength to snowshoe out to the Windcharger to turn it on. He went back to kerosene lights, and with the water pump out, he bathed in a washtub with water heated on the woodstove, the old way, the way they did forty-five years ago. The shape his body was in told him something had happened in all that time.

He hung on till summer took a good hold. June sun sponged into the pale aspen leaves. He wasn't getting out of bed anymore. We only figured out later he had cut off his intake of food, liquids, and medication. Jorie was house-cleaning for him—he hadn't cleaned all winter and it was depressing. As she dusted, careful to replace exactly each object, she tried to keep up a cheerful chatter of news and questions.

Lyle said, 'Hand me that box'—the one she was putting back after dust-ing the bureau. She handed it to him. He turned it over, studying it. He hand-ed it back. 'Ain't that pretty?'

Jorie sat down in an overstuffed chair that was bathed in windowlight. She looked at the box, one Lyle had made. He had carved it from a single block of apple wood so that with the lid on all the grain lined up and made its two-partedness disappear. The sides of the box were as thin as the sides of a violin. It was finished simply, with oil. On the lid were carved three cattail leaves, all gently bending.

'Yes,' she said, 'it's beautiful.'

She took off the lid. There was nothing in the box. Woodgrain. Woodsmell. She started to cry. She covered her eyes and tried to stop.

'You'd best take that if you like it,' Lyle said. He waited, hoping she would stop. He said firmly, 'Jorie.' She looked at him. His eyes were looking straight out of good weather.

'What?'

'It's no big deal, you know.'

———

Nowadays the meadow isn't considered worth haying. Machinery is cost-prohibitive in relation to annual yield. No one will winter here anymore. We are a different breed of Westerners. Snow always looks good to skiers.

Someone from Denver bought Lyle's place for the fishing, a summer retreat. Without irrigation much of the meadow has regressed to native side-hill pasture and sage. The rest is frumpy-looking, matted under the yellow thatch of last year's uncut growth. Along the east fence, where Pat and Lyle used to bet on whether the snowdrift would last till the Fourth of July, short lengths of snowbroken wire sink into the earth, sink down with the roots.

Underneath its feral pelt, the meadow is still the meadow, entire, lying in wait for winter. Wildflowers still joy in its swells and hollows. And do the ruined, sage-choked irrigation ditches feel sorry for their intricately patterned uselessness?

Between the sky and the egg-shaped, egg-smooth granite boulder that floats out in the middle of the meadow's widest field, everything has its own green: cattails, willow leaves, the flip side of an aspen leaf, the gray-green sage, the yellow-green native pasture, the loden timber, all circling around, with the boulder at the center, as if the meadow were a green ear held up to listen to the sky's blue, and there is an axis drawn between the boulder and the sun.

Elsewhere on the mountain, most of the green stays locked in pines, the prairie is scorched yellow. But Lyle's meadow is a hemorrhage of green, and a green clockwork of waterways and grasses, held up to the sky in its ring of ridges, held up for the sky to listen, too.

The granite boulder is only there to hold it down.

# TOM GRIFFITHS

## Cooper Dreaming

Angus Emmott and his wife Karen and their two children Amelia (nine) and Fergus (six) live in the Channel Country of southwestern Queensland on 'Noonbah', a property (about 130,000 acres) owned for sixty years by the Emmotts. Angus's father and mother live there still in the old homestead. So Angus has never had to move from home. He finished school at Year 10 and never went away to boarding school. As a child he collected everything, alone in his family with this passion for natural history, and so he learnt by observing and from books. His home now is like a museum. He has cabinets with smoothly sliding drawers in which are beetles and butterflies and insects of every kind, carefully pinned and labelled. On his coffee table is a basket of dried seeds and nuts and fruits, a still life of local, casual nature. On his verandah, if you're hungry, you have to watch out which refrigerator or deep freeze you open, for two of them are given over to the preservation of roadkill and other animal specimens. On the table there is a dugong skull and a camel skull, as well as the nests of birds. This is where I slept in my swag, amongst the roadkill and beside a death adder in a terrarium, the dingoes circling the house at dawn and howling. One of my companions would come and say goodnight to me on the verandah each night and, as he did so, peer into the death adder's lair beside me and exclaim: 'Oh, it's gone!'

When Angus drives, he leans forward, both arms resting along the wheel, gazing up and forwards, naming every bird he sees, each a quiet achievement, and sometimes he brakes and turns, jumps out of the truck, crouches on the road and returns with a fan of wings or a wounded bearded dragon which he places beside you. He has many specimens in museums, especially in Australia, but some overseas too, and has contributed substantially to the Australian Wildlife Collection in Canberra. It is his greatest pride that he has, I think, three species named after him, the latest a wren (*emmottorum*). In his study, amid the piles of paper, are many books of natural history and exploration, Australasian and Antarctic, and American too, amid bottles of snakes and jars of frogs. I told Angus that he was the person I wanted to be when I was growing up, and he replied, sincerely and quite simply: 'I've never grown up.'

And that's true in the nicest way. He is 38, wears shorts, his pockets are full of things he picks up, he has an infectious giggle, never left home, and he has Mum and Dad next door. Belonging to a place is important to him. He doesn't want to move from here. Karen wants to retire to the coast, nearer the sand dunes of her upbringing, but I think she knows she'll never get him there. (As he drives towards the Simpson Desert, she warns: 'Now don't find a retirement block out there, will you? ... They're not the dunes I have in mind!') 'Noonbah' is home, and every thing that he collects, names, pins, secures, is an act of homage to this place, a way of knowing and loving it better. Jane Carruthers, a South African historian travelling with us, commented that this is not evidence of 'ecology and empire', of possession by conquest. Instead it is a way of belonging by knowing a place, scientifically, intellectually; a way that perhaps we underestimate and too often categorise as imperial. His way of knowing is generous and loving and humble, an act of respect, never complete. He's a 'national treasure' and we know this is true because television's *7.30 Report* told us so this year, and we watched the video of it in the treasure's own lounge room.

The next day, Amelia and Fergus take me for a walk to Sandy Gully, just a few minutes from their house, one of their play areas and fantasy lands. Amelia treads lightly in her bare feet through the dry and spiky grasses, and Fergus wields a compass. This makes him boss.

Each morning—or so I have read in a glossy magazine—Angus can be found 'sleepily devouring his bowl of muesli in the modest homestead'.[1] His business has just abandoned sheep in the face of the severe global depression in wool prices. Angus has decided to sell them all and to rely on cattle, which will be 'the first time Noonbah is sheep-free since the early 1940s' when his father Bruce Emmott started the family operation. *Truckin' Life* told this story in April 2000. In the article, the sheep appear as no more than an amorphous mob of 'woolly wethers', 5000 of them, but the trucks used in the operation emerge as colourful individuals: 'a Louisville hitched to two trailers', 'a Kenworth pulling its three trailer 12-deck rig', 'a big old Mack Superliner'. And these vehicles have poetry and history, too: 'The trucks are the tallest shapes on the flat landscape' and they are managed by a third generation descendant of a local Cobb & Co driver, a truckin' family that did the mail run for nigh on sixty years till 1999.

In her book *The Territory* (1951), Ernestine Hill wrote of northern Australia: 'its human interest and natural history are superhuman interest and unnatural history'.[2] 'Superhuman' and 'unnatural': these are the adjectival dimensions of northern histories. Culture is larger than life, heroic, legendary, epic. And nature is somehow corrupted, deficient or unrealised. Explorers and settlers did not describe the land as it was; instead, they divined what it lacked or imagined what it might become. They described not so much its features as its shortcomings and redeeming potential.

We are certainly in a country of legends. I've met people called Crackers and Chumpy and Dude and Bub and Bud. We even saw some drovers on horses with 2500 head of cattle on the final stages of a journey from the Gulf to near Windorah. I think I've noticed one or two thumbnails dipped in tar and we've certainly driven around some overflows, and the Cross turns over every night. Bush poetry is an idiom: Karen Emmott showed me some of hers (after some urging), and young Fergus (distantly related to Banjo Paterson) whispered to me several times a prize-winning poem he wrote for school. There is the Stockman's Hall of Fame, of course, and a Waltzing Matilda Centre, and the Tree of Knowledge where the Australian Labor Party seeded.

I'm interested in the special challenge of writing environmental history in a country of legends, where the adjectives are indeed 'superhuman' and 'unnatural'. The Stockman's Hall of Fame fails to do it, constrained as it is by its legendary mission. We learn a lot about the imported stock but nothing about the native grasses. Are an heroic history and an environmental history incompatible? I don't think so. Here goes.

———

The Mayor of the Barcoo Shire, Bruce Scott, uses words like 'braided' and 'anastomosing' and 'ephemeral'. They don't always quite fit in his mouth and sometimes mutate in the process, but he knows their power and meaning and politics better than any lexicologist.

The locals happily embellish their language now with these scientific terms, eagerly adopting and adapting the words of urban professionals to advocate the special attributes of their water system. One Cooper pastoralist, full of genuine wonder, called the channels 'anastomazing'.

This is one of the legacies of an extraordinary and effective alliance since 1995 between pastoralists, greenies and some Aboriginal people to defend Cooper's Creek from regulation for irrigation. The language superbly captures the meeting and melding of cultures. Windorah pastoralists, I found, often begin sentences with the words: 'I'm not a radical greenie, but ...' Their rivers are not only unregulated but also unpolluted. 'There's no pee in our river,' they say of the (frequently mis-spelt) Thomson!

There are the floods—or I should say, the flow. It's not a flood but a flow; it's not a river but a creek. The braided channel system. As the stockman Ron Pagett, put it, it's not like you cross the Cooper and that's it. You cross the Cooper, and then you cross it again, and then again, and then again. And the flow swells to a sea. It is the largest inland draining system in the world. Inflows.

The system is at such a whole-landscape scale that you simply cannot ignore it. Its rhythms are overwhelming. Debris in trees and on fencelines records the last height of flow.

I had this simplistic idea that the country got more marginal the further one went out. But the Channel Country and large swathes of central and western Queensland—particularly the mitchell grass country—defy that expectation. There is an ownership mosaic of large company holdings and smaller private landholders, the companies gradually winning. But many families here date themselves back to the Duracks and Costellos of the 1860s, providing a social continuity that is unusual, quite unlike large areas of western NSW where social instability and land degradation have been tragic partners. And although some of the signs of historical mismanagement are still evident, there seems to have been no single devastating period of gross overstocking and long-term environmental damage such as western NSW experienced so cataclysmically in the 1880s and 1890s. Many of the pastoralists here now talk of pasture management as much as stock management, of firing the grasses, of huge paddocks kept only for emergency feed, of planning for drought and accepting flood as a bonus, of going with the flow.

In 1995, four farmers from the Macquarie Valley of NSW proposed an agricultural development on the Cooper. They had all been involved in irrigation for over fifteen years and two of them also had long experience with sheep and cattle. Their proposed 'Currareva' development included the growing of cotton and wheat, followed by more intensive horticultural and viticultural activites, as well as a fish farming enterprise.[3] Cotton production, with its chemicals and thirst for water, is far more disruptive of ecological processes than pastoralism has ever been.

The debate about irrigation on the Cooper is a revealing moment in the catchment's history and it made locals articulate their history and their pride, and see the political as well as environmental advantages of talking 'sustainability'. In the face of corporate cotton, pastoralists mobilised in defence of their social as well as natural environment. It's a reversal of the more usual situation where a rural shire might be found advocating development and being restrained by government on behalf of an urban environmental sensibility. One of the leaders of the campaign was Bob Morrish, a local pastoralist with a background in psychology who writes referenced academic papers on the natural rhythms of the Cooper system, and gives them titles like 'Aliens in the Ecosystem: The Strange Behaviour of Human Beings'. He acknowledges a lineage of Australian perspectives on 'the global ecocrisis' which includes Jock Marshall's *The Great Extermination* (1966), Leonard Webb's *The Environmental Boomerang* (1973) and Tim Flannery's *The Future Eaters* (1994). 'Small wonder,' writes Morrish, 'that the Australian novelist Xavier Herbert described humans as the most savage and brutal animals on this earth.' In this pastoralist's mind, the win for Windorah is placed in an historical context of international ecopolitics and a timeless and despairing psychology of humanity.

On the ground it translates into local advocacy for the Cooper as a national resource. The link between embedded locals and an educated, travelling, urban populace therefore becomes crucial, and tourism is increasingly tolerated not only for its economic promise, but because of the expanded electorate it offers to an outnumbered and defensive few living downstream in a fragile catchment.

We are now staying at a property thirty kilometres out of Windorah, beside Cooper's Creek. It is owned by Bruce (the Mayor) and Maureen Scott, who have two children, Karly (aged nine) and Courtney (five). Karly has just skipped into her little classroom to put on her headphones and begin school, and Courtney is getting a painting lesson from Mandy Martin, our artist, on the verandah of the house where we are staying, opposite the homestead. Bruce Scott and Guy Fitzhardinge, a fellow pastoralist, spent most of breakfast

discussing the intricacies of acetylene gas bottles and later I had some marvellous, intense conversations with Bruce, too, about Aboriginality and bioregionalism and education. Guy slips easily into the idiom of whoever he is with,
drawing them out on their home ground, and so he and Bruce were talking
fast and low, mouths barely opening, exploring the full range of their shared
pastoral lingo. Later in our stay we were joined at dinner by neighbouring gra-
ziers, Brian and Ross, and the rhythm of the repartee, the laconic humour, and
the extreme economy of lip movement, rendered Jane (our South African) a
non-speaker. The words merged into a fascinatingly foreign sound, as if it were
another language. An anastomazing night.

Such is the pace of adventure and the number of new people and places and
ideas that we are encountering that Jane and I sometimes both feel a little overwhelmed and temporarily (but happily) exhausted. At times we have been
almost asleep at the dinner table, making brave, pathetic efforts to look attentive, and Mandy has saved us with thoughtful excuses. Jane and I have wondered
if the congestion of our brains might also be put down to coffee deprivation.
This is certainly tea-drinking country. Basically, there's tea and beer and rum
and tea. I think this is one of the deepening divides in Australian culture,
between rural tea drinking and urban coffee drinking. 'The caffe latte set'—
which I now realise I clearly belong to, more completely than I ever knew—is
not an idle label, nor is it just a cultural slur; it contains a brutal biological
insight.

Bruce says that people come here and are almost disappointed that they
do not find it more barren, even in drought. They expect just red dust and
tumbleweeds. I asked him what he wanted them to learn. He said he would
like them to see how the country is still habitable after 100–150 years of settlement, that people have learned to live with the land, with the ecosystems
because they have no choice. Few of the towns here are on artesian or sub-
artesian water supplies; they rely on the surface water in all its unreliability.
People live with that. The pulse of life that enlivens the ecosystems is what the
people, too, must live off. He did not think that there should be more people
out here, or that development should entail meddling with the water supply.
He talked self-sufficiency and integrity of systems, the economy of Cooper
water spilling over into all his politics.

As I write these words, I am reminded of the visiting British biologist
Francis Ratcliffe and the letters he wrote home from the Queensland frontier
in the late 1920s and 1930s. These letters later evolved into *Flying Fox and Drifting
Sand*, a book much loved by Australians that was first published in London in

1938, Sydney in 1947, and reprinted many times since. The Cooper disturbed Ratcliffe. He felt a formless fear there, and found the endless flat bed of grey clay 'menacing'. 'The dry bed of that dead river,' he wrote, '... was one of the most eerie and haunted spots I have ever visited.' He called Cooper's Creek a dead river not only because it did not have water in it when he first saw it in 1935—it had not flowed in its lower reaches for seventeen years—but also because it could never know the sea. It seemed that it did not have water and and never reached water. Even when it did run, it could not fulfil the destiny of a river and release into the ocean. It was dry and landlocked and frustrated. It was a parody of a river. It epitomised the irony, the menace, the waywardness of Australian nature. 'I can never think of the Cooper and the Diamantina as mere rivers,' Ratcliffe reflected. 'They have spirits of their own, which are not friendly to man.'

But Ratcliffe also saw this land animated by water. When he returned to the Cooper the following year, 1936, he felt that it was like returning to 'the tiger's paws from which I had so recently escaped ... The tiger, moreover, was no longer slumbering, for the drought had broken, and the great inland rivers had come down in flood.' 'In the end it took us three weeks to get over the wretched "creek",' he said of the Cooper. A fresh flood came down and blocked him at Windorah.

Although Ratcliffe was on a scientific mission—to investigate the causes of soil erosion ('drifting sand') in inland Australia—he had much more to say about people and politics than about ecology and wildlife. Or perhaps it is more accurate to observe that he saw them as interrelated. He came as much to study society as nature, to listen more than to teach. He looked for whole landscape solutions, bravely argued the reality of environmental limits and the shocking consequences of overstocking, and he took seriously his duty to communicate his findings to a general public. He regarded people not only as components of the ecosystem, but also as sources of knowledge about it. Ratcliffe listened. He did not just hand down scientific knowledge from on high. He derived it from the people who lived it, as well as from his own expertise. He spun his letters and his book and his science out of conversations in paddocks and at homestead tables.

Like Ratcliffe, I am simply observing the tallest vertebrates in this landscape. As Angus (*emmottorum* sp.) says, it is wrong that in our species lists of various regions we do not include *Homo sapiens*.

———

Last night we stayed in the most beautiful place imaginable. We unrolled the swags on a gentle knoll beside Cooper's Creek. It was at the Cullyamurra Waterhole, the deepest in the system, the place which has the largest peak flow of any river in Australia. Just above the waterhole is 'the choke' where the flare of the Cooper channels narrows, and there—above a flood line on the rocks—is an Aboriginal quarry and gallery, every boulder an artefact, every rockface a canvas. It's worth remembering that Burke and Wills died not of heat and thirst in the middle of nowhere, but of malnutrition, exhaustion, thiaminase poisoning (from raw nardoo) and the cold (Burke accidentally set fire to their wurley and burnt most of their spare clothes) in a watered and inhabited place of art and industry.

Large graceful coolibahs spread their limbs above us, and the creek was a chortle of bird noise, especially the grunting and grinding of pelicans as they sailed the waters majestically or flew in formation or glided in to land on the pond like Hercules aircraft. There were egrets, and pacific herons and night herons and hardhead ducks and black kites. After the big wet earlier this year, the banks of the Cooper were green with native spinach, with which we supplemented our evening campfire meal. It was delicious—and ironic, too, to live off the land even in this small way in a setting of such European hopelessness. There was a sense of such abundance, of rippling waters, dense bird life, bush tucker, an inland Eden, and yet it was here that Burke and Wills perished. Without any doubt they spent their last weeks near our campsite, would have walked over it several times. The Yantruwanta people brought the explorers food every day, looking after them tenderly, but Burke knocked the nets of fish out of their hands and ordered King to fire over their heads because he was 'afraid of being too friendly'.[4]

As night closed in, I read aloud two chapters of Alan Moorehead's account of the expedition, *Cooper's Creek* (1963). It was haunting and eerie to read it there, around a campfire on the Cooper, to learn of their despair, their camel swallowed by the clay, their hopeless chasing of branches of the waterhole, looking for a watered route out, knowing that they dragged their feet over this very ground, under these trees, stared at this sky. Guy said he was spooked all night. A place of such beauty and capricious bounty needs only an epic tragedy to deepen and complete its significance. This it has, bequeathed unwillingly by an expedition leader chosen for his romance rather than his sense. Again the moon was extraordinarily bright, dazzling, hanging above us there like a street lamp, and I lay awake for long, contented periods under the stars, listening to the land, thinking of fate and circumstance, of history and the future, dreaming with my eyes open.

## NOTES

1   'End of an Era', *Truckin' Life*, April 2000, pp. 22-26.

2   Ernestine Hill, *The Territory*, 1951, p. 2.

3   Bert Hawkins, John O'Brien, Paul O'Brien and Hans Woldring, *Initial Information Statement: Proposed 'Currareva' Agricultural Development*, September 1995.

4   Tim Bonyhady, *Burke and Wills: From Melbourne to Myth*, David Ell Press, Sydney 1991, p. 140.

# JOHN
# HAINES

## Pieces of a Place

### SNOW

To one who lives in the snow and watches it day by day, it is a book to be read. The pages turn as the wind blows; the characters shift and the images formed by their combinations change in meaning, but the language remains the same. It is a shadow language, spoken by things that have gone by and will come again. The same text has been written there for thousands of years, though I was not here, and will not be here in winters to come, to read it. These seemingly random ways, these paths, these beds, these footprints, these hard, round pellets in the snow: they all have meaning. Dark things may be written there, news of other lives, their sorties and excursions, their terrors and deaths. The tiny feet of a shrew or a vole make a brief, erratic pattern across the snow, and here is a hole down which the animal goes. And now the track of an ermine comes this way, swift and searching, and he too goes down that white shadow of a hole.

A wolverine, and the loping, toed-in track I followed uphill for two miles one spring morning, until it finally dropped away into another watershed and I gave up following it. I wanted to see where he would go and what he would do. But he just went on, certain of where he was going, and nothing came of it for me to see but that sure and steady track in the snowcrust, and the sunlight strong in my eyes.

Snow blows across the highway before me as I walk—little, wavering trails of it swept along like a people dispersed. The snow people—where are they going? Some great danger must pursue them. They hurry and fall; the wind gives them a push, they get up and go on again.

———

I was walking home from Redmond Creek one morning late in January. On a divide between two watersheds I came upon the scene of a battle between a moose and three wolves. The story was written plainly in the snow at my feet. The wolves had come in from the west, following an old trail from the Salcha River, and had found the moose feeding in an open stretch of the overgrown road I was walking.

The sign was fresh, it must have happened the night before. The snow was torn up, with chunks of frozen moss and broken sticks scattered about; here and there, swatches of moose hair. A confusion of tracks in the trampled snow—the splayed, stabbing feet of the moose, the big, furred pads and spread toenails of the wolves.

I walked on, watching the snow. The moose was large and alone, almost certainly a bull. In one place he backed himself into a low, brush-hung bank to protect his rear. The wolves moved away from him—those moose feet are dangerous. The moose turned, ran on for fifty yards, and the fight began again. It became a running, broken fight that went on for nearly half a mile in the changing, rutted terrain, the red morning light coming across the hills from the sun low in the south. A pattern shifting and uncertain; the wolves relenting, running out into the brush in a wide circle, and closing again: another patch of moose hair in the trodden snow.

I felt that I knew those wolves. I had seen their tracks several times before during that winter, and once they had taken a marten from one of my traps. I believed them to be a female and two nearly grown pups. If I was right, she may have been teaching them how to hunt, and all that turmoil in the snow may have been the serious play of things that must kill to live. But I saw no blood sign that morning, and the moose seemed to have gotten the better of the fight. At the end of it he plunged away into the thick alder brush. I saw his tracks, moving more slowly now, as he climbed through a low saddle, going north in the shallow, unbroken snow. The three wolves trotted east toward Banner Creek.

———

What might have been silence, an unwritten page, an absence, spoke to me as clearly as if I had been there to see it. I have imagined a man who might live as the coldest scholar on earth, who followed each clue in the snow, writing a book as he went. It would be the history of snow, the book of winter. A thousand-year text to be read by people hunting these hills in a distant time. Who was here, and who has gone? What were their names? What did they kill and eat? Whom did they leave behind?

## SPRING

The sun is warm in my yard this spring afternoon. It is the first clear day without wind. I am sitting on the sawhorse, doing nothing. Looking out over the Tanana River, looking at the ground, watching and thinking. My mind sleeps and awakens. I think how good the sun feels on my back and shoulders. Goodbye to so much darkness and frost, to the long night. I watched the sun barely clear a mountain in the south; its spent light without heat threw long, blue shadows over the snow. And then the days slowly lengthened and brightened.

The sun has come back. It has been a good winter after all, with little snow after the first deep fall in October. A warm winter. For a few days in January the temperature fell to thirty-five and forty below. After that the wind blew, a mighty and blustering force out of the south, sweeping across the hills, shaking the birches; the deep cold was gone. Now, in April, meltwater seeps and drips from every cornice and clay bank, and pools of water deepen in the yard.

Flies buzz around me, their green bodies shining in the sunlight. They light on the woodpile, and on the wall of the house nearby, drawn there by the warmth. If a shadow passes over them, they move away into the light again. Flies awakened early this spring, trapped behind the glass of the storm windows. They fumed and droned there, to die or sleep again. A little sunlight, some warmth finding its way into the housewalls, and they return to life. After long silence they are welcome.

I watch a carpenter ant crawl about a chunk of split firewood at my feet. The wood is dry spruce from an old snag up the creek. The ant has lived there all winter in the honeycomb passages. Now he is out here in this strange, new place of warmth and passing shadows. His black skeleton glistens in the light. He feels his way along.

Wet snow and sawdust underfoot. Wood dust from my saw fell here all winter under the sawhorse, mixing with the snow. Now the snow melts, and the sawdust settles in a sodden heap. If I push it aside with my boot, I see that it darkens toward the ground; it is turning itself slowly to soil itself.

An odor, strong and sharp with ammonia, comes off the low band where my dogs are chained to their houses. It is too wet for them on the ground; they lie on top of their houses, blinking, sleeping in the sun. They like this warmth and stillness.

All around me I see the debris of winter, long hidden by snow. The scattered woodchips, the gnawed bones; part of a moose jaw, a hoof, a lost spoon. Bits of trash, moose hair, peelings thrown out and forgotten; urine stains in the rotting snow. The ground smells sour.

This morning I worked in the greenhouse, loosening the soil, turning it over, setting it free to the sun and air. The plants I have cared for all spring stand here in their flats and boxes: tomatoes, peppers and cucumbers; cabbages and broccoli. I took them from the house this morning to let them harden for a while outdoors. It will soon be time to set them in the garden.

Already the earth is warm where the snow has gone. Patches of dead grass have been visible for several days. I see a few shoots there above the roots. Shoots of fireweed and wild rhubarb have begun to break through the banked soil by the porch. They are the first things up in the spring, good to eat until they grow tall and bitter.

———

I look away from my yard to the river glittering below me in the sunlight. There is ice yet in the channels, and drifts of snow on the islands. And far across to the south, much snow in the foothills. But that too is melting, like the snow here in my yard and on the hillside above me. And soon water will be rushing down through the ditches, under the culverts and bridges, away downhill to the river. Water brown as tobacco, stained with tannin, strong to drink.

I know that ice is still thick on the creek below the house. Much overflow came last winter, the springwater seeping somehow through the frozen soil, flowing out over the ice and freezing again. It will take a long time to melt; there will be ice there in shaded places well into June. And back in the woods, on the side-hill, stumps of the birches I cut last winter are pink and wet. Sap is rising, flowing away into the soil again. At night it freezes over the stumps in a glaze of clear pink ice.

I hear geese out there on the river bars, small groups of them wherever there is bare soil and open water. Last night I heard them flying through the darkness overhead; the sound came to me in my sleep. Snow buntings have passed through and flown west, like flocks of small, black and white pigeons wheeling over the snowfields. I have seen longspurs and rosy finches on the roadside toward Delta, picking seed and gravel, bursting away as the cars approach. They are bound west and north to the open tundra and the high, bare summits.

I found a butterfly this morning, the first one I have seen this year. I found it resting on the wet, half-frozen road, motionless in shadow. I knew it for a mourning cloak: the brown and violet, smoky darkness of its wings, their pale flame-edges pulsing. I picked it up and held it in the sunlight, warming it with my breath, until its wings loosened and it flew away.

———

To do nothing, to be nothing: that would be a good life. Be still, like a stone in the sun. All this running after life, this chasing of things: felling trees, cutting wood to keep warm, melting snow and ice for water; there is no end to it. Hunting down meat, hauling it home for miles with the sled and dogs; learning the ways of an animal in snow, that I may lift the fur from its back. Eating, washing, finding time to sleep; waking in the cold, half-light of dawn, hungry and thinking.

Our sleep is not long enough. How much better to be a bear, and snore from November through February, those months of darkness and uncertainty, when it seems that the world will never be warm again, that even the ravens must fall frozen from the sky, and chickadees and redpolls drop from the aspen twigs like feathery lumps of ice. To awaken again when the sun comes back, and water drips from the eaves. Sunlight in the mouth of the cave says it is time once more.

This clarity and distance and light. It is almost too much, the gift we have waited for, this loosening and freeing of the spirit. All things must feel it now; everything that was cold and gripped in darkness, shredding itself, bit by bit letting go, falling to the ground. I hear a sound like thunder, a heavy splash, as another half-acre of ice collapses on the river.

Two weeks more, and our fox sparrow will come again to the thicket below the house. He will sit on the same branch of the same birch, and sing the song he sang last summer. As long as I have lived here a fox sparrow has sung from that tree. Many generations of sparrows have nested there in the alder thicket and learned that song, a sweetness never forgotten.

I saw a cow moose on the hillside last evening, half-hidden in the reddish, twiggy growth of the birches. She will soon have a calf, perhaps more than one, and feed all summer along the river. There, in the sloughs and on the islands, she and her calf may be safe from bears. When snow has gone from the high country, the bulls will move to the upper slopes of Banner Dome, above timber. They will not be down again until late August.

———

A fly settles on my hand, then moves away. Soon the big, furry bumblebees will be fumbling the larkspur and fireweed blossoms. And all too soon the mosquitoes will come. First, the old ones wintered over from last fall. They are heavy and slow in flight, but they still want blood. Then, in the first week of June, the new crop, tiny and ferocious, swarming out of every ditch, pond, and pool of meltwater. For a few weeks life here in the woods will not always be pleasant. But now the air is mild and clear, and we can sit like this, soaking in the warmth and stillness. If a mosquito comes near us, solitary and wandering, we will brush him quietly away.

There is much to be done; it is nearly May, the buds on the poplars will be swollen and sticky. I have the garden to spade and plant, the greenhouse to heat and water. When all that is done, I will start work on a new boat. I have drawn a sketch for it, a rough plan. I will build it twenty feet long, narrow and flat-bottomed, with plenty of flare and a shovel nose. I am without money again this spring, but somehow the material will be found: a few boards and nails, some paint and tar. When the boat is built, I must find a new place to fish, perhaps upriver at the mouth of the Tenderfoot. Last fall I watched the eddy there; it was deep and slow.

I can think of a thousand things, and some of them I may never do. I want to build a root cellar; not this year perhaps, but soon. Summer will be crowding me; the salmon will come in July, and for three weeks or so I will be busy packing and cleaning fish, and mending my nets. There will be berries to pick and wood to cut; the days drawing close again, the time for gathering up the garden and potatoes, as the year slopes down the far side of the summer. They will come soon enough, the hunting and the short days once more.

A shadow crosses my mind, and then it goes. The air feels cooler: a cloud shadow passes overhead, and a little wind comes off the river. I must bring my plants indoors. I move from where I have been sitting, and stretch like someone just awakened. I turn and look behind me toward the birchwood. I will be up there on the hillside soon, spading the ground for potatoes. A wind will blow from the northwest, a brief and chilling gust, bringing sleet and cold rain. But that will pass, and sunlight will be warm again. For a while, a few weeks, summer will stay.

## OTHER DAYS

It is evening, early in November. I am sitting on the closed porch of the cabin at Richardson, making snares. Working with a few strands of cable and a pair of pliers, I make a sliding noose seven to eight inches in diameter; it will be for lynx, or coyote if I am lucky. The wire is tough and springy, and I find it hard to make the knots hold.

I have spent part of this day cutting wood. Out in the yard by the sawhorse there is a pile of freshly sawn birch, and slabs of it already split to be stacked against the outside wall of the cabin. The woodflesh, the sawdust and chips, are a pale yellow on the evening snow.

The cabin is warm; a fire smolders and sparks in the big black woodrange in the room behind me. Something is cooking there on the stovetop; the big kettle hums in the silence. Out the window, in the southwest, a cloudy light fades slowly over the mountains. The river channel at the foot of the hill is frozen, but downriver I see a dark streak in the snow: open water.

The land changes slowly in a thousand years. The river has shifted from one side of the valley to another, worn its bed deeper in the sediment and rock. Islands have formed, grown grass and willows, and then been washed away, to be drift-piles buried in sand. The spruce forest on these slopes gave way to fire, to birch and aspen, and in the spaces among these now the spruce came slowly back. The birch will die, stand punky, and fall, and moss thicken once more on the drowned and rotting trunks.

Of all I can see from this hillside, the only recent things are the narrow roadway below the house and my own cluster of cabins and sheds. Everything else is as it has been for thousands of years. It was colder then, or warmer. Brown coalbeds were forming in the swamps to the south. Animals and birds very like those here now roamed the windy meadows, made their way south, and flew north again in a far springtime. Enormous herds left tracks in the snow, browsing the willows and lichens. And others no longer here, huger, with hairy sides and heavy tusks. They were hunted, pursued by shadows on the snow. They have passed through, they have eaten and killed.

———

Days and years run together. It is later and colder, past the middle of December, the shortest days. The sun has gone down behind Mount Deborah, a cold, pyramidal slab in the southwest. I am fitting together a new harness for the pup I am training. I have cut the leather from strips of tanned moose, made from the back of the animal, the thickest part of the hide. By the light of this window I sew the collar seams with an awl and heavy flax thread. I have already punched holes for the bellyband and the collar buckles.

A large piece of hide taken from the hindquarter of moose is soaking in a tube behind the stove. The hair has slipped, and I have scraped the hide clean. It soaks in a solution of soap and snow water. Stirred and wrung out once or twice a day, it will be ready in a week or two to be washed clean, then pulled and stretched until it is soft and dry. Later I will hang it in the smokehouse and smoke it with dry alder until it is a light or deeper brown. I will cut new moccasin soles from it.

———

I remember things. Names, friends of years past, a wife far off. Last week I saw a magazine article on contemporary painters in New York City, photographs of people I once knew. I wrote one of them a letter, telling of myself here in the north. There will be no answer, and all that seems very far and ages distant.

In that same magazine—or it was another sent to me, or borrowed from the roadhouse—I have read something of the politics of this nation and the world. Names again: Truman, MacArthur, Eisenhower, a place named Korea. But these too are distant and unreal. My life is here, in this country I have made, in the things I have built. In the world of Richardson and Tenderfoot, of Banner Creek, and the Tanana at the foot of the hill. I do not want more than this.

Winter comes dark and close; there is snow, and wind on the hills. It is a lean year, and there are few rabbits in the country now. Two years ago they were thick in the willows and alders; when snow went off in the spring, the gnawed bark showed pale near the height of the snowfall. Lynx followed the rabbits everywhere, and it was no trick at all to catch a dozen or so of the big cats in a few weeks' time. Now the snow in the woods shows little sign of anything, only dust and leaves, the occasional track of a fox or squirrel. I may catch a few marten on the ridges over behind Redmond Creek, a lynx in Banner flats, or a fox here along the river.

I have a small cabin at the mouth of Tenderfoot, six miles upriver. I built a new dogsled this fall, and I am eager to use it. I have dried fish stacked in the shed, potatoes and cabbage in the cellar, and wood in the yard. A moose, shot late and none too fat, hangs from the tall rack behind the cabin, frozen like a rock. Little by little I am learning the ways of the north. In the darkness and cold that is coming, we will not go hungry.

———

I put down my work; the light is poor, and I listen. A car drives slowly by and is gone over the hill. There are not many now so late in the year.

Seasons, years. The sun will rise over the hill next spring, the cold will come again, and more or less snow will fall. If I live here long enough, I may see a new migration of people from Asia. Here below me is the corridor, the way into the continent, a way still open until stopped once more by ice.

I am alone in my thirty-third year, strange to myself and the few people I know. In this immensity of silence and solitude, my childhood seems as distant as the age of mastodons and sloths; yet it is alive in me and in this life I have chosen to live. I am here and nowhere else.

———

It is dark in the cabin now, the fire in the stove is going out. I am done with these snares. I hang those I have finished on a nail by the doorway to the porch; I put away my tools and the lengths of unused wire. It is time to feed the dogs, and begin supper for myself. Tomorrow I must be up early, and out on the trail before light.

A breath of wind pulls smoke down across the south window. Out on the river, there is fog on that open water.

# ASHLEY HAY

## Ultramarine

This island, this shape: like an oblong squeezed hard in the middle and left—all oranges and golds, sandstone from chocolate to rose, green edges—to make up its own plants, its own animals, its own people. With a lap of deep blue all around it, an arc of blue stretching over it, and the sharp line where they meet.

This place has different shapes, different colours that mark it as special, as what it is, depending on who's telling its story. It's gum-tree shaped, ashy-green. It's desert-open, rich reds. It's inner-city, flat grey pavement. It's opportunity, gold piled up. It's dispossession, black and white. It's stripes on a football scarf, whatever colours. It's summer sun, the feeling of sand.

For my story, it's a blue line that runs a hundred miles along a grid laid over the top of the first white people who came to stay and took over the stories of the place. From the beaches north of Wollongong, where Cook tried to make his landing. Over Bell's Point, through the Royal National Park, past Cape Banks and Cape Solander and the hug their two arms of land make around Botany Bay. Up to Coogee and the path that runs along the cliffs to Bondi. And on to South Head, where Arthur Phillip's men built their first lighthouse, as if it might make ships come faster from the rest of the world to Port Jackson. Its hopeful yellow flare pushing east into the Pacific, pushing west into the great deep bubble of ultramarine that is now called Sydney Harbour.

My blue line runs this hundred or so miles. It flows and shifts, turning in less than twelve hours, striping the edge of the country, the space out to the horizon under the height of the day's sky, running against sand and rocks. This blue that I stand and watch and fall into, running up the coast. That I crave when I'm not here. That I guzzle when I come home.

It's this colour—not wide brown or sun burnt or that monotonous khaki that used to be pinned on the eucalypts: it's this colour that holds my place in its shape.

A friend gave me this story.

A man arrives in Australia from Holland, a couple of years ago, with tubes of artists' paint in his bag, and a roll of brushes. He enrols himself in a class, sits down in front of his first Australian landscape, and smears stripes of colour across his pallette. He looks around at the other people in the class, at the rainbows of pigment they have on their boards. There's something different, he thinks, but he can't put his finger on what it is. He begins to paint.

At the end of the morning he steps back from his canvas. The scene in front of him runs replicated around the circle of stretched frames. Still something. He squints at his picture. He squints at the sky. The teacher comes over to him. She points to his cold, unmixed Antwerp blue. We're a much more cobalt country, she says. Or ultramarine.

This place has blue in its soul.

Arthur Phillip brags of his harbour. The finest in the world, he says, and he skites about the extraordinary number of ships that could be comfortably moored in its waters. So deep. So blue. They have sent him to set up a life on the other side of the world. The antipodean side. The inverted side. They have sent him there to try to survive on the edge of the harbour's richness.

He does feel, he writes a little plaintively, the want of several people who may have helped him make sense of this new place. He can't help but comment that he is without anyone with any notion of coal and mining, making him completely ignorant of half the resources he may be walking around on, and more and more dependent on the ungiving timber these gum-trees yield. And he can't help but remark that it might have been useful to pack him a botanist—even a gardener. Botany Bay, the place where Cook landed, was teeming with the stuff it was named for.[1] Yet here he is, 12,000 miles away from Kew Gardens and with only the garden-bed horticultural knowledge of a couple of surgeons and officers available, and a bunch of natives—who have been living off the plants forever and could tell him the use of everything growing up from the harbour's edge—with whom he can't communicate.

The gulfing space between black and white, crouched together around the harbour's blue.

The harbour itself is all about blue. Specifically, it's about ultramarine. More specifically, it's Winsor and Newton ultramarine: 'Winsor and Newton Deep Ultramarine oil colour,' Brett Whiteley salivates on the harbour's edge almost 200 years after Phillip drops anchor, 'has an obsessive ecstasy-like effect upon my nervous system quite unlike any other colour.'[2] The colour of the harbour: rich, inky, sensuous.

Naturally occurring ultramarine had always been precious—so precious that halos used to be painted this colour to demonstrate the capaciousness of the Church's resources, and contracts between patrons and their Renaissance artists specified how much extra funding would be provided for the all-important blue. The first ultramarine known in the new colony of Sydney— pure, precious—is sent in 1812 to John William Lewin by his friend and former student Alexander Huey.[3]

And then, in 1828—when Sydney has stepped from simply surviving to feeling itself established, settled, contemplative—someone on the other side of the world works out how to fake that blue: you no longer need to grind vast quantites of lapis lazuli into pigment. You can take, instead, clumps of china clay, quartz or sand (for silica), sulfur, charcoal or coal (to burn for carbon) and any spare anyhydrous sodium sulfate and/or carbonate you have lying around. Your grind them, take them up to red hot and keep them there—in an airless atmosphere—for a few hours to create a mess; grind the mess, wash it, dry it, and reheat it to 500°C to bring out the blue colour.[4]

And then you may consider the precise painting of Sydney's harbour and the inky line of its coast's horizon—at a starting price (in the 1830s) of 400 francs per pound as opposed to the 2500–3000 francs you would need for a pound of the real stuff. England's Winsor and Newton has it parcelled up and ready for Brett Whiteley's ecstasy by 1832—although they're still selling oil colours in pigs' bladders, a decade or so away from the invention of metallic tubes.[5]

———

Think about ecstasy. Think about the way the light plays on the navy of the water on a clear day, about leaning towards it, mouth open to it slightly, head tilted slightly to open your throat as you try to inhale it. This place that pulls you up every time you see it, laid out under full shine.

Sit here on this eastern edge of Australia's land, facing the horizon, anywhere along my hundred-odd miles. Let the sides of your gaze register the warm golds and oranges and roses and chocolates of the cliffs. Let the top of your gaze register how high and blue and clear the sky is, its apogee so far up against the blackness of space that you can't quite focus on it. Pour the rest of yourself towards that point where the solid ultramarine of the ocean meets the diffuse cobalt of the sky.

This thing is constant: this horizon is hypnotic. An eye gazing at an infinite point tells its brain to release lithium, and a brain releasing lithium feels happier. Does this make a line of seascape compelling? Is it what makes me sit looking over the water, watching its water rise and fall, swell and turn? Is this what Goethe means when he says that blue is a strange paradox of a colour which pulls away from you, receding, yet draws you after it, compelled?

The horizon is hypnotic: the horizon is fixed. Someone arriving on this point of the Australian coast in 1788, someone possessing it and surviving in it, and changing and losing and trampling all the things that are already there—someone then would have seen the same point that you see now. Someone would have seen that same point two days, two years, two millennia before those ships arrived.

It is a constant.

Under this blue, the blue that arches over Arthur Phillip's fine, deep water and Brett Whiteley's ecstasy, there used to be a language that called the sky *burra*.[6] It's one of the first words someone writes down. *Burra*: sky. *Minak* for darkness. *Mulumulu* for stars that fall in a cluster. And *birrung* for stars that stay where they are.

---

I meet a man who builds rockets for NASA. This is the only story he knows about Australia.

When the Americans build the first spaceships that they trust to fly men, they send an astronaut up to orbit the Earth and come back down again. Yuri Gargarin has done this already, and has come back to say that the planet is really the most extraordinarily lush blue you can think of. The Americans want their own vision splendid. And because they are America and are used to performing things for the world, they make this man's flight an international event—where the Russians have crash-landed Gargarin in a field somewhere hoping no one will notice until they make him look like a hero. Can you please ask the people of your cities, the Americans say, to turn all their lights on as the spaceship goes over, to hang out a bit of a welcome for our guy?

The world obliges.

And he passes over the huge bulk of his own continent, on over the huge empty black-blue of the Pacific Ocean, over the top of Brisbane, on over central Australia. 'Can you thank the people of Brisbane for all that light?' he radios back down to the ground. 'And then the next city in to the west from that, in the middle of Australia—the really huge one: whatever they did,' says the American astronaut, 'was just so pretty. I'm flying over with this deep blue around me and they're pushing up so much light that it's like I'm surround-ed by fireflies or crackers or something.'

This is the only story the man who works for NASA knows about Australia. He wants to know what the big, big city—west of Brisbane, in the middle of the country—is called, the one that put on such a show for that rocketman. He's always thought he'd like to go there, he tells me.

I say to him: but there is no big city in the middle of Australia, west of Brisbane. There's country, space, some towns, and a huge thickness of histo-ries and stories. No big city.

———

Under this blue, on the edges of Sydney Harbour, there was a language that was gentle enough to have this word: I will warm my hands in front of the fire, and then I will squeeze your fingers with mine, and you will feel the warmth. *Buduwa*.[7] Linguists say that blue is one of the last colours to be given a word in most languages: it occurs less frequently in the natural world—there's the sea, there's the sky, but if you have words for them you don't really need a blue-word to describe anything else. Better, maybe, to have a word for sharing warmth.

I try to make sense of my blue. I try to make sense of why I carry it. In the middle of words about colour from the other side of the world, I find this: a Frenchman suggesting that blue, between black and white, indicates an equi-librium.[8] After all, people from Aristotle to Leonardo da Vinci have believed that blue is really a lovely composite of black and white.

It means something, I think, carrying this strip of coast and the water that runs out from it as many miles as I can see, that runs in towards its centre, up the harbour. Watching it change through light twice every day. Watching the impossibility of water hitting land, of sky falling sharply into ocean. Of these things coexisting, the clear blue lines of one brushing against the other.

Blue, between black and white.

## NOTES

1   Governor Arthur Phillip, *Historical Records of New South Wales*, vol. i, pt 2.

2   Sandra McGrath, *Brett Whiteley*, Sydney: Bay Books, 1992, p. 214.

3   Erica Burgess and Paula Dredge, 'Supplying Artists' Materials to Australia 1788–1850', in Ashok Roy and Perry Smith (eds), *Painting Techniques: History, Materials and Studio Practice*, London: The International Institute for Conservation of Historic and Artistic Works, 1998, p. 199.

4   Ashok Roy (ed), *Artists' Pigments*, Washington: Oxford University Press/National Gallery of Art, 1993, p. 56.

5   R. L. Harley, *A Brief History of Winsor and Newton*, Wealdstone: Winsor and Newtown, 1982, pp. 3–4.

6   Jakelin Troy, *The Sydney Language*, Canberra: Panther, 1994, p. 50.

7   Troy, *The Sydney Language*, p. 70.

8   Bachelard, in J. E. Cirlot, *Dictionary of Symbols*, London: Routledge, 1993, p. 54.

# PETE
# HAY

## The Red Steer at Rat Bay

In the last hot days of summer—really the first weekend of autumn—the red steer came to Rat Bay. We saw it from the other side of D'Entrecasteaux Channel as we drove south to the ferry. Sighting down the axe-head bight of North West Bay and over the Channel to our acreage of coastal woodland ('the land'), barely nine kilometres distant though still an hour's travel away, my wife noted a benign wisp of smoke. Then we forgot about it.

Coming at Rat Bay from the north, though, the red steer's gambolling path was suddenly in evidence—a blackened swathe paralleling the coast behind the shacks and, up ahead, a no-longer-benign bank of smoke. And so it was that I turned the corner at precisely the moment that the red steer hurdled the road to kick its heels through the bracken and black peppermint of our 'upper acres'.

When Australians write of fire, this omnipresent threat of summer hell, the language is typically graphic and harrowing. But it would be dishonest of me to write thus. The day was hot but the breeze light, and the fire angled past the shack ('the property') and down to the coast—though the oblique widening of the front as it did so was certainly a threat, as was the possibility of a wind shift into the southeast. But we had time for an unhurried evacuation, and the local brigade was promptly on the scene and backburning, so that even when the threatened wind shift occurred later that evening, 'the property' was secure. The steer itself kicked along to within fifty metres of the back door and took out about three-quarters of our bush, but the old vertical-board shack still stood.

I should tell you of our coastal woodland.

Half of it is an unremarkable sea of bracken and a sparse upper story of black peppermint with some *E. viminalis*—white gum. The other half is species-abundant, an oasis within farmland and understorey-impoverished eucalypt woodlot. Sheoak, blackwood, native cherry, bottlebrush, teatree, the glorious *Xanthorrhoea*. Honeyeaters, parrots, bronzewings, robins, whistlers. Shrike-thrush, cuckoo-shrike, cranky fan (my favourite), firetail, tree martin. The endangered '40-spot'. Sometimes wood duck flock, a ludicrous study, in the trees. Black cockies, too, joyously cacophonous. Penguins in the holes at the base of the cliff. Echidna. Potoroo. Quoll, bright-spotted pelt and soft face hiding a murderous soul. A genetically embattled colony of pademelon. At night I listen to the mournful call of a hunting owl.

Tasmania's two leading authorities on coastal woodland have separately conducted species counts. 'I prefer this to rainforest,' says Steve Harris, 'it's much more species-rich; the most diverse habitat we have.' The other, Jamie Kirkpatrick, enthuses similarly. But he adds a caution: 'coastal woodland is poorly reserved and, precisely because it's on the coast where everyone wants to be, it's under threat'. Then he fair wets himself. He has just discovered two straggling specimens of *Acacia gunnii*, only known to exist from a mere dozen other sites. I have not checked to see whether my two *Acacia gunnii* survived the red steer.

But this is fire-*adapted* bush. It needs fire every fifteen years—though not *regularly* every fifteen years—and to ensure maximum seed recruitment, it should be burnt in patches. That's the advice of Adrian Pyrke, fire management officer with Parks and Wildlife. Adrian and I were set to burn a patch this autumn—the sector we were going to burn equates almost exactly with the tract left *unburnt*. The two straggly *Acacia gunnii* are (were?) right on the rim of our intended burn—and, thus, close to the edge of the territory claimed by the red steer as its own.

I have written of the red steer. I have written of 'the land'. But these are only instrumental to my purpose, because, the risk of self-indulgence and narcissism notwithstanding, I am myself the subject of my essay. The red steer's visitation sharpened in my mind several deep ambivalences attaching to my ownership/stewardship of this small acreage of Bruny Island coastal woodland and, these dis-eases being, I think, of somewhat greater import than mere personal conundrum, it is of these I wish to write.

See how confidently I discuss bush management. With what irresistible authority I catalogue the life of 'the land'. Well it's all for show. It's all for this counterpoint—that, concerning the embattled coastal woodland over which I hold a steward's charge, I really haven't a clue. Without Steve, Jamie and Adrian, I am lost, bereft, hopeless. As it is I wander about like a lost soul, their field lists in hand, in forlorn endeavour to match name and plant. The catalogue above, you'll have noted, consists entirely of the large and easy. Where are the lower shrubs, the groundcover plants? Not listed, because I can't, for the most part, tell the one from the other. And my bird list? Well, those aren't nearly the half of it; just the very obvious ones that any dunderhead, this one included, might identify.

It's the same with bush management. For years I shied away from that regeneration burn. It was too daunting. In the 'upper acres', where the range of species declines in the face of a ubiquity of bracken, I had long wanted to embark on a project of restoration, gradually clearing the bracken and planting out seeds gathered elsewhere on the block. Others do it. I have read the relevant literature—Steve and Jamie prominent therein—and it seems straightforward enough. But each time I contemplate it I am overwhelmed.

You will likely think this pathetic. That's as may be. In a moment I intend to defend myself after a fashion. There is a larger sense, though, in which the question of my personal adequacy hardly matters, because the cards are, in any case, stacked firmly and officially against those landholders who would exercise ecologically responsible citizenship. In Tasmania productive farmland is exempt from land tax—but 'mere bush' is not. How's that for an incentive to clear! Similar administrative impediments to land management for natural values can be found, in my experience, in most jurisdictions.

But these can be removed in the stroke of a legislative pen. Other impedimenta are less tractable. Let's return to the visitation of the red steer. The local brigade, comprising volunteers all, was most effective as it swung into action in defence of 'the property'—which is to say, in defence of the shack (a weekender is known hereabouts, however grand or humble, as 'the shack'). That is the brigade's purpose; its *telos*. To ensure the survival of 'property', construed as human artefact. All regimes bend to this purpose. Each spring, the local council issues 'fire abatement notices'. Never mind that 'the land' is an isolated tract of threatened coastal woodland. In the accepted scheme of things its natural values are—implicitly but emphatically—accounted far less than jerry-built weekenders and pre-fab outhouses. And 'burning off' is a spring activity in these parts, because that is the time of quickening; it is when the bush generates the 'fuel' that may, under human agency, combust in the parched weeks of summer. But the management imperatives of fire control and bush regeneration stand opposed in important respects. Adrian's unequivocal advice was to burn in late autumn, not spring. Natural reseeding is thereby maximised—and ours was to be a regeneration burn, not, in its prime purpose, a 'fuel reduction' burn.

The head of the local brigade is a 'permanent'; he owns the farm and is my nearest neighbour. He's a big and a powerful man, a man's man, brusque, not given to small talk. His presence is a whimsy-free zone. He holds 'greenies' in contempt. I like him. We have cricket and Australian football in common and, like me, he's killed many a beer.

We fell out for the first time a week after the fire. He rang me at my home in Hobart, wanting, there and then, to take to the environs of the shack with a 'dozer. His arguments were impeccable. This is fire-prone and adapted bush. 'The property' is, as things stand, at risk. He needs access for the fire truck where currently none exists. He and his crew run the risks and do the work, and they do so on my ungrateful behalf. The least I can do. I found his arguments impeccable; still do. And I said no.

How to explain to him that mine is a paradigm in which it is not uncomplicatedly self-evident that 'the property' is of greater inherent worth than 'the land'? I do not—desperately do not—want to see the shack go up in smoke. But, if I am to be honest, still less can I countenance the prospect of the natural values of this tract of coastal woodland irredeemably impaired.

It can be objected that, if all this were properly sorted out, these imperatives would *not* be in irreconcilable conflict. That the problem here is still me. I can see, the structural bias against the natural interest notwithstanding, that that's true. It is a problem of love.

I hold for 'the land', the mysteries of its rich brew of botany, its secretive, soft-eyed fauna, a passionate, unreasoning —not to be read as 'unreasonable'—love. For years I have immersed in the writings of radical environmental philosophy, and there I have learned that deep empathetic identification with our home range is the antidote to nature-impoverishing interventionism. I have learned the lesson well. I have deep empathetic identification in spades. The real—the 'deep'—reason for my rejection of the fire chief's offer is that his exercise in prudent fire control would destroy several venerable

*Xanthorrhoea* that were already in existence when Captain Cook first dropped anchor down the road in Adventure Bay. I couldn't do it. As it is, my need to distinguish this species from that does not sit well with my intellectual mentors. The act of naming, I have read (many times) is an essentially colonial act, an appropriating act, the essential prelude to despotism and a comprehensive mastery. It is also a process of differentiation, of individuation, and it takes the mind away from the relationality of living process. It is not an act of deep love, of humbling, unselfconscious immersion, of giving oneself to the cosmic dance. It is an act of imperialism.

Before the coming of the red steer I was already suppressing uneasiness over the practical implications of these intellectual positions. But the red steer brought them vividly, uncompromisingly, into focus. I now believe that there is no choice but to name, to know, to benignly intervene, to 'steward'. Left unattended, this small tract of coastal woodland will suffer inevitable encroachment, impoverishment, obliteration. And so it is, given the human's reach and the destructive power of his tools, for the natural world everywhere. There is no choice. We must be stewards—whatever the consequences for noble ideas of ecological democracy and biospherical egalitarianism. We must be stewards because the alternative to benign management is, in these times at least, a remorseless and accelerating decline of the natural estate. Destruction by neglect.

Two problems occur. One is what we might call, using the coy and cutesy terminology of management-speak, a 'knowledge deficit'. We can apply principles of scientific ecological management. I have already lamented my personal 'deficit' in this regard. I think it important, nevertheless, that such knowledge be extended and put to work. To do that a prerequisite is to 'name', to know the qualities and needs of individual ecosystem components, as well as the relational dynamics that make synergies of living systems rather than mere summed agglomerations. The scientific insights thus acquired are the knowledge gift of my western intellectual heritage, in its benign and minor tributary. I would be foolish to eschew them.

But there is another relevant knowledge, and to this I am denied access— the saturated vernacular knowing of the Aboriginal peoples who belonged here. This was the territory of the Nuenone, the Bruny Island people, the first of Tasmania's indigenous peoples to have their ancient social ways torn apart. I have been told, though I cannot confirm it as true, that one of a handful of inscribed tokens given by Cook to Aborigines at Adventure Bay in 1777 was found right here on 'the land'. George Augustus Robinson, on God's and

Governor Arthur's mission to save the 'savages', often came to Rat Bay, landing here for Woodcutter's Point, now ten minutes walk to the south, and the site of Robinson's first Aboriginal 'facility'. And somewhere out there in the Channel an abused and captive Truganini watched as the hands of her intended husband were hatcheted off by convicts as he clung to the gunwale of their boat. This is potently Aboriginal land, redolent with hints of ancient ways and yesterday's horror.

I do know, of course, that tribal Aboriginals were active managers of the land. They fire-stick farmed, and the fire-adapted coastal woodland of 'the land' is their cultural artefact. And I know, too, that there's was a storied existence—they would not have abstractly intellectualised love of place in the way that I have done. I can never know this coastal woodland with the intricate detail of an Aboriginal knowing and so I have to concede that I can never be 'native' in their deep and unbounderied way. Generations hence that may be possible—then again it may not. I can only tread the smallest distance down an uncertain path. And in the treading, I must take most of my signposts from the baggage of my westerner's *Weltanschauung*. It is not as if I have a choice.

The second problem? Well, it remains me. It is one thing to acknowledge the need for an interventionist management of natural areas. But I remain a prisoner of those pathetic shortcomings detailed above. I cannot change. I cannot even find an effective way of rendering my stance plausible. Where are the words that work? My perspective finds no sympathy with friends of more prosaic proclivity, for whom any 'going lightly' management regime that might, as a by-product, impair the status of 'the land' as tradable commodity—such as the installation of a conservation covenant—constitutes absolute folly. Even my children are without interest in 'the land', visiting it only under parental duress. To them my position is bizarre, incomprehensible.

Yet I am assuredly not alone. Throughout the Australian bush other people, motivated by a deep biophilia, and armed with nothing more tangible than love, are undertaking bush stewardship roles for which they are blissfully inadequate. I would not apologise for the impulse to love the diversity of life that is now so much at risk. At day's end we do need it in spades. It is necessary. But, the red steer showed me as it kicked its heels through the upper acres, it is not sufficient.

# LINDA HOGAN

# Creations

We were told by the Creator, This is your land. Keep it for me until I come back.

THOMAS BANYACA, HOPI ELDER

We are traveling toward the end of land, to a place called Ría de Celustún, Estuary of Heaven. It is a place where clouds are born. On some days they rise up above the river and follow water's path. On those days, from across the full length of the land, Río Esperanza, the River of Hope, can be seen as it is carried up into the sky. But today, the late morning clouds have formed farther out, above the ocean.

It is the day after spring equinox, and as we near the ocean, whiteness is the dominant feature. Salt beds stretch out at water's edge. Beaches, made of sea-worn limestone and broken-down coral, are nearly blinding in the early spring light. Water, itself, wears the sun's light on its back, and near a road sign several young men are at work, throwing buckets of salt-dried fish into the bed of a pickup truck.

It has been a long, narrow road through the Yucatán. We have passed jungle, brush, and villages created from bone-colored limestone. A woman in an embroidered white huipil walks along the road carrying a bundle of firewood.

Smoke from a household fire rises above thatched roofs. Two boys with small rifles step into the forest in search of food. In spite of the appearance of abundance in the Yucatán, it is a world endangered, not only by deforestation, but by other stresses to the environment, by human poverty. It is a hungry place with dwindling resources.

In some villages, the few livestock—a single horse, a solitary cow—are bony of rib. People, too, in many towns are thin with a poverty that as it grows diminishes the world about it.

Many of the people in and near Ría de Celustún are new people. Previously, they were farmers of henequen, a plant used to make hemp rope, but since the introduction of plastic and nylon rope, the people have been relocated without consideration for what their presence would mean in this region, or how they would stretch a living out of the land. In order to build houses, swamps were filled in with garbage. There are sewage problems, contaminated water, and the cutting of trees has destroyed the watershed. With the close-in waters now overfished, the farmers-turned-fishermen are forced into the dangerous business of taking poorly equipped boats out to deeper waters in search of food.

In geological history, as with that of the people, this is a place of rising and collapsing worlds. There is constant movement and transformation. Some are subtle changes—the way mangrove swamps create new soil, the way savannah grows from the fallen mangrove leaves—but most of the boundaries here are crossed in sudden and dramatic ways, the result of the elemental struggle between water and land, where a water-shaped cave collapses and new water surges to fill the sinkhole left behind, where water claims its edges from land, where swamp becomes ocean, ocean evaporates and leaves salt. The land itself bears witness to the way elements trade places; it is limestone that floated up from the sea, containing within it the delicate, complex forms of small animals from earlier times; snails, plants, creatures that were alive beneath water are still visible beneath the feet. To walk on this earth is to walk on a living past, on the open pages of history and geology.

Now even the dusty road we travel becomes something else as it disappears into the ocean at Celustún. It is a place of endings and of beginnings, full with the power of creation.

Holy Mother Earth, the trees and all nature, are witnesses of your
thoughts and deeds

WINNEBAGO

For the Maya, time was born and had a name when the sky didn't exist
and the earth had not yet awakened.
The days set out from the east and started walking.
The first day produced from its entrails the sky and
the earth.
The second day made the stairway for the rain to run down.
The cycles of the sea and the land, and multitude of things,
were the work of the third day.
The fourth day willed the earth and the sky to tilt
so that they could meet.
The fifth day decided that everyone had to work.
The first light emanated from the sixth day.
In places where there was nothing, the seventh day
put soil; the eighth plunged its hands and feet in the soil.
The ninth day created the nether worlds; the tenth
earmarked for them those who had poison in their
souls.
Inside the sun, the eleventh day modeled stone and tree.
It was the twelfth that made the wind. Wind blew,
and it was called spirit because there was no death in it.
The thirteenth day moistened the earth and kneaded
the mud into a body like ours.
Thus it is remembered in Yucatán.

EDUARDO GALEANO, *MEMORY OF FIRE*

Inside the people who grow out of any land there is an understanding of it, a remembering all the way back to origins, to when the gods first shaped humans out of clay, back to when animals could speak with people, to when the sky and water were without form and all was shaped by such words as 'Let there be.'

In nearly all creation accounts, as with the Maya, life was called into being through language, thought, dreaming, or singing, acts of interior consciousness. For the Maya, time itself is alive. In the beginning, the day sets out walking from the east and brings into being the world and all that inhabited it—jaguar, turtle, deer, trees. It was all sacred.

Then there were the first humans, whose job it was to offer prayer, tell stories, and remember the passage of time. Made of the clay of this earth, the mud people of the first creation did not endure; when it rained, their bodies grew soft and dissolved.

In the next creation, humans were lovingly carved of wood. These prospered and multiplied. But in time, the wooden people forgot to give praise to the gods and to nurture the land. They were hollow and without compassion. They transformed the world to fit their own needs. They did not honor the sacred forms of life on earth, and they began to destroy the land, to create their own dead future out of human arrogance and greed. Because of this, the world turned against them. In a world where everything was alive, the forms of life they had wronged took vengeance on them. There was black rain. The animals they harmed attacked them. The ruined waters turned against them and flooded their land.

In the final creation of mankind, the people were created from corn:

And so then they put into words the creation,
The shaping of our first mother
And father.
Only yellow corn
And white corn were their bodies.
Only food were the legs
And arms of man.
Those who were our first fathers
Were the original men.
Only food at the outset
Were their bodies.

QUICHÉ MAYA, *POPUL VUH*

At first, these care-taking, life-giving people made of corn, the substance of gods, saw what the gods saw. In order to make them more human, less godlike, some of this vision was taken away so there might be mystery, and the mystery of creation and of death inspired deep respect and awe for all of creation.

In most stories of genesis, unwritten laws of human conduct are taught at creation. For the Maya, too, the story of the hollow people is not only part of a beautiful and complex story but also a telling language, one that speaks against human estrangement from land.

Emptiness and estrangement are deep wounds, strongly felt in the present time. We have been split from what we could nurture, what could fill us. And we have been wounded by a dominating culture that has feared and hated the natural world, has not listened to the voice of the land, has not believed in the inner worlds of human dreaming and intuition, all things that have guided indigenous people since time stood up in the east and walked this world into existence, split from connection between self and land

The best hunters of the far north still find the location of their prey by dreaming. In *Maps and Dreams*, by anthropologist Hugh Brody, one informant says, 'Maybe you don't think this power is possible. Few people understand. The old-timers who were strong dreamers knew many things that are not easy to understand ... The fact that dream-hunting works has been proved many times.' Maps of the land and the direction of deer are revealed in dreams.

Like the wooden people, many of us in this time have lost the inner substance of our lives and have forgotten to give praise and remember the sacredness of all life. But in spite of this forgetting, there is still a part of us that is deep and intimate with the world. We remember it by feel. We experience it as a murmur in the night, a longing and restlessness we can't name, a yearning that tugs at us. For it is only recently, in earth time, that the severing of the connections between people and land have taken place. Something in our human blood is still searching for it, still listening, still remembering. Nicaraguan poet-priest Ernesto Cardenal wrote, 'We have always wanted something beyond what we wanted.' I have loved those words, how they speak to the longing place inside us that seeks to be whole and connected with the earth. This, too, is a place of beginning, the source of our living.

So also do we remember our ancestors and their lives deep in our bodily cells. In part, this deep, unspoken remembering is why I have come here, searching out my own beginnings, the thread of connection between old Maya cultures and my Chickasaw heritage. According to some of our oral traditions, a migration story of our tribe, we originated in this region, carved dugout canoes, and traveled to the southeast corner of what is now called Florida, the place of flowers. I have always felt a oneness with this Mexican land, but I know this call to origins is deeper, older, and stronger than I am, more even than culture and blood origins. Here, there is a feel for the mystery of our being in all ways, in earth and water. It is a feel for the same mystery that sends scientists to search for the beginning of the universe. We seek our origins as much as we seek our destinies.

And we desire to see the world intact, to step outside our emptiness and remember the strong currents that pass between humans and the rest of nature, currents that are the felt voice of land, heard in the cells of the body.

It is the same magnetic call that, since before human history, has brought the sea turtles to the beach of Celestún. The slow blood of the turtles hears it, turtles who have not been here since the original breaking of the egg that held them, who ran toward an ocean they did not know, who have lived their lives in the sea, then felt the call of land in deep memory and so return to a place unseen. Forever, it seems, they have been swimming through blue waters in order to return, to lay their eggs in sun-warmed sand, and go back to the clear blue-green waters of their mothers in ancient journeys of creation and rituals of return.

———

The white shoreline stretches around us, wide and open. It is early for the endangered hawksbills and green turtles to be coming to land. Egg-laying usually begins in late April and early May. Because of the endangered status of the sea turtles, members of an organization called Pronatura will arrive to protect the turtles and the eggs. In this region in 1947, there were so many sea turtles that it was said forty thousand of them appeared on one beach to spawn. Now the hawksbills are the second most endangered species in the world. Today, despite the earliness of the season, there are tracks in the white sand, large tracks that have moved earth as if small tanks had emerged from the water and traveled a short distance up sand. Some of the tracks return, but others vanish, and where they end, there are human footprints.

———

In the traditional belief systems of native people, the terrestrial call is the voice of God, or of gods, the creative power that lives on earth, inside earth, in turtle, stone, and tree. Knowledge comes from, and is shaped by, observations and knowledge of the natural world and natural cycles.

In fact, the word 'god,' itself, in the dictionary definition, means to call, to invoke. Like creation, it is an act of language, as if the creator and the creation are one, the primal pull of land is what summons.

Sometimes beliefs are inventions of the mind. Sometimes they are inventions of the land. But how we interpret and live our lives has to do with the religious foundations and the spiritual history we have learned.

The Western belief that God lives apart from earth is one that has taken us toward collective destruction. It is a belief narrow enough to forget the value of matter, the very thing that soul inhabits. It has created a people who are future-sighted only in a limited way, not in terms of taking care of the land for the future generations.

> The Lakota knew that man's heart, away from nature, becomes hard; he knew that lack of respect for growing, living things soon led to lack of respect for humans, too.
>
> LUTHER STANDING BEAR

Not far from here is where Fray Diego de Landa, in the 1500s, tortured and killed the Maya people and burned their books in the alchemical drive of the Spanish to accumulate wealth, turn life into gold, and convert others to their own beliefs. They set into flames entire peoples, and centuries of remembered and recorded knowledge about the land. It is believed that there were considerable stores of knowledge in these people and in their books, not just history and sacred stories but medical knowledge, a math advanced enough to create the concept of zero, and a highly developed knowledge of astronomy whose intelligence continues to surprise contemporary astronomers. It is certain that centuries of habitation on this land yielded more knowledge about the earth and its cycles than has been newly understood and recovered in the brief, troubled years that have since followed. And we are left to wonder if that ancient knowledge would help us in this time of threat, if the lost books held a clue to survival.

This burned and broken history is part of the story of the land. It is the narrative of the past by which we still live. It is stored in the hearts and blood of the people and in the land. Fray de Landa for one brief moment acknowledged such life when he wrote that the land is 'the country with the least earth that I have ever seen, since all of it is one living rock.' These words, this recognition of living rock, might have bridged a different connection, an understanding closer to the way indigenous people see the land, and a life-sustaining way of being.

> The tides are always shifting things about among the mangrove roots ...
> Parts of it are neither land nor sea and so everything is moving from one
> element to another.

LOREN EISELEY, *NIGHT COUNTRY*

A rib of land separates ocean and barrier beach from the red-colored tidal estuary and wetlands area where the river runs toward larger waters. The river is so full of earth that it is red and shallow. In its marshy places, plants grow from its clay. There are places where freshwater underground rivers surge upward to create conditions that are unique to this place, and exist nowhere else.

There is salt marsh, a tidal estuary, and mangrove swamps that contain one of the world's largest colonies of flamingos, birds named after flame, as if they belong, in part, to the next element of creation. This red estuary is alive and breathing, moving with embryonic clay and silt.

It is a place crucial not only to the flamingo colonies and waterfowl but also to migratory birds from as far north as Maine, a connection that closes the miles, another boundary undone.

Traveling into this red water, we are surrounded by the many-rooted mangrove swamps. Mangroves, a network of tangled roots and twisted branches, are a part of creation and renewal in this land. Coastal plants, they live in the divide between land and water. Both marine and terrestrial, these plants are boundary-bridgers that have created islands and continents. Consuming their own fallen leaves, they are nurturers in the ongoing formation of the world, makers of earth, and the mangroves have a life force strong enough to alter the visible face of their world. Rachel Carson called them a world 'extending back into darkening swamps of its own creation.'

The interior of the swamps is dark and filled with the intricate relationships of water with plant, animal, earth, sheltering small lives within them.

Mangroves are plants that reach out to grow, searching for water and mineral with a grasping kind of energy that can be felt. As they send their roots seeking outward, they move forward, leaving behind them the savannah that will become tropical forest. In turn, rainwater flowing underground will break through the forest and create a cenote. No one knows the paths of these rivers. Theirs is a vast underground network. It is only known where they rise. And in some of these sinkholes, or cenotes, are species of fish from one river system not found in other cenotes in the region.

The rain clouds have not yet reached us. Light shines through the leaves. A fish jumps. As we move forward, the path of our disturbance is lighter in color, like a vapor trail, behind us. Then it vanishes, unlike the paths we have left behind in other places. There is a dreaminess here where creation continues to happen all around us in time that is alive.

———

At the far edge of copper-colored water, a white egret steps through the shallows, an eye sharp for fish. On the other side of water's edge stands a solitary blue heron. Herons are fragile birds, and it is not unusual for them to die from stress. I think of them when hearing that Hmong men, forced to leave their country and rootless in America, die of no apparent cause while they are sleeping. I understand the loss that leads to despair and to death. It has happened to us and is happening to the land, the breaking of the heart of creation.

The poet Gertrud Kolmar, a woman who loved animals, died in Auschwitz, one of those lost by whatever other failures of the gods have made men hollow and capable of such crimes. There is a poem of hers that herons fly through. With rigid legs and boomerang wings they fly beneath rolling clouds through a smoke blue sky, flying toward dawn, flying without falling from heaven. But the holocaust began before her time. It began on this continent, with the genocide of tribal people, and with the ongoing war against the natural world. Here is a lesson: what happens to people and what happens to the land is the same thing.

Shape, I think she meant by boomerang wings, although the boomerang is something more than that; it is something that returns. And there is great hope in return. Not just in returned time or history, as the round cycles of the Maya worldview express, but in returned land and animal species. Return is what we are banking on as we attempt to put back what has disappeared, the songs of wolves in Yellowstone, the pale-edged wings of condors in California sky, the dark, thundering herds of buffalo to Indian country, the flamingos along the River of Hope. This colony, once diminished to five thousand birds in 1955, has increased to twenty-two thousand, according to JoAnn Andrews of Pronatura. This, and Ría Lagardos to the north, are the only wintering and nesting areas these flamingos have.

———

And then we see them, these returned flamingos, in their wintering grounds, first as a red line along the darker water, red as volcanic fire breaking open from black rock, revealing its passionate inner light, fire from the center of earth's creative force, lighted from within.

For well over a mile, all along the shore, we see them, like dawn's red path stretched before us. It is almost too much for the eye to see, this great vision, the shimmering light of them. It's a vision so incredible and thick. I know it will open inside my eyes in the moment before death when a lived life draws itself out one last time before closing forever. We are drawn to these birds the way air is pulled into fire. They are proof of how far blood will travel to seek its beginning.

We sit, floating, and watch these lives with their grace and the black lines of their underwings. They are noisy. The birds at the outermost edges are aware of us. We are careful not to disturb them as they eat. Their mission here, at the end of winter, is to fill themselves. Already there are mating displays, though true nesting takes place to the north of here in Ría Lagardos, where they build and guard mud nests.

They are restless. One group begins to fly with a running start across water, red clouds rising across the thin red-brown skin of water, as if water has come undone from itself, lost something to air where clouds, too, are born of water. Other groups are in water and onshore, long-necked, the rose-colored light coming from the marvelous feathers constructed of centuries of necessity and the love that life has for its many forms and expressions.

They are birds glorious and godly, and like us, are an ancient nation.

———

The clouds that were out at sea have moved east and now they reach us. Thunder breaks open the sky and a warm afternoon rain begins. We turn off the engine of the boat and pole into a shadowy corridor of mangroves until we reach a sheltered pool. A faint wind creaks the trees. Above us, in the branches, a termite nest is black and heavy. It is a splendid architecture wedged in the branches of a tree, one come to over time, a creation older than human presence on the earth by millions of years. The nest is contained intelligence, made up of lives that work together with the mind of a single organism.

The word 'termite' was given by Linnaeus and originally meant 'end of life.' That's how young and new our oldest knowledge is, because these, too, are old participants in creation, in beginnings. They break down wood, forming rich soil in a place that would otherwise be choked.

The overhead canopy of leaves shelters us. We watch the drops meet water, returning to their larger country, becoming it, re-creating it out of themselves.

This is one of the places where an underground river has broken through the shelf of limestone and risen to the surface. It is called Ojo de Agua, Eye of Water. Looking into this eye, it seems to gaze back, and in that blue gaze are tiny fish. The water is one of earth's lanterns, the same blue of glacier light and of the Earth as seen from out in space. Beneath us, a larger fish eats algae off a fallen tree, long-legged insects move about the unclosed eye of water.

There is a second eye, and we decide to crawl through roots and dark mud to find it. Frederico, the guide, is barefoot and barefoot is the only way to move here. As we pass through the tangles and intricacies, he offers me a hand and helps me through. His hand is strong and warm, but inspite of it, my foot slips off the convoluted roots. I think it is all right; I see the blue leaves resting on the water's floor, but it is a false bottom, and my leg keeps going until both legs are in to the hip, my foot still slipping down, 'To China,' Frederico says as I find a limb to grasp. Here again the boundaries did not hold. What looked like bottom was merely blue leaves and algae held up by a rising current of boundless water.

And here, where the underground river ends, other beginnings are fed, other species and creations. If it were time, instead of space, scholars would call it zero date, that place where, as for the Maya, the end of one world is the beginning of another. As they interpret the world, time is alive and travels in a circle. There were other creations and worlds before the one we now inhabit; the cosmos has reformed itself.

For those who know only this one universe, to think of its origins is an overwhelming task. It means to think before time, before space, all the way back to the void that existed before creation. And for people of science, as for those of religion, the universe in its cosmic birth originated from small and minute beginnings. There was nothing and then life came into existence. Stephen Hawking says, 'It was possible for the entire universe to appear out of nothing.' There is a place from which all things grew into a miraculous emergence.

'All beginnings wear their endings like dark shadows,' says astronomer-physicist Chet Raymo. And maybe they do. If endings are foreshadowed by their beginnings, or are in some way the same thing, it is important that we circle around and come back to look at our human myths and stories. Unlike the cyclic nature of time for the Maya, the Western tradition of beliefs within a straight line of history leads to an apocalyptic end. And stories of the end, like those of beginning, tell something about the people who created them.

In her article 'What Do Stars Eat?' in *Left Bank*, Lynda Sexson writes:

> We are so accustomed to myths (sacred stories) of extinction, that we are not as practical at imagining that greater gap—continuation … Would the earth or our existence on it be in such peril if we did not harbor a profound desire for extinction? *'They lie down, they cannot rise, they are extinguished, quenched like a wick,'* resonates Isaiah. The crisis of Western culture is ecological. The source of that crisis is in Western culture's own version of reality; the myth of the urge to eradicate: earth and images of earth, body and song.

Without deep reflection, we have taken on the story of endings, assumed the story of extinction, and have believed that it is the certain outcome of our presence here. From this position, fear, bereavement, and denial keep us in the state of estrangement from our natural connection with land.

We need new stories, new terms and conditions that are relevant to the love of land, a new narrative that would imagine another way, to learn the infinite mystery and movement at work in the world. It would mean we, like the corn people of the Maya, give praise and nurture creation.

Indian people must not be the only ones who remember the agreement with the land, the sacred pact to honor and care for the life that, in turn, provides for us. We need to reach a hand back through time and a hand forward, stand at the zero point of creation to be certain that we do not create the absence of life, of any species, no matter how inconsequential they might appear to be.

———

At the beginning, there was nothing and something came from it. We have not been able to map it, except in theory, in mathematical terms. As with the underground rivers, we only see where it surfaces. It is the same mystery of swimming turtles, early morning's new light, the limestone floor of sea that rose up to become land. Every piece fits and has its place, we learned from Darwin. As our knowledge has increased, that fitting has grown infinitely more complex and intricate. There is an integrity, a terrestrial intelligence at work. It's an intelligence far-reaching and beyond our comprehension. As Alan Lightman says: 'Creation lies outside of physics.'

The immeasurable *quality* of this world has depth and breadth we can't measure. Yet we know it's there, and we believe in it; the whole of it has been revealed only a small piece at a time. Cosmologists now surmise there are other universes. Creation is still taking place. As the story becomes larger, we become smaller. Perhaps that is why we shape belief around mystery.

———

We come from the land, sky, from love and the body. From matter and creation. We are, life is, an equation we cannot form or shape, a mystery we can't trace in spite of our attempts to follow it back to its origin.

As Cardenal knew by those words about the want behind our wanting, we do not even have a language to speak words deep enough, strong enough to articulate what it is we truly desire. This is just one hint of our limitations. The real alchemy of our being here is the finest of transformations, and we do not know it except to say that we are atoms that were other patterns and arrangements of form.

We do not know the secrets of stars. We do not know the true history of water. We do not know ourselves. We have forgotten that this land and every life form is a piece of god, a divine community, with the same forces of creation in plants as in people. All the lives around us are lives of gods. The long history of creation that has shaped plankton, and shaped horseshoe crabs, has shaped our human being. Everything is Maker; mangroves, termites, all are sources of one creation or another. Without respect and reverence for it, there is an absence of holiness, of any God.

> All over the earth, faces of all living things are alike. Mother Earth has turned these faces out of the earth with tenderness.

LUTHER STANDING BEAR

> Men talk much of matter and energy, of the struggle for existence that molds the shape of life. These things exist, it is true; but more delicate, elusive, quicker than fins in water, is that mysterious principle known as organization, which leaves all other mysteries concerned with life stale and insignificant by comparison ... Like some dark and passing shadow within matter, it cups out the eyes' small windows or spaces the notes of a meadowlark's song in the interior of a mottled egg. That principle—I am beginning to suspect—was there before the living in the deeps of water ...
>
> If 'dead' water has reared up this curious landscape ... it must be plain even to the most devoted materialist that the matter of which it speaks contains amazing, if not dreadful powers, and may not impossibly be, as Hardy has suggested, 'but one mask of many worn by the Great Face behind.'

LOREN EISELEY, *NIGHT COUNTRY*

The face of the land is our face, and that of all its creatures. To see whole is to see all the parts of the puzzle, some of which have not even been found, as there are still numerous animals and plants that have not been identified. Even here at Celustún there are faces still unseen. What grows within us is the same.

———

In this place are spectacular fish, deep blue ones, green and yellow. But swimming, I see a silver circle of fish, many small ones, swimming in a cluster. All of them turn at one time and hold the circle together. They avoid me, moving away, and still their circle holds. They share a mind, the way termites do, share a common mission of survival, like all the faces turned out of the earth, all part of the one mask of many faces worn by the Great Face behind.

> The lands around my dwelling
> Are more beautiful
> From the day
> When it is given to me to see
> Faces I have never seen before.

All is more beautiful,
All is more beautiful.
And life is thankfulness.
These guests of mine
Make my house grand.

ESKIMO SONG

What does god look like? These fish, this water, this land.

# WILLIAM KITTREDGE

## Reimagining Warner

A scab-handed wandering child who rode off on old horses named Snip and Moon, I grew up with the constant thronging presence of animals. Herds of feral hogs inhabited the swampland tule beds where the waterbirds nested. Those hogs would eat the downy young of the Canada geese if they could, but never caught them so far as I knew.

Warner Valley, tucked against the enormous reach of Great Basin sagebrush and lavarock desert in southeastern Oregon and northern Nevada, was a hidden world. The landlocked waters flow down from the snowy mountains to the west but don't find a way out to the sea. They accumulate and evaporate in shallow lakes named Pelican, Crump, Hart, Stone Corral, and Bluejoint.

Sandhill cranes danced their courtship dances in our meadows. The haying and feeding and the cowherding work couldn't have been done without the help of horses. We could only live the life we had with the help of horses.

All day Sunday sometimes in the summer my family would spread blankets by Deep Creek of Twenty-mile Creek and even us kids would catch all the rainbow trout we could stand.

The late 1930s, when I was a child in that valley, were like the last years of the nineteenth century. What I want to get at is our isolation. We were thirty-six gravel-road miles over the Warner Mountains from the little lumbering and rancher town of Lakeview (maybe 2500 souls). Warner Valley was not on the route to anywhere.

The way in was the way out. The deserts to the east were traced with wagontrack roads over the saltgrass playas and around rimrocks from spring to spring, waterhole to waterhole, but nobody ever headed in that direction with the idea of going toward the future.

To the east lay deserts and more deserts. From a ridge above our buckaroo camp beside the desert spring at South Corral, we could see the long notched snowy ridge of Steens Mountain off in the eastern distances, high country where whores from Burns went in summer to camp with the sheep herders amid aspen trees at a place called Whorehouse Meadows, where nobody but wandering men ever went, men who would never be around when you needed them. And beyond, toward Idaho, there was more desert.

———

By the end of the Second World War my grandfather had got control of huge acreages in Warner, and my father was making serious progress at draining the swamplands. The spring of 1946 my grandfather traded off two hundred or so work teams for chicken feed. He replaced those horses with a fleet of John Deere tractors. Harness rotted in the barns until the barns were torn down.

I wonder if my father and his friends understood how irrevocably they were giving up what they seemed to care about more than anything when they talked of happiness—their lives in conjunction to the animals they worked with and hunted. I wonder why they acted like they didn't care.

Maybe they thought the animals were immortal. I recall those great teams of work horses running the hayfields in summer before daybreak, their hooves echoing on the sod as we herded them toward the willow corral at some haycamp, the morning mists and how the boy I was knew at least enough to know he loved them and that this love was enough reason to revere everything in sight for another morning.

Those massive horses were like mirrors in which I could see my emotions reflected. If they loved this world, and they seemed to, with such satisfaction, on those mornings when our breaths fogged before us, so did I.

Soon after World War Two electricity from Bonneville Power came to Warner, and telephones that sort of functioned. The road over the mountains and down along Deep Creek was paved. Our work in the fields had in so many ways gone mechanical. Eventually we had television. Our isolation was dissolving.

About the time I watched the first Beatles telecast in the early 1960s, the Chamber of Commerce gentlemen in Winnemucca got together with like-minded gentlemen from Lakeview, and decided it made great economic sense to punch a highway across the deserts between those two little cities. Think of the tourists.

The two-lane asphalt ran north from Winnemucca to Denio, then turned west to cross the million or so acres of rangeland we leased from the BLM (we saw those acreages as ours, like we owned them: in those days we virtually did), over the escarpment called the Dougherty Slide, across Guano Valley and down Greaser Canyon, and directly through our meadowlands in Warner Valley.

I recall going out to watch the highway-building as it proceeded, the self-important recklessness of those men at their work, the roaring of the D-8 Caterpillars and the clouds of dust rising behind the huge careening of the self-propelled scrapers, and being excited, sort of full up with pride because the great world was at last coming to us in Warner Valley. Not that it ever did. The flow of tourism across those deserts never amounted to much. But maybe it will, one of these days.

Enormous changes were sweeping the world. We didn't want to encounter hippies or free love or revolutionaries on the streets of Lakeview. Or so we said. But like anybody, we yearned to be in on the action.

We were delighted, one 4th of July, to hear that the Hell's Angels motor-cycle gang from Oakland had headed across the deserts north of Winnemucca on their way to a weekend of kicking ass in Lakeview, and that they had been turned back by a single deputy sheriff.

There had been the long string of lowriders coming on the two-lane blacktop across one of the great desert swales, and the deputy, all by himself, standing there by his Chevrolet. The deputy, a slight, balding man, had flagged down the leaders and they'd had a talk. 'Nothing I can do about it,' the deputy said, 'but they're sighting their deer rifles. These boys, they mean to sit back there three hundred yards and shoot you off them motor-cycles. They won't apologize or anything. You fellows are way too far out in the country.'

According to the legend, the leaders of the Hell's Angels decided the deputy was right: They knew they were way too far out in the country, and they turned back. I never talked to anybody who knew if that story was true, but we loved it.

It was a story that told us we were not incapable of defending ourselves, or powerless in a nation we understood to be going on without us. We never doubted some of our southeastern Oregon boys would have shot those Hell's Angels off their bikes. Some places were still big and open enough to be safe from outsiders.

During the great flood in December of 1964, when the Winnemucca-to-the-Sea highway acted like a dam across the valley, backing up water over four or five thousand acres, my brother Pat walked a D-7 Caterpillar out along the asphalt and cut the highway three or four times, deep cuts so the floodwaters could pour through and drain away north. What he liked best, Pat said, was socking that bulldozer blade down and ripping up that asphalt with the yellow lines painted on it. We were still our own people.

———

But even as huge and open to anything as southeastern Oregon may have seemed in those old days, it was also inhabited by spooks. In autumn of the same year the Winnemucca-to-the-Sea highway came across our meadow-lands, I had our heavy equipment, our Carry-All scrapers and D-7 bulldozers, at work on a great diversion canal we were cutting through three hundred yards of sage-covered sandhills at the south end of Warner, rerouting Twenty-mile Creek.

Soon we were turning up bone—human bones, lots of them. I recall a clear October afternoon and all those white bones scattered in the gravel, and my catskinners standing there beside their great idling machines, perplexed and unwilling to continue. Ah, hell, never mind, I said. Crank 'em up.

There was nothing to do but keep rolling. Maybe bones from an ancient Indian burial ground were sacred, but so was our work, moreso as I saw it. My catskinners threatened to quit. I told them I'd give them a ride to town, where I'd find plenty of men who would welcome the work. My catskinners didn't quit. I ducked my head so I couldn't see, and drove away.

If you are going to bake a cake, you must break some eggs. That was a theory we knew about. We thought we were doing God's work. We were cultivating, creating order and what we liked to think of as a version of Paradise.

What a pleasure that work was, like art, always there, always in need of improving, doing. It's reassuring, so long as the work is not boring, to wake up and find your work is still there, your tools still in the tunnel. You can lose a life in the work. People do.

---

But we left, we quit, in a run of family trouble. I have been gone from farming and Warner for twenty-five years. People ask if I don't feel a great sense of loss, cut off from the valley and methods of my childhood. The answer is no.

Nothing much looks to have changed when I go back. The rimrock above the west side of the valley lies as black against the sunset light as it did when I was a child. The topography of my dreams, I like to think, is still intact.

But that's nonsense. We did great damage to the valley as we pursued our sweet impulse to create an agribusiness paradise. The rich peat ground began to go saline, the top layer just blew away. We drilled chemical fertilizers along with our barley seed, and sprayed with 2-4-D Ethyl and Parathion (which killed even the songbirds). Where did the waterbirds go?

But the waterbirds can be thought of as part of the *charismatic megafauna*. Everybody worries about the waterbirds. Forms of life we didn't even know about were equally threatened.

*Catostomus warnerensis*, the Warner sucker, is endangered. So are eight other fish species in the region, seven plant species, and seven plant communities such as *Poptri corstosalix*, a riparian plant community centered on black cottonwood, red osier dogwood, and willow.

As a child I loved to duck down and wander animal trails through dense brush by the creeksides, where ring-necked Manchurian pheasants and egg-eating raccoons and stalking lynx cats traveled. I wonder about colonies of red osier dogwood and black cottonwood. I was maybe often among them, curled in the dry grass and sleeping in the sun as I shared in their defenselessness and didn't know it.

The way we built canals in our efforts to contain the wildness of the valley and regulate the ways of water to our own uses must have been close to absolutely destructive to the Warner sucker, a creature we would not have valued at all, slippery and useless, thus valueless. It's likely I sent my gang of four D-7 Caterpillar bulldozers to clean out the brush along stretches of creekside thick with red osier dogwood and black cottonwood.

Let in some light, let the grass grow, feed for the livestock, that was the theory. Maybe we didn't abandon those creatures in that valley, maybe we mostly destroyed them before we left. We did enormous damage to that valley in thirty some years that we were there. Countrysides like the Dordogne and Umbria and Tuscany, which have been farmed thousands of years, look to be less damaged. But maybe that's because the serious kill-off took place so long ago.

I love Warner as a child loves its homeland, and some sense of responsibility for what's there stays with me. Or maybe I'm just trying to feel good about myself.

But that's what we all want to do, isn't it? It's my theory that everyone yearns, as we did in Warner, plowing those swamps, with all that bulldozing, to make a positive effect in the world. But how?

How to keep from doing harm? Sometimes that seems to be the only question. But we have to act. To do so responsibly we must first examine our desires. What do we really want?

A few years ago I went to Warner with a couple of film-makers from NBC. Some footage ran on the Today Show. Sitting in an antique GMC pickup truck alongside a great reef of chemically contaminated cowshit which had been piled up outside the feedlot pens where our fattening cattle had existed like creatures in a machine, I found it in myself to say the valley should be given back to the birds, and turned into a wildlife refuge.

It was a way of saying goodbye. I was saying the biological health of the valley was more important to me than the well-being of the community of ranchers who lived there. I had gone to grade school with some of them. It was an act people living in Warner mostly understood as betrayal.

Some eggs were broken, but I had at last gotten myself to say what I believed. Around 1990, when I heard that our ranch in Warner, along with two others out in the deserts to the east, was for sale, and that the Nature Conservancy was interested, I was surprised by the degree to which I was moved and excited. Maybe, I thought, this would be a second chance at paradise in my true heartland, an actual shot at reimagining desire.

What did I really want? A process, I think, everybody involved—ranchers and townspeople, conservationists—all taking part in that reimagining. I wanted them to each try defining the so-called land of their heart's desiring, the way they would have things if they were running the world. I wanted them to compare their versions of paradise, and notice again the ways we all want so many of the same things—like companionship in a community of people we respect and meaningful work.

Then I wanted them to get started on the painstaking work of developing a practical plan for making their visions of the right life come actual, a plan for using, restoring, and preserving the world I grew up in. I liked to imagine some of the pumps and dikes and headgates would be torn out in Warner, and that some of the swamps would go back to tules. That's part of my idea of progress—recreate habitat for the waterbirds, and the tiny, less charsimatic creatures. But nothing like that has happened.

The Nature Conservancy did not end up buying the land. The MC Ranch, our old property in Warner Valley, was stripped of livestock and machinery, and sold to what I understand to be a consortium of local ranchers. I have no idea of their plans—they don't confide in me, the turncoat.

But the world is inevitably coming to Warner Valley. The BLM purchased several thousands of acres of prime hayland in north Warner, and included it in a special management unit in which no grazing is allowed. The idea of the federal government buying land and taking it out of production (out of the tax base) was unthinkable when I lived in Warner. And the old drift fences on Hart Mountain have been torn out. Again, no more grazing.

There's no use sighting in the scopes on deer rifles, not any more. This invasion will not be frightened away. There is not a thing for the people in my old homeland to do but work out some accommodation with the thronging, invading world.

So many of our people, in the old days of the American West, came seeking a fold in time, a hideaway where they and generations after them could be at home. Think of *familia*, place and hearth and home fire, the fishing creek where it falls out of the mountains, into the valley, and the Lombardy poplar beside the white house, and the orchard where children run in deep sweet clover under the blossoming apple tree. But that's my paradise, at least as I remember it, not yours.

We have taken the West for about all it has to give. We have lived like children, taking and taking for generations, and now that childhood is over.

It's time we gave something back to the natural systems of order which have supported us, some care and tenderness, which is the most operative notion, I think—tenderness. Our isolations are gone, in the West and everywhere. We need to give some time to the arts of cherishing the things we adore, before they simply vanish. Maybe it will be like learning a skill: how to live in paradise.

# LAURIE KUTCHINS

## Wind Ensemble

### EXILE. SANDSTONE AND SNOW.

It begins with a sound the night makes knowing I will soon be gone. A determined train thunders across the broad reach of a grass dark prairie. The land bears its grinding round of hard surfaces, its whoosh of change, the engine's low groin whistle, crude oil from windy wells, coal slurry cars from open pits, clanking and rumbling through specks of electricity called cities out here—Sundance, Gillette, Midwest, Casper, Cheyenne. It is a metal growl the coyotes and the grazing antelope don't seem to mind. The land holds its brief passage as it will hold mine.

When the train has gone, the wind sound stays, pushing snow across the bluffs of red-wash sandstone. Wind shaking sage and buckbrush into bristled gnarls. Wind smoothing the rock of names, banishing the human imprint grit by grit where the first wheelruts have long folded into the chapped loam. The Wyoming wind is a cadence always beyond me. It extracts from the land its ruthless music, dust and grit and a dry clamor of snow. Wind sounds I was to learn before any other. Its scrambled song is my story, its directive my own lived paradox. The wind has told me to go: go west where weather always comes from, and then go east where you cannot see the weather coming, where you cannot come home.

This night smells of snow although it is not yet falling. Impending storm. Tomorrow I will drive into it, in a car that is my false chrysalis against the coming weather. The snow and the wind will make me go slowly, and think twice about going, and keep me from looking back or forward, or from seeing the true shape of my journey for a long time. I will creep into the distance snow blind, past the green road sign that says next services 87 miles, past the crouching snow fences, the rangeland, the shale and sandstone outcroppings, the oil patch, into a vertigo of blowing snow.

Erosion is mostly the wind's work, the way it softens and crags at the same time. It carves a good ear out of bedrock, and then it sings to and scolds its own geology. The wind will cradle itself in the very shapes it destroys. The tough buffalo grass, the sandstone, the Absaroka, the granite divide where the Tectonic plate forces a single trickle from one high snowfield and untwines it into separation, Atlantic and Pacific Creeks, the Wind River and the Snake.

There's more here. The startle of some oceanic presence beyond our scope of time. On the surface, imprints of brachiopods, ammonites. Just below, spines of saber-toothed tigers and apotosaurus embedded in chalky Cretaceous bedrock. And just above, the sounds of clouds breathing, breathing. Snow falling only to gust away all hope of summer water.

Exile. Erosion. Sounds that shelter even as they rip open.

## KOAN. HOLLOW AND WHITE PINE.

I live in two places, and more than two places live in me. Writing an evocation of place, conjuring such wild openness as a kind of manifesto, I am pacing like an agitated hen about her nest in a yellow room built inside a once-dilapidated chicken shed. This place—my small brick house, my shed and yard—is squeezed between two insubstantial Virginia hills. Winter days when I wait more than half the morning for the sun to rise up over Green Hill to my east and scratch my windows, and no sooner do I have that sunlight and I must lose it over the hill that flanks my west, I fathom that I am living in a hollow.

This room is tucked among the fertile hills and glens of the Shenandoah Valley. Outside the shed window I watch the breezes of early March tip the long limbs of white pines that have almost overgrown themselves from a surplus of groundwater. The dogwood in my yard has this week borne its tiny buds, drab nubs that will stay tightly locked until the coming season nudges them into a choreography of pink blossoms. In my hand I rub and turn a fossil shard of wrinkled Pleistocene turtle shell—out of habit, yes, but also to elicit placement and direction from a much older, larger story. I live always under the skin of the wind's questions.

This hollow I live in is patterned by Appalachian geology and lore, but these did not bring me here. I came because of the blunt logistics that shape a life: work, income, marriage, and now children who know this place as home. Although it has a lush and pastoral beauty, I do not love the manicured woods and farmland of the Shenandoah. In truth, I get irritable in these densely fenced glens, lethargic among hollows that fill with the stench of manure used to keep the crops abundant, and claustrophobic among hill-folds that shrink the horizon and prevent me from watching weather coming a long way off. My relationship to this place known as Singers Glen is a loveless, but not a worthless, arrangement. It is based on practical sticks and not a music.

The other place, Wyoming, lives in me as an elemental force. It is infant and childhood country; between us, some irrevocable symbiosis has transpired. Because as a young woman I heard Wyoming wind say *I'll stay with you: go now*, the path of my life insisted I depart. The work of rupture is to heal. The work of embodiment is to be all verb, all process, and seemingly as gradual as what we call geology itself. I am learning that I cannot stratify the landscape of spirit from the physical terrain that is its threshold. Nor can I sing of one place without making space for the contrapuntal ache of exile and displacement. The past and the particulars of its geography have formed me as deeply as any human love. Wyoming is a literal, living place to which I'll always come and go. Mysterious and potent as archetype, fierce as any erosional force, it keeps carving me.

Why don't I live where I fit, and why don't I celebrate and love where I live? How to make this place that is not home, home? For now, wind seems to be my image of an answer. Wind in this place, wind in the other. Wind. A riff, a reminder, a connective breathing. Yet I know better than to think this wind on my skin today carries west to east, past to present, the temporal and spatial resolution I ask for. The wind carries only enigmatic directives, like an answered koan out of which break more questions.

My questions stitch a loss and a joy side by side. I am made supple. One moment I am chasing after my lost wind-forsaken hat on an exposed ridge rich in coyote scat, antelope carcass, sage and shalebed fossils, and the next moment I am filling a birdfeeder to attract red cardinals under the fat shade of white pines. Undoubtedly the one place, Wyoming, has marked my life more deeply than any other, but it is Virginia my children now call home. I'm asking how to be present, how to be *here* and not *there* in the moment-to-moment anatomy of daily life. How to alchemize the *there* into *here,* as prescience and as presence. And to make of this alchemy a windmill of arterial power.

## EVOCATION. ESCARPMENT AND COYOTE SCAT.

This is the body naming itself. Mouth, throat, trachea, lungs, iambus of heart pulse, earlobes and lips, so the sounds will have passage, a way to form, to wander in and back out. Canyon-tongue with upper surface rasp-like. Grasp how the body sings its daily, ordinary work, goes about the chores. Clavicle, rib bend, shoulders, elbows, arms, wrists, thumbs, fingers for washing and hanging laundry to flap dry on the line. Knead the bread, bottle-feed the bum lamb, chop and carry wood, fix a fence torn by the same wind that killed the ewe, and dried the clothes.

I was told vocabulary is learned and consumed by the lonely brain. But my belly has vocalized a 'baaah,' and felt the bum lamb turn, come running. The lamb learns the sound of my voice, my smell equals warmth, equals milk. I am not convinced the cerebrum is the mother of all language. My body creates its own visceral instruments and knows it is integral and worthy of what spirit finds here in the dark, limitless braid of things. This is my body under wind, announcing its viscus: here is spare groundwater.

My body knows it is a landscape, capable of invitations and invasions, seduction and violation. Wind pulls across my face, an intricate sandstone threshold. And I know the landscape as a body. Pinnacles and chasms. Vulvus faultlines, breast-round shale, igneous shafts, wrinkled scrotal topsoil. He scatters the seed and the pollen, she bears the world.

Here is my body walking in wind and sagebrush, chasing after my brown hat blown off by a muscular gust. The language of this place finds its home on the edge of my elbow, in my earlobe, in the jaw of an antelope nibbling escarp-ment grass, in hair and fur whirling in the inexhaustible here. In the mild chinook of a late March morning, bent stalks of August, November. Twist of hair and bunch-grass across the hatless eyes of a woman, brain in her heart, syllables happy in her mouth making it palpable: *wyoming i am-home am-home am home wyoming iam.*

Even walking away from it, leeward, the wind is strong and relentless. It shoves my back toward the falling scarp where I watched the hat vanish, brown into a tawny beauty. I walk east along the open spine. How well the whole length of me knows the wind's incessant pushing and pulling across my skin, as if to enter and embody me, spirit into matter.

Stooped as sagebrush or a lone scrub pine, I step upon a femur with white fur. It will not break under me. I cross more dried coyote scat. Looking closer, I see bone, hair, grass and juniper embedded in the scat. The drum of the wind pounds beneath my skin, an arid voice. Almost as echo, I hear my own breathing trying to keep pace with the wind. Yes, what the wind tells me is older than my body. Half a life, and how small I am grown. I have always been so. A human speck in this country made out of wind and sky, and filled with dry light, unappeasable space. Boundaries here are permeable. I cannot tell where the body of this country ends and mine begins, which words belong to me, and which to the wind. This, the only symbiosis I fully trust.

Beyond the scarp, I do not see the end of land or sky, only their confluence far beyond me where they meet and move together at the rising of the Rattlesnakes and the Seminoes. In such country, my breath joins the drift of other voices, the vena cava of something greatly palpable but unseen. When I give up on the hat, turn westerly into the face of the chinook, I am half a circle, the letter 'c' walking windward. Carved thus, I am all the smaller, and the whole world smells like wind on a sleeve.

## ORACLE, CHINOOK AND OUTCROP.

The wind has been blowing since I began. Yesterday it was a sweet breeze laced with snow, sunlight, and a promise of spring. Today it is only cold and dissonant. It hounds the shed metal, lashes the shaggy limbs of the white pines, rips a shutter from the house, and rolls the trashcans all up and down the glen. Such an unruly wind is rare here in the Shenandoah Valley, this polite topography of tucks and folds with so many sheltering pockets from the wind. Wind in the Shenandoah belongs to the month of March. Like a slim genie, it swells out of some uncorked vessel for the inrush of Aries, and then it settles again and is done for the year. This cloistered zephyr in the trees is winter taking its last gasps. No season or event is ever stopped by wind in Virginia. By April the earth is turned and fertilized, no dust sweeps across the horizon. The wide gardens and field corn are planted in the weather of mercy. A verdant, blossoming spring comes on like a prom of colorful gowns without a wind to snarl a hairdo or snap a fresh corsage.

But in my other place, the wind is no tourist passing through. It is a rough, cantankerous resident, a force to be dealt with all year round. Even the name, Wyoming, suggests its erosive openness. It comes from a Delaware Indian word, M'cheuwomink, which means 'place where the plains open.' As a sound, Wyoming embodies the very vowels and sonic energy of its wind.

Across a vast swath of Shoshone rangeland, the wind has namesakes in the state's largest mountain range, and air to water, in the river that comes from a frigid trickle of snow high in the Absarokas.

In Wyoming, the wind is a relentless breathing that gusts down from the Rockies and whips east onto the high plains where there are so few trees to break its concentration. Days and nights with wind are far more common than those without it. To live here you must come to terms with the wind's restless drives, to accept that it will be a constant part of your hair, skin, face and eyes.

I once met a couple from Oregon who told me of their decision to move to Wyoming. After looking over a map, they chose my hometown of Casper because they liked its size, its central location on the state map, and its name reminded them of the friendly ghost. They packed up their car and headed toward a new life. When they got to Bessmer Bend, the wide outcropping west of Casper along the Platte River, they pulled over to admire the abundant country surrounding their new home. But the wind was blowing so hard their little car shook, and they could not get their doors open to get out. They learned from locals that the wind is insistent, infamous, central. A few days proved it true. The wind had already broken a dream. The couple turned around and drove back to Oregon. My brother-in-law, a restless man by nature who has lived in Casper his whole life, was recently so infuriated with the wind that he packed his suitcase as if to spite or threaten it with departure. The suitcase stayed packed and ready until the wind let up for a few days, enough to appease his fantasy gesture of escape.

To be born and come of age in this place is to have the wind own your eardrum. Even when calm, the wind resounds in the blood and bone of your body. It is absent so rarely that stillness begins to hound almost as much as its presence. When the wind is not making a ruckus in Wyoming, it feels like a pause between movements in a great symphony, an epiphanic hush that an audience sometimes unwittingly layers with clapping because after such orchestral energy even the briefest of silence can disarm. The wind will inhabit you as an animal inhabits a place where it knows how to stay alive. Its authority—both within and without the body—will erupt but also comfort, protect as well as plague.

If I speak of the wind as if it were a presence, a parent, even a lover, this is because it is true. Disembodied, bodiless, the wind's whole mission is to reach for the grounded, sensory body. It caresses, stings, and blows to keep me earthly and awake. Perhaps like so many of us, the wind seeks wholeness in what it does not have. Messenger without a body, it is always ripping the fence between hunger and gratitude.

My relationship to the wind, and its country, was first borne out of pre-natal bedrock and childhood. It further grew out of isolation and imagination, symbiosis and then fissure. Because I formed so deeply from wind I fathom the body and land as porous. I feel its urgency as strong, connective tissue. My passionate connection and intimate attachment with such presence refuses to be reduced to terminology known and comfortable to the literate. Personification, anthropomorphism, pathetic fallacy are all terms that presume and depend upon a separation between human and natural elements, but what I long to forge is an intimacy, an ecological symbiosis.

Those terms, and the human structures of power they reinforce, suggest that I am in charge of that other voice, that I am making it up out of fancy or whimsy. But I am not. The wind in harshly open country has swept eyes and ears, voices and cadences into me, and not the other way around. I've given nothing to the wind but a series of lost hats and audible cries. My search for something of the self upon windswept escarpment is an inexplicable truth of my inheritance, my gift from—not *to*—the place.

What is the wind? Embedded in my ear, it is surely the voices of the place, the collective breath of memory, inrush of child, ancestor, animal, fossil imprint in the outcrop that lives between my mountain and my river. It is a great geology of palpable spirit, an integral metamorphosis of water, air, earth and breathing across ages. It is unformed firmament that seeks a form, a pattern, a language. Air pressure hovers always above the earth, so close it is drawn down by the earth's magnetic pulls. North of the equator this air spins clockwise around patterns of high-pressure and counterclockwise around lows. It reverses this pattern in the Southern Hemisphere. North to south, east to west, the wind is a mandala of atmospheric energy moving across unseen contours. On a weather map, the patterned wind creates its own topography of curvy lines called isobars. Its kinesis and its dance beget whole bodies of air. The stronger earth pulls air down to itself, the faster wind's velocity. Our earth is always tugging at the air, and air is always whooshing and rushing down to it. Earth and firmament, it is an unending love story, is it not?

Seen in this way, the wind is a veil of constant change wrapped loosely around the earth. It is the most natural embodiment of spirit, what we cannot see making itself known—witnessed in our skin, hummed as a dry whistling in our ears, a sting of dust or blowing snow tearing our eyes. Inhale to exhale, it is a wild smell indelibly understood by nose and mouth. Breathing is the work of intimacy, of staying close, riveting, even as wind erodes what it cannot live without.

Through our own breath the wind pulls spirit into us. We are stitched to life in motion, to everything sentient: windsock, plastic bag, weathervane, rattlesnake, scrimrock, dust, cloud, floating voice. Wind summons us to be stirred, mussed, into change.

## MEMORY. BEDROCK AND SHADOW.

Flying over the town in a small prop plane the child witnesses and absorbs the encircling land. Her evidence is how a landscape looks like a living body from high above it. How choppy and solid the sky really is when she'd thought it would be smooth and flowing. She is five, and at first loves the odd hour of looking down at home, being so far above it, for once, airborne. From the air she begins to see clearly what shapes coincidence and confluence make. The geology that made the town form as it did, between the North Platte River and the strange, uncharacteristic warp in the Rocky Mountain chain. Casper and Muddy Mountains don't conform, they jut the wrong direction, west to east, not south to north like the others in the great tectonic spine. For once the mountains look insubstantial, nothing more than tucks and wrinkles on a sun-faded blanket.

She thought the plane would allow her to think like a hawk or eagle, what she imagines a large raptor knows when it spreads its wings and floats from here to there, its graceful shadow falling over land. She thought flight would bring on the exhilarations of soaring, the winged freedom of detachment, a potent sort of power in being able to pull so many miles into two small eye-balls. When the plane flies over her street so close to prairie at the rim of town, she sees her house, a red square in a buffed patchwork. She thinks she has seen Pearl, the neighbor, sweeping dust from her front walk, and she sees that Pearl from the air is no different in relative scope than the dust itself when she is sitting beside it on the ground. For the first time she can see the town in relation to its country, how rude the town looks, how insubstantial. How quickly its patterns give way to the curves in the river, how the prairie builds its bench land to the mountains from a long way off, and how with height the known landmarks become the bones and skin of an animal vastly alive.

But beyond her pleasure in the sheer oddity of flying over all that is famil-iar to her, beyond the brief novelty of seeing the world from a great height, comes the shock of relativity itself. She grows aware of a churning that does not feel like freedom at all. It is attachment, the ferocity of connection. She feels a homesickness to be lifted even for only an hour above the familiar ground—the Jelm and Chugwater outcrops, the sandstone hogbacks, the Goose Egg granite, the Alcova limestone, the Lakota mountains. Unknowingly, the dark pit that forms both exile and attachment is taking root in her gut, not yet voiced.

What does the roaming eagle think? How many times did I stand with my feet on the earth at the west edge of the mountain where a canyon is home to a brood of bald eagles, and look up when my father said to? How often did I cluck my tongue and watch them wing and circle, their shadows briefly crossing our upturned faces? Were the eagles attached to their own shadows on the ground, did they look us in the eye?

The child feels the evidence, senses the memory, already there, implicit in the earth, but cannot begin to render or speak of it. Within a few months her family will leave this place, move away only to come back a few years later and start again. She knows nothing yet of her father's dreams and failings, how quickly he will fall from his own calculations of grace, how necessity and longing will return them to the weather of rocks. She does not know that this windy country is the nest of her voice. She does not know that failure, departure and loss will groom a voice in her father that breaks cellos. Rupture will become the hands of him who will overturn tables, shatter dishes, and pull a worn belt from the loops at his waist to lash his children in turn. The child is just beginning to learn what home looks and feels like from the air. How many times she will have to look at her life from such distances, locate the contours of grief in the land, mirrored in the body, the ridges of pleasure that correspond to the all the faults.

Her uncle who pilots the plane shows her the glittering metal of her playground from the air. She waves at the children down below, thinking surely they are looking through the wind to see the small plane cross them. The plane fills with the loud metallic hum of the engine, its fuel overpowers the clean smell of the sky. She marvels how the land has the look of a great-grandmother's nakedness, wrinkled, parched, a testament to wind, water, and time.

In the air she trusts the visiting uncle to keep the plane aloft and land them safely amidst the currents of wind. But she fears how mean he can be, on the ground. She senses something hateful in his trim body. His arms are muscled with anger. He belongs to the air force, and his medals shine in a perfect but incomprehensible order on his blue uniform. Already she has lain awake listening to him beat his only child because she cried from her crib at nighttime. Already her body knows: never let slip a tear or voice a cry in front of the pilot. She sits alert, all smiles and politeness up in the air while he flies the plane. Her stomach turns over and over, her voice in the wind current the plane muscles across.

How does the body know itself except through place? It is a clear day, filled with cirrus and easy breezes. She marvels at how the uncle works the levers and buttons on the plane's control panel. He makes three graceful circles above the town, masters the currents of wind, and then widens the plane out over the rippling plains. She places her fingertips along the window glass and begins to touch and name all that she knows down there—the mountain ranges, buttes, hogbacks and scarps that form the hem of her first world, define it for her. To the north the Big Horns, to the west the Rattlesnakes, the Seminoes, the Owl Creek range and the snow-topped Winds; to the south, Muddy Mountain, Elk Mountain, Laramie Peak. From the air, she can see how one story is enfolded and followed by another, how the high plain-land is really the bottom of a forsaken, wind-swept sea. For the first time it makes sense to her why her father brings home fossils of mollusks and seashells from the oil patch.

Until the plane ride she had not known the land held so many scars, or how ragged the town looks, like a mishap that won't go away. She counts the scars, markings she took for much less on the ground. Here is the switchback road up the mountain, the irreparable hairpin turn halfway up, a gouging one can see long before the canyons and creek drainages that carve the true shape of the range. Here are the gravel pits and storage units beyond the refineries, the glint of round white tanks for keeping oil. Beyond the red rock of Bessemer Bend along the Platte, south and east of the river's path there is the large gash of the Shirley Basin uranium boom, an excavated circle that seems to have no end. The dams that now control the river—more buttes of concrete than she can count from the air. There is the Dave Johnson Power plant with its spouts of smoke, floating like a ship in the prairie, awaiting the next oceanic age. And ever so faint, she thinks she can see even the grassed ruts of the Oregon Trail, the rock of names near Devil's Gate where the Sweetwater forms another path across the sweeps of wind.

With height and distance the child learns the past is a remote and beautiful thing. Even its grief is a beauty. From the air she learns to see the whole, from the windy earth she gathers an ear. But give her space. Give her ages of flight and landing, scattering and gathering, burial and excavation. Over time the girl erodes and forms the woman that will speak of wind and of elegy embedded in the earth. Bless the vast silences. Bless the ages that let me run my fingers again along the whittled sandstone spine, and know it as a succulence, a joy. I receive and release its stories on my tongue—words to give back to the wind: bedrock, groundwater, erosion, eros.

# WILLIAM J
# LINES

## Tangibles

My flesh had grown foreign. I had been several years out of Australia and my corporeal self consisted of material breathed and eaten overseas. But my body retained memories of a sun blasted world. In my body I belonged to Australia—to salt water, sand, sunburn, vast space, and everlasting sky—and I ached to touch ocean, beach, forest, woodland, heath, scrub, desert, and light.

After my return a friend invited me to join his family and friends for a week over New Year in Port Campbell National Park on Victoria's southern coast. I left Melbourne and drove west under a sumptuous afternoon sun. At roadside stops I stretched my legs in the thin shade of mallee trees. Flies swarmed in the still, scalding air. When I reached Port Campbell village withering evening brightness glazed the stippled waters of an aquamarine bay enclosed by pale yellow limestone cliffs. Offshore reefs broke the Southern Ocean swell. Luminous spume rose high above spilt and busted water. A sea breeze carried the ocean's roar onshore. I stood on the beach and tasted salt air. Waves rolled onto the sand and cold, cold water lapped at my feet.

A few kilometres east of Port Campbell I pulled off the Great Ocean Road onto a sandy track to a weatherboard cottage fenced at the front from the coastal heath. Behind, eucalypts and exotic pines grew on the bank that sloped to the shallow, barely flowing Sherbrooke River.

Sherbrooke River is the main watercourse in Port Campbell National Park, a linear littoral reserve of 65 kilometres. From only a few metres to at most two kilometres wide, the park preserves the sheer cliffs—up to 60 metres high—gorges, arches, and offshore stacks that mark this shore line. Elongated bays and headlands reveal sea-cut indents in the cliffs. High tide washes over narrow beaches and, in many places, brings the sea to the base of the cliffs. Erosion is constant. Fragments, slabs, and blocks of rock detach from the cliff face. Several spectacular cliff failures occurred in the twentieth century. The arch of London Bridge collapsed in 1990.

Behind the cliffs a broad, flat to gently undulating and windswept plain retains a thin strip of heath bordering vast paddocks supporting sheep, cattle, and mobs of eastern grey kangaroos. Remnant park scrubland shelters Red-necked Wallabies, orchids, skinks, and birds, including the Rufous Bristlebird.

Towards dusk—after introductions and dinner—most of the household departed for the Twelve Apostles viewing platform. Fifty metres below, Little Penguins paddled ashore on the surf and huddled in groups at the water's edge. En masse they moved up the beach to the dunes at the base of the cliff. Here groups split and penguins waddled on sand pathways to dozens of individual burrows.

Early next morning, after the penguins had returned to the sea, I walked a track that, beginning at Sherbrooke Beach, loops around the headlands and gorges to Mutton Bird Island. The rising sun replenished the day with light, illuminating ocean, rock, and cliff-top tussock grasslands.

The temperature rose and sweat ran down my forehead, across my back and under my arms. I breathed deeply, took in ocean and land, stood erect. I was home. Australia was real, possessed of a physical actuality more authentic and urgent than any spiritual presence we may attribute to the world. Besides, I do not believe there are hidden meanings, or spirit beneath the material surface. And why need there be? The world of substance is full to overflowing with wonder: light pouring out of a vast sky and falling on ocean and beach; the breathing of salt-scented air; the force of wind, gentle or heavy, on flesh; the burning pressure of the sun on skin; the sturdy support of earth underfoot; and, at Port Campbell National Park the green fuse of tenacious life vividly surviving on limestone rock and sand. What else is there?

Many people think of our culture as materialistic. Unfortunately we are not real materialists. We do not actually value the material world for its own sake.

We are fantasists. Most of the material objects we buy and consume are sold on the basis of the fantasy ascribed to them by advertisers: youth, attractiveness, sex, status, power. We buy products not for themselves, but for the fantasies they exemplify. And in our search for essence we destroy the material world.

Australian Aborigines were materialists. They knew their lives depended on an intimate acquaintance with animals, plants, watercourses, seasons, and weather. They did not try to escape corporeal existence. Because they esteemed the incarnate they left few lasting physical monuments to mark their long occupancy of this continent: no settlements or cities, no roadways, dams, swaths of cleared and denuded land, and no great earthworks or religious edifices. What they did leave was the result of daily, individual interactions with the palpable earth. Steps cut in Port Campbell National Park's cliffs mark the path where the Kirrae Whuurong people walked to and from the beach in search of food. Shell middens and charcoal in the dunes mark where they shucked, cooked, and ate shellfish.

After my morning walk I joined my friends at what they called Secret Beach, a 200-metre crescent of golden sand enclosed by a curving, mustard cliff. A few metres offshore, kelp-covered reefs broke the force of the surf. A cave started one end of the beach. Nearby a small creek crossed a cliff edge and formed a hanging valley. Water spilled onto the beach and disappeared into the sand.

That evening, New Year's Eve, we climbed down wooden steps into Loch Ard Gorge and gathered on the beach. We celebrated midnight with sparklers and hugs. Afterwards we lay on our backs on the cool damp sand and gazed at the patch of sky framed by the sheer walls of the gorge. The great, blazing streak of the Milky Way lay directly overhead. We watched for shooting stars.

Loch Ard Gorge takes its name from the ship, *Loch Ard*, wrecked just outside the gorge in 1878. The ship, among the very first iron vessels built, was on its third voyage from Gravesend to Melbourne and carried 51 passengers and crew. On 28 May the captain, believing he was 240 kilometres southwest of Cape Otway, turned the ship north. That night the wind freshened. About 3 a.m., with the *Loch Ard* sailing through a thick haze, the crew heard surf. An hour later the haze lifted. Straight ahead loomed the high, pale cliffs of Mutton Bird Island.

The crew tried desperately to hoist more sail and alter course but it was too late. The ship sailed into the breakers. Sailors let go the anchors but they dragged on the sandy bottom. The anchor cables were slipped. For a moment it seemed the ship might clear the cliffs but suddenly hit a ledge. The ship rolled from the blow and its yardarms struck the cliff above, dislodging rocks and showering the crew with masts, rigging, rock, and debris. Waves broke over the deck.

Eighteen-year-old passenger Eva Carmichael later told a coronial enquiry: 'The concussion was alarmingly loud and all was confusion and terror.' Clad only in her nightdress, she struggled up a companionway: 'It was totally dark and impossible to see what was going on.' She saw streaks of light caused by the friction of the yardarms striking the cliffs and then a wave washed her overboard.

Ship's apprentice Tom Pearce, also 18, and other crew tried to launch a lifeboat, but the *Loch Ard* slipped off the reef and quickly sank. Only floating wreckage and struggling people were left in the waves. Tom's lifeboat capsized, trapping him underneath. He dived, pushed out, and clung to the upturned boat.

Eva, meanwhile, seized a floating hen-coop. The cages, placed on deck during the voyage, had caused considerable inconvenience. 'So at last the despised hen-coops have some use!' Eva remarked to another passenger struggling in the water. But she changed her mind about the hen-coop's buoyancy and took hold of a spar. Two other passengers joined her but swam away from the spar when they thought they were going to be battered against the cliffs. They disappeared. Eva clung on, surrounded by tanks, cases, casks, planks, bales of paper, and wreckage. The spar remained outside the line of breakers and drifted east along the coast.

The tide took Tom's boat out to sea. He also drifted east about 600 metres and then back towards the coast to the mouth of a gorge. High cliffs, just 50 metres apart, compressed the heavily rolling swell. The turbulence righted the boat and Tom clambered in. A moment later waves hurled the craft against the cliffs. Tom fell into the water, which, released from the gorge, subsided and rolled towards the shore. He swam 100 metres through drifting wreckage to the sandy beach.

Tom rested in a cave then walked the 100-metre beach looking for food among the growing pile of ship's debris. At the same time a surge of water flung Eva's spar through the entrance of the gorge and jammed it against the limestone wall. Floundering in the water with her clothing caught on a rock, Eva could see a man on the shore. She screamed for help.

Tom looked up and saw Eva about midway up the gorge. Stripping most of his clothing, he plunged into the sea. When he reached Eva she was semiconscious. Pulling her free and clenching her nightgown in his teeth, he tried to drag her through the wreckage-choked water. An upturned table floated by. He grabbed it and made for shore.

'He took me into a wild-looking cave a few hundred feet from the beach and finding a case of brandy, broke a bottle and made me swallow some, which revived me. He pulled some long grass and shrubs for me to lie on. I soon sank into a state of unconsciousness and must have remained so for hours.'

Tom also went to sleep. When he woke in the early afternoon he decided to seek help. He climbed the cliff and walked along the headland where he met two station workers. They recruited more help and descended the gorge. Eva was not in the cave.

'When I woke up I felt very confused and very sore all over, but after awhile I began to recollect things very clearly and got up to find Tom Pearce. When I got out of the cave I could not see him anywhere. I did not know what had become of him. Before I left England I heard so much about the wild blacks which were out here and I thought the ship had struck against an island that was peopled with blacks, so, before it got dark, I went and crawled under the thickest bush I could find in the gorge. I heard something that sounded like "coo-ee", and when I heard that strange call I thought I was amongst the blacks and kept concealed.' Shortly, Eva heard the English word 'yes' and revealed herself.

Tom and Eva were the only survivors of the *Loch Ard* wreck. Forty-nine people perished. Eva lost all her family: mother, father, and sisters. Several months after her rescue she returned to Ireland. Eva's encounter with Australia had been brief but intensely physical. Tom had been born in Australia but had no great love of the land. He first went to sea at 15 and soon after the *Loch Ard* wreck returned. He spent most of his life at sea and survived several more shipwrecks.

A few days after our New Year's celebrations, Loch Ard Gorge saw another shipwreck drama, Shakespeare's *The Tempest*, mounted by Ozact, a Ballarat-based theatre company specializing in outdoor productions.

Ozact's version opened on scene two, Prospero's cave. The setting was perfect: a grotto at the far end of Loch Ard Gorge. Ferny stalactites hang from the limestone roof and wall. Water drips on to the mossy ground. Birds fly about the scrub at the top of the cliffs. The audience sat in the sand. Settings changed according to the act. The audience followed the actors to the beach and then to a cave (not the one Tom and Eva sheltered in), before returning to the grotto for the final scenes, performed just on dusk.

As written, *The Tempest* opens with an exuberant burst of wild energy: 'A tempestuous noise of thunder and lightning heard.' In a matter of seconds we are in the heart of a raging storm on board a ship at sea.

Amid the uproar, Alonso, King of Naples, and his entourage appear on deck. Alonso questions the seamanship of the mariners but the boatswain dismisses him and orders him below. Alonso's councilor, Gonzalo, takes offence at the boatswain's insubordination and reprimands him: 'Good, yet remember whom thou hast aboard' (I.i. 19–20).

The boatswain replies with a challenge: 'None that I more love than myself. You are a councilor; if you can command these elements to silence, and work the peace of the present, we will not hand a rope more. Use your authority. If you cannot, give thanks you have lived so long, and make yourself ready in your cabin for the mischance of the hour, if it so hap. Cheerly, good hearts! Out of our way, I say' (I.i.21–28).

The boatswain asserts a natural order, represented by the storm, which must be met physically with manual skill, against a human order, represented by Alonso and his scheming entourage, and based on hierarchy, predictability, and security. In this conflict between nature and human order, will human arrangements and conceits prevail over the way of the Earth?

The duplicity and contingency of those human arrangements become clear in the next scene. Prospero tells his daughter, Miranda, how, through foul and perfidious means, Prospero's brother, Antonio, usurped the dukedom of Milan, a position that rightfully belongs to Prospero. But order is about to be restored. Prospero, through his magic powers, has arranged the storm and for the ship's passengers—Alonso, Gonzalo, Antonio, and others—to come ashore on the island where Prospero and Miranda lived. The usurpers are going to confront their own treachery.

During this discourse, Prospero reveals his vision for the world and for the island on which he and Miranda have been exiled. He values honour, order, authority, and book learning. But while Prospero seeks to convey a serene sense of power and control, he also displays rage at his undoing, threatens constriction and imprisonment, and demands unwilling servitude, particularly from his slave, Caliban, whom he describes as a surly brute. Yet Prospero and Miranda cannot do without Caliban. He is capable and energetic and they are neither; he can catch fish, and labour with skill and they cannot. As Prospero concedes:

> We cannot miss him. He does make our fire,
> Fetch in our wood, and serves in offices
> That profit us.

(I.ii.310–12)

Because of this dependence, Prospero resents Caliban and abuses him: 'Thou poisonous slave' (I.ii.318). In reply, in images concrete and earth-bound, Caliban curses Prospero:

> As wicked dew as e'er my mother brushed
> With raven's feather from unwholesome fen
> Drop on you both! A southwest blow on ye
> And blister you all o'er!

(I.ii.321–24)

Caliban's unregenerate nature and his rejection of authority move Prospero to a wrath that he otherwise reserves only for the usurper Antonio. Prospero practises dark magic as well as white and he punishes Caliban with pains that fit his earthy, animal nature, causing him to stumble over hedgehogs and be bitten by apes.

Caliban is undeterred, presses his claim against Prospero's rule and asserts his identification with the island. From Caliban's view, Prospero is the invader and the usurper. His charges have merit. He has been wronged and it is hard to argue with his claim and his accusation:

> This island's mine by Sycorax my mother,
> Which thou tak'st from me. When thou cam'st first,
> Thou strok'st me, and made much of me; wouldst give me
> Water with berries in't; and teach me how
> To name the bigger light, and how the less,
> That burn by day and night. And then I loved thee
> And showed thee all the qualities o' th' isle,
> The fresh springs, brine pits, barren place and fertile.
> Cursed be that I did so! All the charms
> Of Sycorax—toads, beetles, bats, light on you!
> For I am all the subjects that you have,
> Which first was mine own king; and here you sty me
> In this hard rock, whiles you do keep from me
> The rest o' th' island.

(I.ii.331–44)

Prospero does not answer this indictment. How could he? The claim is incontestable. Instead, he changes the subject and accuses Caliban of ingratitude and the attempted rape of Miranda.

Caliban later meets some of the shipwreck survivors. They become his confederates and he hopes they will help him overthrow Prospero. His prospects appear slim but he is not entirely unrealistic. For while Prospero

rules the island through his magic, his learning, and his books, Caliban inhabits the place. He knows every inch of it. He has mapped it with his senses. His
sensual-based knowledge is beyond Prospero's comprehension. And Caliban is
generous with his knowledge. He offers, for example, to share his endowment
with the useless Stephano:

> I'll show thee the best springs; I'll pluck thee berries;
> I'll fish for thee, and get thee wood enough ...
> I prithee let me bring thee where crabs grow;
> And I with my long nails will dig thee pignuts,
> Show thee a jay's nest, and instruct thee how
> To snare the nimble marmoset. I'll bring thee
> To clust'ring filberts, and sometimes I'll get thee
> Young scammels from the rock.

(II.ii.168–9, 174–80)

(Crabs are crab apples; pignuts are tubers, a European wild food never
successfully cultivated; scammels are seabirds; a marmoset is a small monkey;
filberts are hazelnuts.)

Through this and other speeches, Caliban conveys a sense of place,
demonstrates his familiarity with the island's fecundity, and signals his
physical identification with the soil and its life. His offer to dig pignuts with
his nails, for example, shows his tactile, unaffected connection to the earth.
His senses are acute: he feels, smells, and sees. He has a rich, affective, and
tangible apprehension of nature, and an imaginative, poetic power second only
to Prospero's. Caliban can hear and describe the island's music:

> Be not afeard, the isle is full of noises,
> Sounds and sweet airs, that give delight and hurt not.
> Sometimes a thousand twangling instruments
> Will hum about mine ears; and sometimes voices
> That, if I then had waked after long sleep,
> Will make me sleep again; and then, in dreaming,
> The clouds methought would open and show riches
> Ready to drop upon me, that, when I waked,
> I cried to dream again.

(III.ii.140–48)

Caliban's usefulness and his perceptive, poetic nature do not win him any
sympathisers. His detractors and tormentors constantly dismiss his earthi-
ness and liken him to the creatures of the world: fish; tortoise; mooncalf;
snail; and freckled whelp. Insult reinforces Caliban's vital link with the ani-

mal realm. He embodies the life force—sheer drive, raw energy. When Prospero conjures another image, 'Thou earth, thou' (I.ii.313), the identification is complete.

To Prospero, Caliban's corporeal link with the earth, his physical identity with the soil and dirt of life, and his exuberance in his own animal existence, are his most damning characteristics. Whereas Prospero is ascetic and cerebral, Caliban is sensual. He has appetites: he farts and he lusts and he physically suffers. He has a body-based acquaintance with the world and has learnt from experience what Prospero can never teach him from books. Even more uncomfortably for Prospero, Caliban embodies a whole range of qualities manifest in Prospero but which Prospero consistently denies: rage, passion, vindictiveness, hurt-pride and, most disruptively, sexuality.

Prospero preaches self-control and denial. He distrusts feeling, advocates self-discipline and containing one's passions. He believes properly constituted civil process should temper desire. When Miranda meets and falls in love with Ferdinand—Alonso's son and one of the passengers from the shipwreck—and Ferdinand proposes marriage, Prospero warns him:

> Then, as my gift, and thine own acquisition
> Worthily purchased, take my daughter. But
> If thou dost break her virgin-knot before
> All sanctimonious ceremonies may
> With full and holy rite be minist'red,
> No sweet aspersion shall the heavens let fall
> To make this contract grow; but barren hate,
> Sour-eyed disdain, and discord shall bestrew
> The union of your bed with weeds so loathly
> That you shall hate it both. Therefore take heed,
> As Hymen's lamps shall light you.

(IV.i.13–23)

In his reassuring reply, Ferdinand echoes and affirms Prospero's emphasis on restraint and control:

> As I hope
> For quiet days, fair issue, and long life,
> With such love as 'tis now, the murkiest den,
> The most opportune place, the strong'st suggestion
> Our worser genius can, shall never melt
> Mine honor into lust, to take away
> The edge of that day's celebration

(IV.i.24–29)

Ferdinand seeks 'quiet days' and 'long life', a marked contrast to his recent experience aboard ship amidst nature at its most violent and unpredictable where he faced imminent death. In obedience to Prospero's wishes, Ferdinand denies nature's contingency, accepts the necessity of order, and agrees humans have base instincts that must be controlled. His bride, however, possesses a more expansive, vital imagination. Miranda finds the world fresh and bright and full of possibility. Hence her exclamation:

> O, wonder!
> How many goodly creatures are there here!
> How beauteous mankind is! O brave new world,
> That has such people in 't!

(V.i.181–84)

To which Prospero wryly, sardonically, and perhaps sadly, comments ''Tis new to thee.' Prospero's response reflects his world-weariness and ennui and cynicism induced by too much book learning, excessive intellectual and moral Puritanism, and intense self-preoccupation. He cannot escape the exhausted mental world fabricated by his books and his learning and his consuming sense of having been wronged.

Miranda's 'brave new world' is, in part, the ordinary world we all know, it is our world. But perhaps Miranda also discovered something else. Her comment points to other worlds, new worlds, to lands beyond the sea and to the miraculous existence of people out there beyond the known world. Questions are implied. Are the new worlds peopled by innocent, unfallen Adams, or people like other people? And what is their relationship to the Earth? Are they on it (like Prospero) or of it (like Caliban)?

Miranda's discovery also proposes the existence of worlds within our world, worlds overlooked or seen uncomprehendingly. As comedy, *The Tempest* takes us into realms of freedom and imagination that can uncover another of Miranda's brave new worlds: a world of constant renewal, of life begetting life, always burning, never consumed—the world that intellect denies but which our bodies attach us to and that we cannot, just like Miranda and Prospero cannot, do without.

Shakespeare keeps *The Tempest*—which involves much magic and invokes the supernatural—down-to-earth in more direct ways, as well. Characters handle, hold, and grab objects: in the first scene sailors lay hold of ropes and adjust sails; in the second, Prospero clasps a staff, Miranda takes his robe from his shoulders; Caliban fetches wood; later, Ferdinand does the same;

the conspirators wield swords as do Ferdinand and Prospero at different times; Stephano and Trinculo hold a wine bottle, they later pluck clothes from a line; Miranda and Ferdinand move chess pieces around a board. Characters interact with the material world through their bodies.

Tom and Eva were also down-to-earth. When telling their story of the shipwreck to the coronial enquiry, they frequently and repeatedly mentioned handling, holding, and grabbing things—things that saved their lives. They lived outdoor lives, survived in a material world, and never imagined any other existence.

But modern people have come inside. What was obvious to Tom and Eva and to Caliban is no longer obvious to us. We, and the institutions that serve us, seek escape from the material. For example, Parks Victoria's vision for Port Campbell National Park, mirrors Prospero's vision for the world: ordered, controlled, and under human management. The 1998 *Port Campbell National Park Management Plan* cites protection of 'economic values' as one of the primary goals of management. But what are 'economic values'? They are certainly not based on wonder. They are abstractions with no connection to the material reality of place felt through body. They reflect unreal expectations about the utility of the natural world. They are a fantasy of no relevance to the actual land and life along the Port Campbell coast. Unfortunately, the elevation of fantasy as a management goal undercuts conservation as surely as the Southern Ocean undercuts the south coast cliffs. We need a less arrogant, more modest approach to the world.

In *The Tempest*'s Epilogue, Prospero speaks of a new frailty:

Now my charms are all o'erthrown,
And what strength I have's mine own,
Which is most faint.

At the beginning of the play Prospero believes reason and control are the realities of life. At the end he realizes he has only his own body and those affections that, arising from his body, connect him to the world. He abandons magic, illusion, and fantasy. His circumstances are beyond his control. He accepts dependence.

During my last days at Port Campbell a companion and I collected driftwood to make a table for the cottage. We scouted beaches and pulled salt-impregnated posts, planks, and pallets from the sand. We sat by our pile and faced the ocean in wonder of a world that has such life, light, surging sea, and sculptured coast.

# BARRY
# LOPEZ

# The Language of Animals

The steep riverine valley I live within, on the west slope of the Cascades in Oregon, has a particular human and natural history. Though I've been here for thirty years, I am able to convey almost none of it. It is not out of inattentiveness. I've wandered widely within the drainages of its eponymous river, the McKenzie; and I could offer you a reasonably complete sketch of its immigrant history, going back to the 1840s. Before then, Tsanchifin Kalapuya, a Penutian-speaking people, camped in these mountains, but they came up the sixty-mile long valley apparently only in summer, to pick berries and to trade with a people living on the far side of the Cascades, the Molala. In the fall, the Tsanchifin returned down valley to winter near present-day Eugene, Oregon, where the McKenzie joins the Willamette River. The Willamette flows a hundred miles north to the Columbia, the Columbia another hundred miles to the Pacific.

The history that preoccupies me, however, in this temperate rain forest is not human history, not even that of the highly integrated Tsanchifin. Native people seem to have left scant trace of their comings and goings in the McKenzie Valley. Only rarely, as I hear it, does someone stumble upon an old, or very old, campsite, where glistening black flakes of a volcanic glass called obsidian, the debitage from tool-making work, turn up in soil scuffed by a boot heel.

I've lingered in such camps, in a respectful and deferential mood, as though the sites were shrines; but I'm drawn more to the woods in which they're found. These landscapes are occupied, still, by the wild animals who were these people's companions. These are the descendants of animals who coursed these woods during the era of the Tsanchifin.

When I travel in the McKenzie basin with visiting friends, my frame of mind is not that of the interpreter, of the congnoscente; I amble with an explorer's temperament. I am alert for the numinous event, for evidence of a world beyond the rational. Though it is presumptuous to say so, I seek a Tsanchifin grasp, the view of an indigene. And what draws me ahead is the possibility of revelation from other indigenes—the testimonies of wild animals.

The idea that animals can convey meaning, and thereby offer an attentive human being illumination, is a commonly held belief the world over. The view is disparaged and disputed only by modern cultures with an allegiance to science as the sole arbiter of truth. The price of this conceit, to my way of thinking, is enormous.

I grew up in a farming valley in southern California in the 1950s, around sheep, dogs, horses, and chickens. The first wild animals I encountered—coyotes, rattlesnakes, mountain lion, deer, and bear—I came upon in the surrounding mountains and deserts. These creatures seemed more vital than domestic animals. They seemed to tremble in the aura of their own light. (I caught a shadow of that magic occasionally in a certain dog, a particular horse, like a residue.) From such a distance it's impossible to recall precisely what riveted my imagination in these encounters, though I might guess. Wild animals are lean. They have no burden of possessions, no need for extra clothing, eating utensils, elaborate dwellings. They are so much more integrated into the landscape than human beings are, swooping its contours and bolting down its pathways with bewildering speed. They travel unerringly through the dark. Holding their gaze, I saw the intensity and clarity I associated with the presence of a soul.

In later years I benefitted from a formal education at a Jesuit prep school in New York City, then at New York University and the universities of Notre Dame and Oregon. I encountered the full range of Western philosophy, including the philosophy of science, in those classrooms and studied the theological foundations of Christianity. I don't feel compelled now to repudiate that instruction. I regard it, though, as incomplete, and would say that nothing I read in those years fundamentally changed what I thought about animals. The more steeped I became in the biology and ecology of animals, the more I understood about migration, and the more I comprehended about the intricacy of their neural impulses and the subtlty of their endocrine systems, the deeper their other unexplored capacities appeared to me. Biochemistry and field studies enhanced rather than diminished my sense that, in Henry Beston's phrase, animals were other nations.

If formal education taught me how to learn something, if it provided me with reliable structures (e.g. *Moby-Dick*, approaching the limit in calculus, von Clausewitz's tactics) within which I could exercise a metaphorical imagination, if the Jesuits inculcated in me a respectful skepticism about authority, then that education gave me the sort of tools most necessary to an examination of the history of Western ideas, a concept fatally flawed by an assumption of progress. I could move on from Gilbert White's Selbourne to Thoreau's Walden. I could trace a thread from Aristotle through Newton to Schrödinger. Or grasp that in the development of symphonic expression, Bach gives way to Mozart, who gives way to Beethoven. But this isn't progress. It's change, in a set of ideas that incubate well in our culture.

I left the university with two ideas strong in my mind. One was the belief that a person had to enter the world to know it, that it couldn't be got from a book. The other was that there were other epistemologies out there, as rigorous and valid as the ones I learned in school. Not convinced of the superiority of the latter, I felt ready to consider these other epistemologies, no matter how at odds.

When I moved into the McKenzie valley I saw myself beginning a kind of apprenticeship. Slowly I learned to identify indigenous plants and animals and birds migrating through. Slowly I began to expand the basis of my observations of their lives, to alter the nature of my assumptions. Slowly I began to recognize clusters of life in the valley as opposed to individual, isolated species. I was lucky to live in a place too steep for agriculture to have developed, too heavily wooded to be good for grazing, and too poor in commercial quantities of minerals for mining (though the evidence that all three occurred on a small scale is present). The only industrial scale impact here has come from commercial logging—and the devastation in parts of the valley is as breathtaking a sight as the napalmed forests of the Vietnam highlands in the 1960s. Pressure is building locally now to develop retirement real estate—trailer parks, RV parks, condominiums; but, for the moment, it's still relatively easy to walk for hours across stretches of land that have never been farmed, logged, mined, graded, or homesteaded. From where my house sits on a wooded bench above the McKenzie River, I can look across the water into a four or five-hundred year old forest in which some of the Douglas firs are more than twenty feet around.

Two ways to 'learn' this land are obvious: enter it repeatedly and atten-tively on your own; or give your attention instead—or alternately—to its occupants. The most trustworthy occupants, to my mind, are those with no commercial ties, beings whose sense of ownership is guided not by profit but by responsible occupancy. For the valley in which I live, these occupants would theoretically be remnant Tsanchifin people and indigenous animals. To my knowledge, the Tsanchifin are no longer a presence; and the rational mind (to which many of us acquiesce) posits there is little to be learned from animals unless we discover a common language and can converse. This puts the empha-sis, I think, in the wrong place. The idea shouldn't be for us to converse, to enter into some sort of Socratic dialogue with animals. It would be to listen to what is already being communicated. To insist on a conversation with the unknown is to demonstrate impatience, and it is to imply that any such encounter must include your being heard.

To know a physical place you must become intimate with it. You must open yourself to its textures, its colors in varying day and night lights, its sonic dimensions. You must in some way become vulnerable to it. In the end, there's little difference between growing into the love of a place and growing into the love of a person. Love matures through intimacy and vulnerability, and it grows most vigorously in an atmosphere of trust. You learn, with regard to the land, the ways in which it is dependable. Where it has no strength to offer you, you do not insist on its support. When you yourself do not understand some-thing, you trust that the land might, and you defer.

When I walk in the woods or along the creeks, I'm looking for integra-tion, not conversation. I want to be bound more deeply into the place, to be included, even if only as a witness, in events that animate the landscape. In tracking a mink, in picking a black bear scat apart, in examining red alder trunks deer have scraped with their antlers, I get certain measures of the place where I live. In listening to the songs of Swainson's thrushes and to winter wrens, to the bellows of elk, I get a dimension of the valley I couldn't get on my own. In eating spring chinook, in burning big-leaf maple in the stove, in bathing in ground water from the well, in collecting sorrel and miner's let-tuce for a summer salad, I put my life more deeply into the life around me.

The eloquence of animals is in their behavior, not their speech. To see a mule deer stot across a river bar, a sharp-shinned hawk maneuver in dense timber, to watch a female chinook build her nest on clean gravel, to see a rufous hummingbird extracting nectar from foxglove blossoms, to come upon a rubber boa constricting a shrew is to meet the world outside the self. It is to hear the indigenes.

We regard wild creatures as the most animated part of the landscape. We've believed for eons that we share a specific nature with them, different from the nature of wild berries or lightning or water. Our routine exchanges with them are most often simply a verification of this, reaffirmations that we're alive in a particular place together at a particular time.

Wild animals are like us, too, in that they have ancestors. When I see river otter sprawled mid-stream on a boulder in the noon sun, I know their ancestors were here before the fur trappers, before the Tsanchifin, before *Homo*. The same for the cormorant, the woolly bear caterpillar, the cutthroat. In all these histories, in the string of events in each life, the land is revealed. The tensile strength of the orb weaver's silk, the location of the salmon's redd, the shrew-mole's bones bound up in a spotted owl's cast, each makes a concise statement.

Over the years and on several continents I've seen indigenous people enter their landscapes. (I say enter because the landscape of a semi-permanent camp or village, as I have come to understand it, is less intense, less numinous.) Certain aspects of this entry experience seem always to be in evidence. Human conversation usually trails off. People become more alert to what is around them, less intent on any goal—where to camp that night, say. People become more curious about animal life, looking at the evidence of what animals have been up to. People begin to look all around, especially behind them, instead of staring straight ahead with only an occasional look to the side. People halt to examine closely things that at first glance seemed innocuous. People stop simply to put things together—the sky with a certain type of forest, a kind of rock outcropping, the sound of a creek, and, last, the droppings of a blue grouse under a thimbleberry bush. People heft rocks and put them back. They push their hands into river mud and perhaps leave patches of it on their skin. It's an on-going intercourse with the place.

Learning one's place through attention to animals is not solely a matter of being open to 'statements' they make about the physical, chemical, and biological realms we share. A more profound communication can take place. In this second sphere, animals have volition; they have intention and the power of influence; and they have the capacity to intervene in our lives. I've never known people who were entirely comfortable addressing such things.

However we may define 'consciousness' in the West, we regard it as a line of demarcation that separates human nature from animal nature. A shaman might cross back and forth, but animals, no.

In my experience indigenous people are most comfortable in asserting a spiritual nature for animals (including aspects of consciousness) only when the purpose of the conversation is to affirm a spirituality shared by both humans and animals. (They're more at ease talking about animals as exemplars of abstract ideals, as oracles and companions, and as metaphorical relations.) When someone relates something previously unheard of that they saw an animal do, something that demonstrates the degree of awareness we call consciousness, the person is saying the world still turns on the miraculous, it's still inventing itself, and that we're part of this. These observations keep the idea alive that animals are engaged in the world at a deep level.

The fundamental reenforcement of a belief in the spiritual nature of animals' lives (i.e. in the spiritual nature of the landscape itself) comes from a numinous encounter with a wild creature. For many indigenous people (again, in my experience) such events make one feel more secure in the 'real' world because their unfolding takes the event beyond the more readily apparent boundaries of existence. In a numinous encounter one's suspicion, profound, persistent, and ineluctable, that there is more to the world than appearances is confirmed. For someone reared in the tradition of the cultural West, it is also a confirmation that Rationalism and the Enlightenment are not points on a continuum of progress but simply two species of wisdom.

Whenever I think of the numinous event, and how vulnerable it is to the pinchers of the analytic mind, I recall a scene in a native village in Alaska. A well-meaning but rude young man, a graduate student in anthropology, had come to this village to study hunting. His ethnocentric interviewing technique was aggressive, his vocabulary academic, his manner to pester and interfere. Day after day he went after people, especially one older man he took to be the best hunter in the village. He hounded him relentlessly, asking him why he was the best hunter. The only way the man could be rid of the interviewer was to answer his question. He ended the assault by saying, 'My ability to hunt is like a small bird in my mind. I don't think anyone should disturb it.'

A central task facing modern Western cultures is to redefine human community in the wake of industrialization, colonialism and, more recently, the forcing power of capitalism. In trying to solve some of the constellation of attendant problems here—keeping corporations out of secondary education, restoring the physical and spiritual shelter of the family group, preserving non-

Western ways of knowing—it seems clear that by cutting ourselves off from nature, by turning nature into scenery and commodities, we may have cut ourselves off from something vital. To repair this damage we can't any longer take what we call 'nature' for an object. We must merge it again with our own nature. We must reintegrate ourselves in specific geographic places, and to do that we need to learn those places at a greater depth than any science, Eastern or Western, can take us. We have to incorporate them again in the moral universe we inhabit. We have to develop good relations with them, one that will replace the exploitative relations that have become a defining characteristic of twentieth-century Western life, with its gargantuan oil spills and chemical accidents, its megalithic hydroelectric developments, its hideous weapons of war, and its conception of wealth that would lead a corporation to cut down a forest to pay the interest on a loan.

In daily conversation in many parts of the American West today, wild animals are given credit for conveying ideas to people, for 'speaking'. To some degree this is a result of the pervasive influence of Native American culture in certain parts of the West. It doesn't contradict the notion of human intelligence to believe, in these quarters, that wild animals represent repositories of knowledge we've abandoned in our efforts to build civilizations and support ideas like progress and improvement. To 'hear' wild animals is not to leave the realm of the human; it's to expand this realm to include voices other than our own. It's a technique for the accomplishment of wisdom. To attend to the language of animals means to give yourself over to a more complicated, less analytic awareness of a place. It's to realize that some of the so-called equations of life are not meant to be solved, that it takes as much intelligence not to solve them as it does to find the putative answers.

A fundamental difference between early and late twentieth-century science in the cultural West has become apparent with the emergence of the phrase 'I don't know' in scientific discourse. This admission is the heritage of quantum mechanics. It is heard eloquently today in the talk of cosmologists, plasma physicists, and, increasingly, among field biologists now working beyond the baleful and condescending stare of molecular biologists.

The Enlightenment ideals of an educated mind and just relations among different people have become problematic in our era because the process of formal education in the West has consistently abjured or condemned non-Western ways of knowing, and because the quest for just relations still strains at the barriers of race, gender, and class. If we truly believe in the wisdom of Enlightenment thought and achievement—and certainly, like Bach's B-Minor

Mass, Goethe's theory of light, or Darwin's voyage, that philosophy is among the best we have to offer—then we should consider encouraging the educated mind to wander beyond the comfort of its own solipsisms, and we should extend the principle of justice to include everything that touches our lives.

I do not know how to achieve these things in the small valley where I live except through apprenticeship and the dismantling of assumptions I grew up with. The change, to a more gracious and courteous and wondrous awareness of the world, will not come in my lifetime, and knowing what I know of the modern plagues—loss of biodiversity, global warming, and the individual quest for material wealth—I am fearful. But I believe I have come to whatever I understand by listening to companions and by trying to erase the lines that establish hierarchies of knowledge among them. My sense is that the divine knowledge we yearn for is social, it is not in the province of a genius anymore than it is in the province of a particular culture. It lies within our definition of community.

Our blessing, it seems to me, is not what we know, but that we know each other.

# The South Fork

Two humpback whales, the first I have seen in a decade, roll softly on the surface, like black shining rocks in the silver ocean. Great whales were once so common off the coast at this far east end of Long Island that shore whaling was an industry, but I have seen them from the shore only a few times in my life, and, feeling elated, walk with them along the beach a little way. They move slowly to the east, off the narrow strip of sand that separates Georgica Pond from the Atlantic.

The wind is out of the northwest, and the day is cold, but already the sea breathes its sweet stink of regeneration. The great animals spout thinly in the cold clear light, and the wind fans the spume to mist on the huge horizon.

A few years ago, on another day of spring, a Sagaponack neighbor brought a fish into my yard that had turned up in the nets early that morning. For several years I had hauled seine with the beach crews, and this farmer-fisherman had done so for much longer, and neither of us had ever seen this beautiful silver fish, ten pounds or better, that he held before him with both hands in instinctive ceremony.

I turned toward the house to fetch my book of fishes, then turned back, grinning. It was not the arrangement of the fins that told me what it was but a pang of intuition. Perhaps this rare fish from the cold Atlantic was on its way to the ancient mouth of the Connecticut River, which fifteen thousand years ago (before the melting glaciers raised the level of the seas, separating Long Island from the southern New England coast) was located at what is now Plum Gut, off the North Fork of this great fish-tailed island. Like the great whales, the Atlantic salmon—once so abundant in the fresh clear rivers that the Massachusetts colonists were forbidden to feed it to indentured servants more than once a week—had been reduced to these wandering survivors, to be wondered at in the cold spring sun like emblems of a New World prematurely old.

———

Here within sight of the blue shadow of New England's industrial seaboard ten miles to the north, moving at daybreak on back roads, the fishermen go their traditional way down to the sea. They are tough, resourceful, self-respecting, and also (some say) hidebound and cranky, too independent to organize for their own survival. Yet even their critics must acknowledge a gritty spirit that was once more highly valued in this country than it is today. Because their children can no longer afford to live where their families have harvested the sea and land for three hundred years, these South Fork baymen—old-time Americans who still speak with the Kentish and Dorset inflections of Elizabethan England—may soon become rare relics from the past, like the Atlantic right whales, a cow and calf, that in the winter of 1984–1985 have been appearing here and there off the ocean beach.

———

With windy weather, as Indian summer turned to fall, the scallops became scarce in shallow water. We turned to heavy labor with the dredges, dumping the wet loads of eelgrass and codium, or Sputnik weed,[1] onto the culling board. The load was never twice the same. The elegant scallops, snapping their shells, were occasionally accompanied by an unwary flounder, together with an indiscriminate assortment of crabs, horsefoots, sand worms, glass shrimp, sea horses, sponges, whelks, stones, bottles, sneakers, dead shells, and—not uncommonly—a clump of wild oysters.

Later that autumn, when the scallops thinned out inside the harbors, we went prospecting for virgin scallop beds as far away as Napeague, Montauk

Lake, and Gardiners Island, putting in at Promised Land for our supplies. One day of late October, as we scalloped off the western shore of Gardiners Island, a cold front came in toward midday, with a stiff wind out of the northwest. Though heavily crusted with quarterdecks, or boat shells, the scallops on this rocky bottom were plentiful, and we were hurrying to complete our twenty-bushel boat limit and head home when the one-cylinder motor on my old boat conked out and would not revive. Hoisting the *Vop*'s patched gaff-rigged sail, we beat upwind toward the mainland.

Already a hard gale was blowing; despite her deep keel, the boat was banging into white-capped waves. Halfway across the channel the pine mast broke off at the deck, and mast, boom, and canvas crashed upon our heads. Not saying much, we sorted out the mess as the wind carried us back toward Gardiners Island. (Years ago, an old-timer named Puff Dominy broke down off Lion Head Rock and drifted back east to Gardiners on this same course. Told to throw over the anchor, his retarded crewman cried, 'No twing! No twing!' Impatient and uncomprehending, Puff hollered, 'Let 'er go, goddamn it, "twing" or no "twing"!' Thrown overboard with no 'string' attached, Puff's anchor disappeared forever, but 'twing or no twing' has survived in local lore.)

Nearing the island, we threw over an anchor, but by the time the grapnel finally took hold, the *Vop* was scarcely two hundred yards offshore in Bostwick Bay, buffered by wind and seas in the growing weather. It was midafternoon of a swift day of late autumn, and a cold sun was sinking fast, with no boat in sight, nothing but whitecaps and wind-blown gulls and long black ragged strings of cormorants beating across the wind toward the southwest. Not only was the boat wide open, but the hatch covers of the fish holds forming her deck were only three inches lower than the gunwales, which provided no shelter from the wind. On this north end of Gardiners Island, never inhabited, the view from the sea was as wild as it was three centuries before when the Algonkian people known as Montauks escorted Lion Gardiner to his New World home.

In 1676, by the Dongan Patent, Gardiners Island—roughly seven by three miles, or about thirty-three hundred acres—had been deemed a manor, and it is, in fact, the last of the old English manors to remain in the same New World family to the present day. In the 1690s, Captain William Kidd, a minister's son and retired sea captain pressed into service as a privateer by a syndicate that included the English governor of Massachusetts, was arrested in Boston and sent to England. There he was hanged for disputed reasons,

among them, it is said, the protection of the reputations of those who had
benefited from his voyages, including the hard-living 'Lord John' Gardiner,
son of the incumbent Lord of the Manor, David Lion Gardiner, who had first
welcomed Kidd to Gardiners Island. Captain Kidd's only known treasure of
gold dust, gold coin, jewelry, and the like, retrieved from the pond behind the
beach in Cherry Harbor off which we had been scalloping when the boat
broke down, was turned over to the authorities by Lord John, who escaped
unpunished. In 1728 the manor was commandeered for three days by real
pirates, causing the family to look for safer lodgings in East Hampton Village.
Since then, Gardiners Island has been occupied intermittently by the
Gardiner family, which has often leased it to other people.

In the 1950s the island was inhabited by an estimated five hundred pairs of
ospreys, by far the largest colony of these striking fish hawks in North America
and perhaps the world. High cliffs to the eastward (a source of clay for the early
settlers) slope gradually to low fields in the west, with broad lowlands, salt
marshes, ponds, and sand spits, north and south. Where we were anchored was
the windward shore of the northern sand spit, in Bostwick ('Bostic' to the fishermen) Bay, where a bad storm in 1879 had overturned a lobster boat out of
New London, drowning two crewmen. Another storm in 1892 parted this sand
spit, creating an islet out at the north point where a lighthouse had been built
in 1855;[2] the shoddily constructed building, weakened by storms, collapsed two
years later, and the light was abandoned. During the Spanish-American war, a
round structure called Fort Tyler was built upon this shored-up islet, part of a
whole string of forts on Plum, Gull, and Fishers Islands designed to protect
Long Island Sound from unfriendly gunboats.[3] Since its abandonment in 1924,
Fort Tyler has been much diminished by erosion and bombing practice, and is
usually referred to as 'the ruin.'

Twilight had come, and a sharp autumn cold. To the north the old fort, in
dark and gloomy silhouette on a cold sunset, rode like a ship in the running
silver tide against the lightless islands and the far black line of the New
England hills where the last light faded in the sky. Our young wives would not
worry about us until after nightfall, so no help could be expected until next
day.

Eight miles to the northeast lay Fishers Island, the easternmost point of
Suffolk County, where I had spent most of my first fifteen summers;[4] five miles
to the southwest lay Three Mile Harbor in East Hampton, where I visited first in
1942. Now it was 1953, I was in my midtwenties, and had moved permanently to
the South Fork. Thus I had lived in Suffolk County all my life, on or about the

edges of these waters; this wild and lonely place where our small boat washed up and down on the high chop lay at the very heart of my home country.

On this cold rough October evening, hunched knee to knee in a cramped anchor cubby, we ate raw scallops from the upright burlap bags that hunched like refugees on deck, and listened to the waves slap on the hull; if the anchor dragged during the night, our small wood boat would wash ashore on Gardiners Island. It was already gunning season, and we wanted no night dealings with Charlie Raynor, the caretaker and dangerous enemy of enterprising young gunners such as ourselves who would sneak ashore at the south end while out coot shooting around Cartwright Shoals and be reasonably sure of snagging a few pheasants along the airstrip. Raynor's reputation as a man who would shoot first and talk afterward saved him a lot of trouble on the job. Especially in the hunting season, he made no distinctions between castaways and trespassers, and anyway he lived too far off to be of help.

At daylight the cold wind from the northwest had not diminished, and there were no signs of boats or sail. All Gardiners Bay was tossed in a white chop, crossed by the strings of cormorants, the hurrying scoters and solitary loons, the wind-tilted gulls, hard wings reflecting a wild light that pierced the metallic clouds.

Toward midmorning a Coast Guard plane came over; when we waved our arms, the plane went away, and still there were no boats on the rough horizons.

In early afternoon a black fishing boat appeared. Its hardy skipper was Fanny Gardiner Collins of Three Mile Harbor, a member of the island clan and avid fisherwoman who knew much more about Gardiners Island and its waters than her wealthy kinsmen. Fanny took us in tow and hauled us back to Three Mile Harbor.

———

On Sunday afternoon, May 12, Lindy Havens and Eddie Trufanoff went out on Gardiners Bay in Lindy's sharpie to try out Lindy's new outboard motor and perhaps pick out some locations for his gill-nets. Lindy wore knee boots, and ET wore the heavy black waders he had used on the beach the previous spring. A southeast wind was blowing, and the day was cold, but in the lee of Hedges Bank, between Cedar Point and Sammis Beach, where the Northwest Woods overlooks the water, the bay was calm.

Lindy must have been teasing ET as usual, for the two were heard shouting and laughing by people in the housing development above. The motor, which had apparently cut out, now started up again, and a few moments later, a man standing on the stair that leads down to the rocky beach heard the sharpie suddenly accelerate. Glancing over, he saw both men floundering in the boat's wake.

The man on shore was casually acquainted with Ed Trufanoff, and reported that ET had gone over first, since he saw his reddish head twenty or more yards farther back in the boat's wake than Lindy's dark one. Though Lindy was a veteran boatman, it appeared that he had lost his balance and gone over the side when he spun the boat hard to retrieve the other man. Since the two were less than two hundred yards offshore, the onlooker considered swimming out to help them—he told me he had once been a lifeguard—but he knew from recent experience, out clamming, that he would go numb in this cold water once he was in over his waist and would never reach them.

The man with the dark hair was treading high in the water with his shoulders out, dodging the sharpie, which was making tight circles. A few seconds later, when the witness ran to telephone for help, Lindy seemed to be making his way toward ET, who was flailing desperately without making a sound. Glancing back just once, the witness thought he saw them both, but he wonders now if what he thought was ET's head, low in the water, was actually a pot buoy, and if ET went under before Lindy reached him. Perhaps Lindy never got there at all, for when the witness got back to the stair less than three minutes later, both heads were gone.

During those three minutes, a second witness who had come to the cliff edge saw one man—almost certainly Lindy—waving his arms and crying out for help. Then the bay was still but for the empty sharpie, which spun in tight circles until she ran aground, an hour later.

Apparently the balky motor had been started up in gear and at full throttle, kicking the skiff out from beneath the upright Eddie. Apparently ET knew how to swim, but even a strong swimmer would have had trouble staying afloat in heavy waders, which are difficult to take off in deep water. He appears to have resurfaced only briefly, whereas Lindy seems to have been in good control. Perhaps Lindy hollered when he felt himself growing paralyzed in the cold May water, and very likely his heart stopped, since if his lungs had filled in drowning, it seems unlikely that he would have floated. Yet he went under at least briefly, since both men on the cliff edge say he disappeared. By the time his body was recovered about twenty-five minutes after the accident (by a private boat out of Three Mile Harbor that answered a 'May Day' emergency call on its ship-to-shore radio), the southeast wind had drifted him several hundred yards to the northwest, off Tom Lester's fish trap.

'Salt water and drinkin just don't mix,' said a bayman on the Dory Rescue Squad, which tried to coordinate the search for ET's body. The police divers worked mainly in the offshore stretch where the drifting body was recovered, despite the first witness's strong feeling, relayed over the baymen's radio, that Trufanoff must still be on the bottom at the inshore spot right off the cliff stair where he disappeared. 'I clam there all the time, and there's no current, not inshore,' the unhappy man told me a few days later, still upset by the thought that there was some way he might have helped. 'I feel sure he's right there now. I liked ET; you couldn't help but like him. He didn't have anything much to say but he was always smiling. It gives me a funny feeling about going clamming, knowing he's out there.' Eddie Trufanoff's body washed up on Sammis Beach two Sundays later.

A memorial service for Sidney Lindbergh Havens, one of the best fishermen on the East End, was held in a funeral home on Newtown Lane in the late morning of May 16, an hour which permitted most baymen to attend. There were copious flowers and floral wreaths, some in the shapes of fish and anchors, and the room was crowded. The Amagansett Fire Department, of which Lindy was a member, carried his flag-draped casket to the Oakwood Cemetery, where he was buried toward midday of a soft spring morning. Three old friends from the haul-seine crews, Don Eames, Sr., Pete Kromer, and Milt Miller, were among his pall-bearers, and Milt was chewing on his lip as the casket was lowered into the Bonac earth.

Leaving the cemetery, Milt put his arm around my shoulder, and we walked along a little. 'Kind of a sad day,' I said. 'Old Lindy had a lot of spirit.' But Milt had grieved and made his peace with his friend's death and was on his way back to the bay, which is just what Lindy would have wanted. He nodded politely at my glum remark before cocking his head to look at me with that wry squint. 'Well, I don't guess *none* of us are goin to get away with it, now are we, Pete? Try as we might.' I laughed quietly, and he laughed, too, shaking his head. It was what Lindy might have said at Milt Miller's funeral, and we both felt better.

On December 4, 1984, finishing the first draft of these journals, I walked down to the ocean for a breath of air. The day was cold, with a northwest wind shivering the rainwater where ice was broken in the puddles. Rising and falling in flight along the dunes, a flock of gulls picked up the last ambient light from the red embers in the west. The silent birds, undulating on the wind, shone bone white against massed somber grays, low over the ocean; the cloud bank looked ominous, like waiting winter.

From the beach landing, in this moody sky and twilight, I saw something awash in the white foam, perhaps a quarter mile down to the eastward. The low heavy thing, curved round upon itself, did not look like driftwood; I thought at first that it must be a human body. Uneasy, I walked east a little way, then hurried ahead; the thing was not driftwood, not a body, but the great clean skull of a finback whale,[5] dark bronze with sea water and minerals. The beautiful form, crouched like some ancient armored creature in the wash, seemed to await me. No one else was on the beach, which was clean of tracks. There was only the last cold fire of dusk, the white birds fleeing toward the darkness, the frosty foam whirling around the skull, seeking to regather it into the deeps.

By the time I returned with a truck and chain, it was nearly night. The sea was higher, and the skull was settling like some enormous crab into the wash; I could not get close enough without sinking the truck down to the axles. I took careful bearings on the skull's location, and a good thing too, because four hours later, when the tide had turned, the massive skull had sunk away into the sands, all but what looked like a small dark rock in the moon-white shallows. I dug this out enough to secure a hawser, then ran this rope above the tide line, as a lead to the skull's location the next morning. But fearing that an onshore wind or storm might bury it forever, I went down at dead low tide that night, under the moon, and dug the skull clear and worked it up out of its pit, using truck and chain. Nearly six feet across, the skull was waterlogged and heavy, five hundred pounds or better. Not until one in the morning—spending more time digging out my truck than freeing the bone—did I hitch it high enough onto the beach to feel confident that the tide already coming in would not rebury it. By morning there was an onshore wind, with a chop already making up from the southwest, but the whale skull was still waiting at the water's edge. Bud Topping came down with his tractor and we took it home. When Milt Miller, who was raised by the old whalers, had a look at it a few weeks later, he said it was the biggest skull he ever saw.

## NOTES

1    Codium was introduced accidentally in Greenport harbor in the twenties or thirties from Japan, and is now widespread on the East End; it is called Sputnik weed because it seemed (and looked) as if it might have dropped from outer space.

2    Lighthouses were installed on Little Gull Island in 1806 and on Plum Island in 1827; both of these lights are still in operation, though no longer manned.

3    The construction of this problematic chain, out of date so long before its own completion, eliminated an obscure species of mouse called the Gull Island vole, but an uncommon bird called the roseate tern still nests in the crumbling ruin of the gun emplacements on Gull Island, which is now owned and administered by the American Museum of Natural History.

4    It is sometimes said that Fishers Island was named after a certain Vischer, who served the Dutch navigator Adriaen Block as cartographer, but more likely it refers to an isle of fishers, or fishing Indians, who called the island Munnatawket (very likely these Indians were the seagoing Montauks).

5    The finback, largest whale on earth except the blue whale, attains a length of seventy to eighty feet.

# MICHAEL McCOY

## Home Ground

I feel like I have spent this 37 years travelling on a boardwalk—like those con-structed through some delicate piece of wetland, so that one can look, with-out touching. I am suspended above my surroundings. The few times my feet have touched the ground have been joyous, but have later left me more acute-ly aware of the lack of contact I experience most of the time. I long for some sense of being partially buried, at least up to the ankles—of being planted, somehow. But I have spent my life on the landscape, rather than in it.

I suspect this is not a unique experience for an Australian. Most of us are yet to belong. One could argue that this is a natural consequence of living in this hostile land—the driest continent on earth, and unable to support human life without modification. But living in a relatively gentle and moist part of this diverse landmass, I don't think that alone explains my alienation.

The experience that comes closest to comfort for me is that of being dwarfed by my surroundings. I have such a conviction of my insignificance that I look for evidence of this in the landscape. Registering the impact of my own presence as vertical (that I was until recently always dramatically skinny may have something to do with that), I am only dwarfed by vertical extremes. To stand amongst the aggressively vertical, untapering cream candles of

Australian Mountain Ash (*Eucalyptus regnans*), for instance, is the closest I come to being absorbed. My own presence is totally overridden—obliterated—by this massive upward force, which works intensely against gravity.

Horizontal extremes, on the other hand, make me very uncomfortable. To stand atop a peak in the mountainous south of Zambia, which feels like a vast eroded plane, is to be surrounded by more sky than feels either natural or safe. The dome overhead fish-eyes to far more than the usual maximum of 180 degrees, making any human painfully conspicuous.

It may be that our senses are just so satiated with the cloying abundance of our Western lifestyle that only the most extreme stimulus will register any response. I suspect that the true character of our common, everyday surrounds will only be detected with a humility and silence that are almost impossible to achieve.

Not long ago I was looking for a house just to live in—nothing more. We didn't have the money to seek anything special. Even the lowest end of the market looked like stretching the budget. When we found the house that we eventually purchased—the ugliest and cheapest of the lot, incidentally—we stepped into a house awash with light. Having lived for too long in a gloomy house in a misty, light-deprived spot not far from here, we recognized good natural lighting as being the most precious thing a house can possess. Then we walked around to the back yard, and stepped into the base of a bowl, three sides made of trees in this and surrounding yards and the fourth provided by the house. It was a bowl sufficiently large that I was a reassuringly minor presence. My partner and I both stated, simultaneously, that we could make a garden here.

Garden designers these days pay great lip service to a 'sense of place'. We are meant to be sensitive to it, and make decisions that will enhance and draw attention to it. But its relevance is questionable in most suburban locations. One tries to listen and look, sensitively, to what it is saying, then decides that the only real option is to cover up what one hears and sees.

My own garden did not have any real sense of place borrowed from the wider landscape. It had, perhaps, a sense of location, provided by the nearby mountain, which served to anchor it in position. But its greatest value, by far, was that it was an enclosed and introspective space of very appealing proportions—to me. It was sufficiently cut off from the world that I could make a garden here without having to work in with the wider landscape. Thinking that we would find living in an ugly little house intolerable, we didn't expect to stay long, so decided that the garden I created here would have to be

fabulous in the first year so as to maximise our pleasure from it. And not seeing any reason why such a goal couldn't be achieved, I committed myself to
opening it to the public a year later, though the garden was only just begun.

I spent most of that year like some crazed alchemist of old, throwing
together every life-giving force I could muster—every possible vital ingredi-
ent—in unrestrained, and possibly quite dangerous, quantities. The ground
quickly began to rumble, to rise, boil and foam, and what exploded beneath
my feet was a vegetable sculpture for my indwelling. It surrounded, then swallowed me. I was dwarfed again. Magic.

Or at least that is how it seems in my memory, now that a few years have
passed. In fact it was a lot of very hard work. I'm a fanatic when it comes to
garden soil preparation, so with double digging, 45 cubic metres of compost
to incorporate and ten tonnes of gravel to spread, there was much hard, brain-
less labouring. And that didn't seem anything like magic. I wasn't so much
responding to my surroundings, or even listening to them, but actively working against the prevailing conditions to force this space to meet my own needs.

But that is so with virtually all gardening.

The early Persian gardens are an extreme example. Their appeal is that of
the oasis, splashing water about with abandon in otherwise parched conditions. They sought to totally mask the hostile conditions outside their walls,
and in doing so were spectacularly inappropriate to their surroundings.
Nowadays we'd be preaching to Persian garden designers about their responsibility to save water and feeding them with propaganda about the subtle
beauty of xeroscaping.

The oasis I was creating was one of scale, rather than of water. The wider
landscape is on a massive scale provided by the aforementioned mountain. I
needed to work with a foreign sense of scale, to sculpt and mould the space in
keeping with the domesticity of my subdivision, and my six-foot frame.

And I needed it to be an oasis of fertility. The landscape beyond is of largely woody plants that reveal a minimal response to the seasons, and I wanted to
dramatically exaggerate seasonal change. I love that seasonal rise and fall—the
slow climb through spring and summer, then the crash in autumn. Fertility
also ensures vigour, and vigour is one of the things I respond to most in gardens, much more so than carefully contrived colour schemes, or pretty foliage
combinations.

So to this end I laboured. And, curiously, it was in the hard work that I
found my greatest connection with my surrounds, and most frequently when
the weather conditions were hostile, or at least had me braced against them.

There came a point when my body was in autopilot, and my mind just sufficiently occupied to retain a single focus. It was at these times, and when I least expected it, that I stepped into some new relationship with my surrounds. I was suddenly a part of them, no more foreign for my consciousness than a weed seed blowing in; an inhabitant as valid as the old trees around me and the microbes under my feet; a creature doing what is needed to survive or thrive as had other inhabitants for millennia before me but whose length of stay, though minute on any eternal scale, had perhaps given them more validity than I normally felt.

These were moments when time blew out, my face to the cold drizzle and my body still braced for the next thrust of the spade.

But these feelings were only ever momentary. Most of the time I was a foreigner, inflicting my inappropriate demands on this unfortunate bit of ground. And this feeling was greatly exacerbated when I gave in to the baser desires of wanting to 'show it off'. While I was working for myself and for my own needs there was some reciprocation of benefit. I was nurtured as I nurtured. But the integrity of this experience was undermined when I began to consider how I might impress my visitors, who were to come to find out what I'd achieved in this experimental garden. I began to think in the shortest of terms, making decisions that placed the emphasis upon a show for one day, and compromised the garden's ongoing development. A day or two after opening, I stood in the garden just looking, then suddenly heard myself, saying 'What? What have I done?' In the future I need to garden entirely for myself. And others can enjoy the results—or not, as they please.

Within this rectangular prism that is my own space, and parallel with one of its long sides is the smaller prism of my office, and there I sit and observe this explosive, boiling, erupting, then cooling cycle, largely unaware of what's beyond.

But then on occasion a small and lonely group of black cockatoos passes, arrow-like overhead, and one will release its distant, horizontal call. The effect in my garden is like that of the French horn in a movie soundtrack—blowing out cinema walls to infinite distance. The cockatoo calls and the paling fences fall like dominoes. The trees are levelled and I am left sitting alone on a vast, gently undulating plane. Like the bird, I am aware of no boundaries, and like the bird I wait in the silence to see if this yawning open space will return any reply.

# RICHARD NELSON

## Island of the Rain Bear

A hushed, damp, cool August evening, embroidered with the sighing calls of mew gulls, the chiming of varied thrushes, the murmur of distant waterfalls. Our skiff glides easily into a narrowing estuary where the stream from Lake Eva swirls into Peril Strait. With my friend Don Muller, I've come 70 miles from Sitka, navigating the complex tidal channels of Baranof Island, in the Tongass National Forest of southeast Alaska.

A lone merganser duck paddles on the silky water, cutting a wake through reflected mountain walls. Her crested, cinnamon head turns this way and that, as if she's looking first at us, then at something else. Following her gaze, I pick out a hulky shape beside the far bank, shadowed by the boughs of an enormous spruce. It looks like a half-submerged boulder uncovered by the falling tide, yet there's something strange ... a softness at the edges, a tangible ephemerality. As we idle closer, the rock seems to breathe and gently rise, triggering a crescent of tiny ripples.

For a moment, I'm distracted by a marmalade-colored jellyfish drifting beneath us, big as a basketball, trailing hundreds of threadlike tentacles. And then—looking back at the rock—I see the truth of it: sloping shoulders, neck as wide as a young tree trunk, and a broad, densely-furred, tawny brown head.

'Bear!' I whisper. Don nods intently. I can only imagine his pleasure: a dedicated advocate for wildlife and forests, his face is absolutely beaming.

The animal peers our way, showing the humped shoulder and dished face of a grizzly, or brown bear, as it's called locally. I expect the bear—apparently a young male—to retreat, but instead he casually swims out into the lagoon, ducking his head underwater at intervals, searching for spawned-out salmon. Finding none, he heaves up onto the opposite shore. And there he stands, at the hard seam joining water and land: an upright bear perfectly balanced on the splayed paws of an inverted bear shimmering on the liquid mirror.

After a contemplative pause, the bruin shakes himself dry and rambles along the bank, stopping occasionally to sniff the air, still oblivious to our intrusion. He also ignores a yodeled voice tumbling from the high mountainside. I glance up to see a raven, black as the eye of night, soaring beneath latticework clouds.

Although I first came to southeast Alaska thirty years ago, the immense wildness and tranquility of this place still sets my heart thundering. It makes a child of me—an avid, eager, excited, impatient child, seized by a perpetual rage for discovery. Even in midsummer, when the daylight spans twenty hours, I mutter about the time lost to darkness and wish for a way to evade sleep. If only I had come to southeast Alaska much earlier in life ... but more than anything, I'm grateful for the blessed serendipity of being here at all.

I had dreamed of this place—imagined myself living in the company of ravens and brown bears—long before I left the family nest in Wisconsin. As a college student majoring in anthropology, I became fascinated by Indian cultures of the north Pacific coast, and especially by their lavish temperate rainforest environment. In my class notebooks, I'd sketch an imaginary cove with a cabin among tall conifers, a simple garden, a skiff drawn up on the beach, a storehouse for venison and dried salmon and wild berries.

But instead of coming to southeast Alaska, I traveled much farther north and lived for some years with Iñupiaq Eskimos, Gwich'in Indians, and Koyukon Indians, learning about their ways of hunting, fishing, and gathering. Eventually, I made a trip to Juneau, where I saw, for the first time, the snow-covered mountains, the deeply-incised fjords, the great towering forest. Despite all the books and pictures and fantasies, I had no sense of encountering the expected or familiar—just the bewildering, incandescent elation of coming to a place where I *belonged*.

Years later I owned a homestead cabin just like the one in my sketches, overlooking an inlet on Chichagof Island near the village of Tenakee Springs. Together with my partner Nita, I fished and hunted for food, cut firewood, helped to raise a growing boy, explored the valleys and waterways, and savored a life wholly imbedded in wild nature. Then one summer, chainsaws and logging trucks entered the surrounding Tongass National Forest and over the following years clearcuts spread across the slopes facing our inlet. Our dream was slipping away, so Nita and I moved to the town of Sitka, on nearby Baranof Island, where the forest, waters, and wildlife seemed less in jeopardy.

The front window of our little house faces an open-mouthed bay, with a palisade of mountains on the east and south, rocky breakwater islands toward the west, and the open Pacific sprawling beyond. The line between town and wild is indistinct here: cormorants, gulls, loons, and bald eagles frequent the bay; harbor seals, river otters, sea lions, and humpback whales are common off our shore; millions of herring swarm along the beach each spring, followed by the summer runs of salmon; black-tailed deer visit our haphazardly-gardened back yard and brown bears haunt the forest just beyond.

But however much we relish the company of wild creatures, it's the human community, above all, that keeps us here. Our town stretches along 14 miles of crenelated shoreline, pinched between steep mountains and the sea. Most neighborhoods clump on either side of the single main road which terminates abruptly at both ends. To go any farther, you need a boat or plane. This brings a particular quiet and measure to the pace of daily life. Remoteness also tightens the bonds between people, reminds everyone of how much they need each other, and enhances the tendency for small towns to nurture big hearts.

Most of us came here from somewhere else, and to compensate for the severing of home ties, we've developed intricate webs of friendship, much like an extended family. An older social tradition persists among us: we visit constantly, thriving in the companionship of like-minded souls; we share foods from the wild and the garden; we watch out for everyone's safety in times of travel and storm; we take care of each other's children; we fish and hunt and gather together; we are united in our common love for this place and our concern for its wellbeing.

I think of my relationship to these home grounds as a kind of marriage— a commitment of body and heart. Although I enjoy the flirtations of travel and relish the beauty to be found elsewhere, I'm always drawn powerfully home, always excited to see this familiar coast again. Although I was not born *in* this place, I believe I was born *for* it. When I return from a long trip, I'm reminded of the urgent thrall that brings salmon back to their natal streams, and of the predators and scavengers whose hunger for fish draws them to the same locale each year.

On this summer evening, our Lake Eva brown bear is apparently so focused on hunger that he cares little about our presence. I wonder why he doesn't move farther upstream where he could snatch salmon almost at will from the riffles. Danger, I suspect. The best fishing spots are often defended by heftier bears—mothers with cubs, or especially the prime males weighing as much as 800 pounds. A smaller bruin edging into their territories risks being chased off ... or worse.

And we know there are plenty of bears around. Earlier today, Don and I joined some friends hiking along a tributary streamlet that meanders through a stand of ancient forest. We'd all come to assist the Landmark Tree Project, a search for the biggest trees remaining in the Tongass National Forest, with a goal of working for their protection. And we did pretty well, threading our way between massive trunks, peering into the perpetual gloom beneath over-spanning boughs, and feeling as if we had entered a forest sanctuary guarded by a congeries of brown bears.

We followed heavily worn trails inscribed with the signatures of their makers: bear tracks, everywhere—imprints of broad leathery soles squashed far down into the mud, each pocked along the front by five toes and the probe marks of formidable claws. Our own bootprints looked puny and ridiculous beside them. Almost certainly there were bears listening to our voices as we passed, perhaps even scrutinizing us from hidden places; but we never glimpsed a tawny flank or heard a scuffle in the underbrush.

Tongass brown bears are seldom aggressive toward people, but there's always the danger of startling a bruin at close range or intruding on a mother with her cubs. For this reason, while hiking some of us put up a noisy banter, a few carried pepper spray, and everyone kept a nervous watch on the thick-ets. Never had I come across such an abundance of bear sign in one place. The thrill of it set my whole body jangling, like being rumbled awake by an earth-quake or watching a tornado reel across the plains. But let me confess right now: I was incredibly grateful not to be alone.

Scattered everywhere along the stream were partially eaten salmon—most of them cankerous with rot. A rich aroma of decay lay heavy in the supersat-urated air, clinging to our skin and flooding down into our throats. I'd occa-sionally see a salmon that looked so fresh it might have been plucked from the water minutes before. These carcasses were like messages from an unseen overlord, lest visitors forget about the one who holds sway here.

Many of the fish were partly skinned—or rather peeled the way a child takes off socks—with chunks of rosy flesh torn away, bellies gaping open, innards trailing out. Sometimes only the back of the head was nipped off, as if the brain were a delicacy, and the rest abandoned to scavenging ravens, gulls, eagles, mink, and otters. There was blood and offal strewn over the rocks, strewn on the cushiony moss, strewn beneath the parasol leaves of devil's club bushes, strewn in the murky basins of bear tracks.

The tributary was mostly narrow enough to jump across and so shallow it wouldn't cover a salmon's back, but there were plenty of fish circling aimlessly in deeper pools, skittering across riffles, bursting away as we came near, throwing sheets of spray with their tails. They had no place to hide or escape, so a hungry bear could simply choose a fish and swipe it out onto the bank. But the bears couldn't catch them all, especially since they spent much of their time hunting along the main river just a hundred yards off, where incalculable thousands of salmon were heading upstream.

When salmon reach their gravelly spawning beds, the slender-bodied females swash out shallow nest depressions; then they quaver in a mating dance beside the humpbacked, hook-jawed males, who engulf the crimson eggs in chalky clouds of milt. Late into the fall, waves of salmon pour up into the river—pinks, chums, sockeyes, and finally silvers. Some fish spawn in the lower reaches, some carry on into Lake Eva, and others lay their eggs far up in the feeder streams.

I knelt beside a crystal pool containing five or six pink salmon. After a few minutes they settled down, nosed into the current, and languidly sculled their ragged tails. It was hard to imagine the journey they had undertaken since hatching in this same river system two years ago. They emerged as yolk-bellied alevins in late winter, grew into minnowy smolts, flushed down to saltwater with the spring runoff, and then spent a couple months in the estuary feeding on plankton. By late summer they made their way to the open sea, following an immense, circling gyre into the far reaches of the north Pacific, slashing through clouds of prey, fattening themselves from the riches of the distant ocean. Now, at the end of their second summer, they had returned to their home waters for the final miracle of their life cycle: mass procreation coinciding with synchronized, collective death.

————

Just as the northern sea nurtures prodigious numbers of fish, it also gives life to the sky, spawning an oceanic mass of clouds and igniting powerful storms that charge up against the coast. This collusion of sea and sky dominates southeast Alaska's weather: overcast is the norm, rain is likely on most days, and sunshine in the forecast is rare enough to make a steadfast workaholic phone in sick. Most parts of the Tongass National Forest average about 100 inches of precipitation yearly, about three times that of notoriously-drenched Seattle. Even the profusion of streams channeling rainfall down off the mountains—these coalescing waters so vital to the lives of salmon—are a gift from the ocean.

During the fall and winter months, convergence of arctic and oceanic air fuels a steady progression of storms, which often rumble through every few days, sometimes reaching hurricane strength. There are few things I'd rather do than run outside into the full, throaty rage of a north Pacific gale, to watch it flail the forest like a wheatfield, tear off branches and pitch down trees, shake houses until they creak and groan, thrash the seas to a frenzy, and beseige the shore with explosions of whitewater.

To truly love southeast Alaska, you must learn to love clouds and storms and rain. You must accept that the human body, being mostly water on the inside, can thrive while constantly wet on the outside. But the truth is, most newcomers settle here for a while and then leave, like pilgrims questing for the desert, their palms opened to the sun. The few who stay can thank the rain for our mercifully small population, our luxuriously rich forest, our miraculously pristine environment.

For all the fierceness of its storms, southeast Alaska's winter temperatures are surprisingly mild, often above freezing and seldom below zero. But snow may come with a vengeance, piling up waist high in the meadows, sending avalanches down the slopes, turning the trees into billowing white colonnades. Winter can be tough on wildlife, especially the black-tailed deer, who survive in the old-growth forest where a dense canopy of boughs intercepts the snow and limits accumulation on the ground underneath. Only in these sheltered places can deer find the low-growing plants they rely on for food, and during severe winters death from starvation hits hardest where the forest has been cut down.

———

Winter seems like an illusion on this August evening, as we drift lazily on calm water, watching the young brown bear wallow in a field of lush beachside grass. Even the high mountain tundra, where brown bears hibernate in cave-like dens deeply buried by snow, is clothed in brilliant green. But summer is already on the ebb——the hunters and foragers and scavengers gathered along Lake Eva's stream are feasting not just for the pleasure of overindulgence but also to allay the coming trials of winter.

A slow current carries us parallel to the bear's bankside wanderings, bringing us within close range; but he remains almost alarmingly nonchalant about our presence, as if the skiff were nothing more than a floating log. At last, when we've come near enough to hear his scuffling footfalls, the bear finds a lifeless salmon in the grass. He nuzzles the carcass, flips it over, holds it down with one platter-sized paw, and deliberately tears off hunks of meat. I'm struck by the powerful musculature in his shoulders, the brawny span of his chest, and the delicate precision with which he uses his long, burnished, scimitar claws. The rhythmic crunching of his jaws comes clearly to us on the still air.

Every time I see one of these island bears, I feel the privilege of encountering a creature unique to our tiny fragment of the world. According to biologists, brown and grizzly bears came into North America from Asia during glacial times, then spread widely across this continent. When the ice sheets withdrew, a small population of ancestral brown bears became isolated on three adjoining islands in southeast Alaska——Admiralty, Baranof, and Chichagof. These Tongass island brown bears, distinctive for their dark color and compact size, have now been separated from their kin for many thousands of years and have changed relatively little from their ancient predecessors. Studies of mitochondrial DNA reveal that brown and grizzly bears everywhere else have evolved much more rapidly and have become genetically quite different from the island bears (even though all are still grouped within one species: *Ursus arctos*).

There is another remarkable fact about these singular bears. Hundreds of thousands of years ago, the brown bear family tree separated into two branches: one leading to the modern brown and grizzly bears of North America and Asia, the other leading toward both our Tongass island brown bear and to its arctic cousin——the polar bear. Because of this common ancestry, the Tongass bear is more closely related genetically to the polar bear than to other members of the brown and grizzly bear clan.

Tlingit Indians, who are native to southeast Alaska, call the brown bear *Xoots* (pronounced khoots), and as a gesture of respect for its physical and spiritual power they also address the animal as 'Grandfather.' This honorific name seems all the more appropriate when we recognize the *Xoots* bear's status as a living ancestor.

It takes our young bear only a few minutes to finish eating his salmon and then lick every scrap from the grass. Relegated to the poorest fishing spots, he doesn't have the luxury of nibbling only the best parts of a fish and abandoning the rest. But like the other bears, he'll wander into the woods and bed down to digest his meal. Nutrients from droppings he leaves on the forest floor will dissolve into the soil, to be absorbed by the roots of spruce and hemlock trees, huckleberry and menziesia bushes, foamflower and goldthread plants, mosses and ferns. Many other mammals and birds who feed along the stream will contribute to this same process, as they've all done for millennia.

In this way, the forest has been nourished by salmon, and by the ocean from which they came.

As each season passes, thousands of salmon die in the stream, where their bodies decay and dissipate, endowing the water and the spawning gravels with rich organic material. These nutrients help to sustain billions of microscopic organisms, foundation of an aquatic food chain on which the growing salmon fry depend. And so, over a vast reach of time, each generation of fish has bequeathed their own bodies as sustenance for the following generation. In this way, the stream has been nourished by salmon, and by the ocean from which they came.

Insects, birds, small mammals, and large herbivores like the black-tailed deer depend on the forest plants fertilized by salmon. People also come here—as they have since ancient times—not only to explore and observe, but also to gather plants, catch fish, and hunt animals in the forest. In this way, humankind has been nourished directly and indirectly by salmon, and by the ocean from which they came.

The forest and sea flow inside my veins. I cherish them for the sustenance they provide, as much as I cherish them for their beauty. Venison, salmon, berries, and greens are among the staple foods in our home, foods we have harvested and processed ourselves. For me, it's important to know where they come from; to know they've grown in a clean, wild place free of pollutants and toxins; to take personal responsibility for the deaths of plants and animals by which my life is nourished; and to fully participate in the organic process that sustains all creatures on earth, including humans.

When I lived with Koyukon Indian people, the elders passed along traditional ways of showing gratitude toward the living things that give us life. Success in hunting, fishing, and gathering depends not only on skill, they explained, but also on showing respect toward the game animals and toward all of nature, because everything around us is aware of our behavior, infused with spirit, and pervaded with a power far greater than our own. Koyukon people also believe it's essential to treat the environment according to principles of conservation and sustainable use handed down through the generations. These Koyukon teachings have been extremely valuable in my own life, alongside the similar wisdom being rediscovered today through Western science, philosophy, and religion.

Hunting, fishing, and gathering—which I first learned from Eskimo and Indian people—have become elemental to my sense of relationship with the place where I live. This is how I engage myself fully in the living community, recognizing that I am not merely an external observer here, as if the surrounding world were only significant as scenery. I am an omnivorous predator, an active member of the food chain, engaged in the most ancient of all human lifeways. These things undergird my spiritual relationship with the surrounding natural world, my physical connections with the sustaining environment, my sense of belonging within this mosaic of land and waters, and my love for the animals and plants from which my body is made.

Most people who live in Tongass communities eat wild food, which they harvest themselves or receive as gifts from their neighbors—a tradition rooted in the cultures of Tlingit and Haida Indians native to southeast Alaska, persisting strongly today among both native and non-native people. There are few other places in the United States where subsisting from the wild is such a vital part of the modern economy and culture; where navigating the remote waterways by boat is no less important than traveling the roads by car; and where townspeople discuss fishing or hunting or sea conditions more often than they talk about national events.

Subsistence livelihoods in southeast Alaska blend comfortably with another kind of wild harvest—commercial fishing. Trollers, seiners, gillnetters, and longliners crowd the harbors with brightly painted hulls and forests of labyrinthine rigging. The natural environment also attracts huge numbers of tourists who throng north in summer, hoping to experience the towns and their people, and to witness a spectacular landscape where much of the environment remains as it was before Europeans set foot in North America, and where not a single native plant or animal species has yet disappeared.

The natural diversity and abundance of southeast Alaska is a gift of incomparable magnitude. In return for this gift, I feel a responsibility to give something back, by working to protect the peace and beauty, shelter and sustenance, uniqueness and diversity that so abound here. Because the Tongass

National Forest is public land, I have the freedom to experience one of America's greatest wild places; the freedom to hike, camp, kayak, fish, hunt, gather, watch wildlife, photograph, and study here; the freedom to find peace and solitude in an open, accessible, unfettered land. And because the Tongass is a part of our national heritage, belonging equally to every American, my work as a conservation activist is volunteered in service to my country—a kind of patriotism for the American land.

On our way to Lake Eva, Don and I had passed many fishing boats working the waters, a few local folks in skiffs catching salmon for their freezers, and several tour ships crowded with visitors. We also saw a logging camp, and there were fresh clearcuts splayed across the mountainsides for many miles along Peril Strait, some very close to the Lake Eva estuary. The future of wild animals like our young bear heavily depends on our efforts to protect all of the remaining forest, because Tongass island brown bears often fare poorly around logging operations and the associated roads, where they're susceptible to overhunting and poaching, and where they suffer nearly complete loss of habitat when the forest is cut down.

These weighty thoughts vanish from my mind as I watch the bear shamble along a muddy shore uncovered by the tide until he's come within fifty feet of us. At this point he stops, peers around for a moment, lifts his nose into the air as if he's searching for a scent, then eases down to the water and swims straight toward the skiff. Don's expression is one of complete amazement and mine is surely no different.

As the bear paddles closer, I realize that he may not be a behemoth but he's still a formidable creature. The breadth of his back, girth of his head, and thickness of his neck are astonishing; and I know the true bulk of him, like an iceberg, is hidden underwater. He swims slowly, almost lazily, looking back and forth, as if he has no destination in mind and might easily decide to clamber aboard the skiff. Instead, he passes less than fifteen feet ahead of our bow.

It seems that the estuary has lapsed into a complete, almost oppressive silence, broken only by the powerful, deeply resonant huffing of the bear's breaths. I can see his nostrils flare and constrict, his jowls loosen and tighten. I can almost feel the sultry mist of his exhalations. When he swims by, he glances up and holds us in a momentary gaze, showing the creamy white crescents around the edges of his eyes. I have no doubt that this is a thinking animal and that he is thinking right now about us. Does he know us far better than we know him, as Koyukon elders would say?

For myself, I am only certain that I've never been so close to a brown bear, that I'm amazed and euphoric, and that an encounter like this scarcely seems possible at a time of such jeopardy for wild nature.

When the bear approaches the opposite shore, I start the engine and gently ease the boat away toward Peril Strait. Don shakes his head and smiles, as we both look back, reluctant to let this end but feeling we should give the bear his time alone. The last we see of him, he's lounging contentedly in the grass, a dark silhouette beneath the sheltering wall of forest.

I switch the engine off and we drift on a cloud of glassy water, listening to the sighs and whispers of the trees.

# PATRICE NEWELL

## A Rogaine

Putting the farm truck into 4WD, I drive across the river flats, detouring around drowsy Angus and Herefords, and manoeuvre over the cattle grid into Dam Paddock. Most of our paddocks are named for a physical feature or a memory—Stump Paddock for the scars of ancient timber cutting, Timmy's Paddock in honour of a beloved cattle dog. The dam in Dam Paddock is one of our biggest, collecting the runoff from a gully that cleaves a steep hill, with a black-soil road leading up to a plateau paddock called Airstrip—for the simple reason that it used to be used by planes spreading superphosphate across the property. This is not a procedure we approve of, so the signs of aviation, apart from a pile of old tyres used to weigh down the tarps that kept the phosphate dry, have disappeared. The time when we'd reluctantly accede to neighbours' requests to use the airstrip, as flat and straight as if it had been carefully bulldozed, are behind us. Ours is a certified bio-dynamic farm, so spreading super, let alone facilitating crop-dusting, is out of the question.

Now I drive through the long grass, following the route where roaring aircraft used to take off and taxi. It took just seconds for the sturdy planes to land, hoover up another load of super and lift off again. Now, to the delight of our nine-year-old, I accelerate along the rutted runway while she calls out, 'Fasten your seatbelts! Fasten your seatbelts!'

On either side of Airstrip the road is so steep that it feels as if you're flying, either climbing towards the clouds or descending from them. The big dam shrank in size as we gained altitude and now, a few minutes later, the canopies of old eucalypts rise to meet us, like clouds on an airport approach. Down in the valley there's the blur of sheoaks, their fuzzy branches marking the course of a creek beloved by cattle, kangaroos and ourselves. We're on our way to a favourite waterhole where, hearing our arrival, wild ducks will scatter, tortoises will plop from rocks and goannas scarper up trees.

But what's this? A human is striding down the hillside ahead of us. 'On our land,' I hear my mind shout. 'Without permission.' This trespass is unprecedented—something that hasn't happened in 15 years. As I steer the truck carefully down the rough track, avoiding the larger rocks dislodged by cattle, he hears us and half turns. Our trespasser is from another century with a face that might have been etched on a piece of whaler's scrimshaw. He's a crewman, with one of those Lincolnesque beards fringing an otherwise clean-shaven face. I notice a compass dangling from his neck, a folded map in one hand, a pen in the other and before he acknowledges us, he takes the pen and makes a cross on the map. At this instant I remember him. He knocked on the homestead door months ago, to tell us he was organising a rogaining event and would like permission to conduct it on our property. Rogaining? He explained that it was an Australian version of orienteering that had been developed by a couple of university people and was now a national and international sport. If we agreed, over three hundred people would arrive in the little township at the edge of Elmswood, camp out on the local oval and then spend twenty-four hours trying to find the checkpoints he'd hide in difficult, almost inaccessible places. The sport requires great skills at map-reading and enormous resources of energy—with the most ambitious competitors walking through the night, augmenting their torches with moonlight and navigating by the stars.

We found the prospect alarming. I was concerned that some of those hundreds of people would pass judgment on our land, on the way we farm it, holding us responsible for a dilapidated fence, criticising a thriving weed, a thin cow, an overgrazed paddock. Our farm manager was more concerned that someone might boil a billy and start a fire—or leave open a gate and let bulls in with the wrong cows or simply muddle the herds. But being a lover of maps, someone who likes to read them as much as novels, I also wanted to agree, to help. In any case, our eighteenth-century whaler was so charming, so open-faced and innocent, that we couldn't say no. So having been reassured that his rogainers would behave responsibly, and that there'd be no fires, we invited him in for a cup of tea.

We spent a few hours together, scanning his maps, the most marvellous I'd seen, detailing the contours of our property. With his magnifying glass and compass, we could plot and plan. I felt an affinity with this gentle man and his shy enthusiasms. He showed me how he'd hide the checkpoints in folds in the hills, behind fallen trees, in the shadows of giant rocks. We'd already come across some of his handiwork—signified by pieces of ribbon tied to trees or fence posts. And here he was, just days before the event, adding the last pieces to his puzzle.

Discussing the prospect, the family realised that at no time in history, not even in the millennia before white settlement, would so many people have been on our farm at the same time. We'd often felt the presence of the long-gone Aborigines, the ghostly sense of their belonging, but knew that their communities had always been small. Perhaps a hundred may have gathered for a major ceremony. But three or four hundred. Never.

The idea of the farm becoming an endurance course for a weekend began to excite me. It would be a strange imposition on the landscape. A brief impact, involving no saws, axes or earth-moving machines. Unlike a golf course that changes everything forever, rogaining is about secret codes, involving dots on a map, ribbons on trees.

The brochure inviting entrants talked about the beauty of the place, the views that competitors would see, and I couldn't help but feel proud and proprietorial. After all, I'd been seeing, feeling these views for fifteen years, enjoying the freedom that came with ownership. I could drive, ride my horse or walk wherever I liked, owning the solitude. The variations of familiar scenery were like variations on a musical theme. There were changes created by the passage of the sun, by the shadows of the clouds, by the change of the seasons, by the great pendulum swings of rain and drought. Nonetheless I wondered whether I could gain anything new out of the experience of rogaining. Would it help me see differently, feel differently? Might it deepen my sense of belonging?

So that is how I came to spend a weekend with hundreds of other walkers trying to find points on a map. I'd convinced a friend that he should team up with me, which he did reluctantly, paraphrasing the old joke about golf being a game that destroys a good walk. 'I love exploring your farm, but why ruin it with a map, a compass and a competition?' On the day, we were expecting to see the hundreds sharing the hills traipse up Dam Paddock, cross Airstrip and descend into the sheoaked creek in convoy. In fact, no sooner had the event started than everyone disappeared. Rogainers headed off in all directions, trying to out-do and out-smart each other. The multitude had melted away, and only occasionally could we glimpse a few in the distance. We only met entrants at check-ins, where they'd quenched their thirst with water left by the organisers.

Any anxieties about them passing judgment on the property were quickly forgotten, along with concerns about carelessness with gates. The rogainers were far too intent on reading their maps, interpreting the fingerprint swirls of the contours, planning their strategies to maximise their point score, to be critical of paddocks, feral plants or cattle. Rogainers are map-readers and athletes, not agricultural inspectors. Nor are they poets, although later they'd talk of favourite places and one reported hearing koalas high in the gumtrees. Koalas? In all our years on the farm we'd never seen one, or even heard of them being in the district.

First and foremost, rogaining is a personal test. It's them against the elements. It's speed and precision in a strange place. And for me, it was discovering another way of walking across the land I thought I knew so well. And it made me realise that most of the walking I do is very different. I'd stride across the hills, my hills, to reach a vantage point, a point of history. Heading off with the purpose of visiting familiar places—so that I could check the activity of a rabbit warren, an eagle's nest, see how one of my beehives was doing, the levels of water in a hilltop tank or a distant dam, or how much clover there was in a pasture. Whereas, as a rogainer, my task was to work out the quickest, easiest way to get from A to B to F to T to Z—all the time trying to locate where the map's As and Bs and Fs and Ts and Zs were in the flesh and blood of the farm.

What I discovered was humiliating. I realised I wasn't half as fit as I thought I was and my map-reading skills, of which I'd been so proud, were really pretty lousy. Again and again I'd drag my partner up a hill or through thick bush to what I believed was the next point on the map—only to find that I was wrong by one hill or two valleys. Even worse, sometimes we'd be just a few yards from the orange flag that marked a checkpoint, yet I'd fail to locate it.

The rogainers' march wasn't for me. It was too emphatic, too confident, too unflagging. I had none of their certainty. How could they know where they were going, in a landscape they'd never been before? How could I feel so repeatedly lost in a place I thought I knew as well as the faces of friends?

It was a strange feeling, that mixture of being lost amidst the familiar. Over the years I've come to recognise thousands of specific trees and boulders and nooks and crannies—I like to botanise as I walk, enabling a greater understanding of the microclimates you find near a rockpool or on the shaded side of a mountain. Over the years I've felt myself on familiar terms with kangaroos, wallabies, wallaroos, clouds of cockatoos and galahs. Even with specific snakes that habitually bask in the sun by this grid or that creek. But all of that familiarity disappeared in the momentum of the rogainers' march.

To rush so purposefully across the landscape defeated, for me, the purpose. My solitary trips demanded an equally intense observation—but of the finest of fine details. Otherwise I'd never have discovered the tiny orchid at the top of a north-facing slope that the experts at Sydney's Botanic Gardens would tell me had only been recently discovered and remained unnamed. Had I found it a few months earlier, they told me, I'd have earned the right to christen it. And I had ten thousand acres to explore slowly, patiently, curiously. How many more unknown, undiscovered plants were out there? After the rogainers had gone, I returned to my slow, unhurried walking. The one thing they taught me was to break from my old habits of following familiar paths. Now I'd follow the tracks of cattle or kangaroos, wherever they led me. Enjoying the conversation between the creeks and rocks, the unhesitating movement of water, the scent of crushed grasses and native blossoms, the kaleidoscope of greens, let alone all the other colours, too subtle to describe. And I know that I'll do it over and over again, as long as I live, with every exploration leading to a different discovery, with even the most accessible parts of the property being endlessly transformed. That is the greatest joy. That nature, like ourselves, is forever changing. So I walk to the hills for different reasons now. Never to reach a point for the sake of it. While I like to prove that I can follow a map and not get lost, the fact is, I can't get lost here. This is my home and to dawdle in the valley is like reciting a loved poem that gets better the more you know it.

The rogainers come back from time to time. We've agreed that the checkpoints be left in situ on the farm, so others can try their skills in reading maps and breaking records. But I'll be happiest simply reading the landscape, from the mountains to the moss.

# DAVID QUAMMEN

## Synecdoche and the Trout

It's a simple question with a seemingly simple answer: 'Why do you live in Montana?'

Repeatedly over a span of some years you have heard this, asked most often by people who know you just well enough to be aware of the city where you grew up, the tony universities you attended, and a few other bits of biographical detail on the basis of which they harbor a notion that you should have taken your place in New York café society or, at least, an ivy-adorned department of English. They suspect you, these friends do, of hiding out. Maybe in a way they are right. But they have no clear sense of what you are hiding from, or why, let alone where. Hence their question.

'The trout,' you answer, and they gape back blankly.

'The trout,' they say after a moment. 'That's a fish.'

'Correct.'

'Like lox.'

'In some ways similar.'

'You like to go fishing. *That's* why you live out there? *That's* why you spend your life in a place without decent restaurants or bookstores or symphony orchestras, a place halfway between Death Valley and the North Pole? A place where there's no espresso, and the *Times* comes in three days late by pontoon plane? Do I have this straight, now? It's because you like to go *fishing*?'

'No,' you say. 'Only partly. At the beginning, that was it, yes. But I've stayed all these years. No plans to leave.'

'You *went* for the fishing, but you *stayed* for something else. Aha.'

'Yes. The trout,' you say.

'This is confusing.'

'A person can get too much trout fishing. Then it cloys, becomes taken for granted. Meaningless.'

'Again like lox.'

'I don't seem to fish nearly as much as I used to.'

'But you keep talking about the trout. You went, you stayed, the trout is your reason.'

'The trout is a synecdoche,' you say, because these friends are tough and verbal and they can take it.

———

A biologist would use the term *indicator species*. Because I have the biases of a literary journalist, working that great gray zone between newspaper reporting and fiction, engaged every day in trying to make facts not just talk but yodel, I speak instead of synecdoche. We both mean that a trout represents more than itself—but that, importantly, it does also represent itself.

'A poem should not mean/ But be,' wrote Archibald MacLeish, knowing undeniably in his heart that a good poem quite often does both. Likewise a trout.

The presence of trout in a body of water is a discrete ecological fact that nevertheless signifies certain things.

It signifies a particular complex of biotic and chemical and physical factors, a standard of richness and purity, without which that troutly presence is impossible. It signifies aquatic nutrients like calcium, potassium, nitrate, phosphate; signifies enough carbon dioxide to nourish meadows of algae and to keep calcium in solution as calcium bicarbonate; signifies a prolific invertebrate fauna (Plecoptera, Trichoptera, Diptera, Ephemeroptera), and a temperature regime confined within certain daily and annual extremes. It also signifies clear pools emptying down staircases of rounded boulders and dappled with patterns of late-afternoon shade cast by chrome yellow cottonwood leaves in September. It signifies solitude so sweet and pure as to bring an ache

to the sinuses, a buzz to the ears. Loneliness and anomie of the most whole-
some sort. It signifies dissolved oxygen to at least four or five parts per million. It signifies a good possibility of osprey, dippers, and kingfishers, otters
and water shrews, heron; and it signifies *Oncorhynchus clarki, Oncorhynchus
mykiss, Salmo trutta*. Like a well-chosen phrase in any poem, MacLeish's included, these creatures are literal and real. They live in imagination, memory, and
cold water.

For instance: I can remember the first trout I ever caught as an adult
(which was also the first I ever caught on a fly), and precisely what the poor
little fish represented to me at that moment. It represented (a) dinner and (b)
a new beginning, with a new sense of self, in a new place. The matter of dinner was important, since I was a genuinely hungry young man living out of my
road-weary Volkswagen bus with a meager supply of groceries. But the matter
of selfhood and place, the matter of reinventing identity, was paramount. My
hands trembled wildly as I took that fish off the hook. A rainbow, all of seven
or eight inches long. Caught on a Black Gnat pattern, size 12, tied cheaply of
poor materials somewhere in the Orient and picked up by me at Herter's
when I had passed through South Dakota. I killed the little trout before it
could slip through my fingers and, heartbreakingly, disappear. This episode was
for me equivalent to the one in Faulkner's 'Delta Autumn,' where blood from
a fresh-killed buck is smeared on the face of the boy. *I slew you*, the boy thinks.
*My bearing must not shame your quitting life*, he understands. *My conduct for ever
onward must become your death*. In my own case, of course, there was no ancient
Indian named Sam Fathers serving as mentor and baptist. I was alone and an
autodidact. The blood of the little trout did not steam away its heat of life into
the cold air, and I smeared none on my face. Nevertheless.

The fish came out of a creek in the Bighorn Mountains of north-central
Wyoming, and I was on my way to Montana, though at that moment I didn't
yet know it.

Montana was the one place on Earth, as I thought of it, farthest in miles
and spirit from Oxford University, yet where you could still get by with the
English language, and the sun didn't disappear below the horizon for days in a
row during midwinter, and the prevailing notion of a fish dinner was not lute-
fisk. I had literally never set foot within the boundaries of the state. I had no
friends there, no friends of friends, no contacts of any sort, which was fine. I
looked at a map and saw jagged blue lines, denoting mountain rivers. All I
knew was that, in Montana, there would be more trout.

Trout were the indicator species for a place and a life I was seeking.

I went. Six years later, rather to my surprise, I was a professional fishing guide under license from the Montana Department of Fish, Wildlife, and Parks. My job was to smear blood on other young faces. *I slew you. My bearing must not shame your quitting life.* Sometimes it was actually like that, though quite often it was not.

———

*Item.* You are at the oars of a fourteen-foot Avon raft, pushing across a slow pool on the Big Hole River in western Montana. An August afternoon. Seated in front of you is an orthopedic surgeon from San Francisco, a pleasant man who can talk intelligently about the career of Gifford Pinchot or the novels of Evelyn Waugh, who is said to play a formidable game of squash, and who spends one week each year fishing for trout. In his right hand is a Payne bamboo fly rod that is worth more than the car you drive, and attached to the rod is a Hardy Perfect reel. At the end of the doctor's line is a kinked and truncated leader, and at the end of the leader is a dry fly that can no longer by even the most technical definition be considered 'dry,' having been slapped back and forth upon and dragged through several miles of river. With this match of equipment to finesse, the good doctor might as well be hauling manure in the backseat of a Mercedes. Seated behind you is the doctor's wife, who picked up a fly rod for the first time in her life two hours earlier. Her line culminates in a fly that is more dangerous to you than to any fish in Montana. As you have rowed quietly across the glassy pool, she has attacked the water's surface like a French chef dicing celery. Now your raft has approached the brink of a riffle. On the Big Hole River during this late month of the season, virtually all of the catchable trout cluster (by daylight, at least) where they can find cover and oxygen—in those two wedges of deep still water flanking the fast current at the bottom of each riffle. You have told the doctor and his wife about the wedges. There, *those*, you have said. Cast just across the eddy line, you have said. Throw a little slack. We've got to hit the spots to catch any fish, you have said in the tactfully editorial first-person plural.

As your raft slides into this riffle, the doctor and his wife become tense with anticipation. The wife snags her fly in the rail rope along the rowing frame, and asks sweetly if you would free it, which you do, grabbing the oars again quickly to avoid hitting a boulder. You begin working to slalom the boat through the riffle. The wife whips her fly twice through the air before sinking it into the back of your straw cowboy hat. She apologizes fervently. Meanwhile, she lets her line loop around your right oar. You take a stroke with the left oar to swing clear of a drowned log, then you point your finger over the doctor's shoulder: 'Remember, now. The wedges.' He nods eagerly. The raft is about to broadside another boulder, so you pull hard on both oars and with that motion your hat is jerked into the river. The doctor makes five false casts, intent on the wedges, and then fires his line forward into the tip of his own rod like a hand-ful of spaghetti hitting a kitchen wall. He moans. The raft drops neatly out of the riffle, between the wedges, and back into dead water.

*Item.* You are two days along on a wilderness float through the Smith River canyon, fifty miles and another three river-days from the nearest hospital, with cliffs of shale towering hundreds of feet on each side of the river to seal you in. The tents are grouped on a cottonwood flat. It's dinner hour, and you have just finished a frigid bath in the shallows. As you open your first beer, a soft-spoken Denver architect walks back into camp with a size 14 Royal Wulff stuck past the barb into his lower eyelid. He has stepped behind another fisherman at precisely the wrong moment. Everyone looks queasily at everyone else, but the outfitter—who is your boss, who is holding his second martini, and whose own nerves are already frazzled from serving as chief babysitter to eight tourist fishermen—looks pleadingly at you. With tools from your fishing vest (a small pair of scissors, a forceps, a loop of leader) you extract the fly. Then you douse the architect's wound with what little remains of the outfitter's gin.

*Item.* Three days down the Smith on a different trip, under a cloudless July sky, you are drifting, basking comfortably in the heat, resting your oars. In your left hand is a cold Pabst Blue Ribbon. In place of your usual T-shirt, you are wearing a new yellow number that announces with some justice, 'Happiness Is a Cold Pabst.' On your head, in place of the cowboy straw, is a floppy cloth porkpie in a print of Pabst labels. In the bow seat of your raft, casting contentedly to a few rising trout, is a man named Augie Pabst, scion of the family. Augie, contrary to all your expectations, is a sensitive and polite man, a likable fellow. Stowed in your cargo box and cooler are fourteen cases of Pabst Blue Ribbon, courtesy. You take a deep gulp of beer, you touch an oar. Ah yes, you think. Life in the wilderness.

*Item.* You are floating a petroleum engineer and his teenage son through the final twelve miles of the Smith canyon, which is drowsy, meandering water not hospitable to rainbow trout but good for an occasional large brown. The temperature is ninety-five, the midday glare is fierce, you have spent six days with these people, and you are eager to be rid of them. Three more hours to the take-out, you tell yourself. A bit later you think, Two more hours. The petroleum engineer has been treated routinely with ridicule by his son, and evidently has troubles also with his wife. The wife is along on this trip but she doesn't fish; she doesn't seem to talk much to her husband; she has ridden a supply boat with the outfitter and spent much of her time humming quietly. You wonder if the petroleum engineer has heard of Hemingway's Francis Macomber. You are sure that the outfitter hasn't and you suspect that the wife has. The engineer says that he and his son would like to catch one large brown trout before the trip ends, so you tell them to tie on Marabou Muddlers and drag those billowy monstrosities through certain troughs. Fifteen minutes later, the boy catches a large brown. This fish is eighteen inches long and broad of shoulder—a noble and beautiful animal that the Smith River has taken five years to grow. The father tells you to kill it—'Yeah, I guess kill it'—they will want to eat it, just this one, at the hotel. Suddenly you despise your job. You despise this man, but he is paying your wage so he has certain prerogatives. You kill the fish, pushing your thumb into its mouth and breaking back the neck. Its old sharp teeth cut your hand.

The boy is a bad winner, a snot, taunting his father now as the three of you float on down the river. Half an hour later, the father catches a large brown, this one also around eighteen inches. You are pleased for him, and glad for the fish, since you assume that it will go free. But the father has things to prove to the wife as well as to the son, and for the former your eyewitness testimony of a great battle, a great victory, and a great act of mercy will not suffice. 'Better keep this one too,' he says, 'and we'll have a pair.' You detest this particular euphemistic use of the word *keep*. You argue tactfully but he pretends not to hear. Your feelings for these trout are what originally brought you out onto the Smith River and are what compel you to bear the company of folk like the man and his son. *My conduct for ever onward must become your death.* The five-year-old brown trout is lambent, spotted with orange, lithe as an ocelot, swirling gorgeously under water in your gentle grip. You kill it.

———

I don't guide anymore. I haven't renewed my license in years. My early and ingenuous ideas about the role of a fishing guide turned out to be totally wrong: I had imagined it as a life rich with independence, and with a rustic sort of dignity, wherein a fellow would stand closer to these animals he admired inordinately. I hadn't foreseen that it would demand the humility of a chauffeur and the complaisance of a pimp.

And I don't seem to fish nearly as much as I used to. I have a dilemma these days: I dislike killing trout but I believe that, in order to fish responsibly, to fish conscionably, the fisherman should at least occasionally kill. Otherwise he can too easily delude himself that fly fishing is merely a game, a dance of love, played in mutual empathy by the fisherman and the trout. Small flies with the barbs flattened are an excellent means for allowing the fisherman's own sensibilities to be released unharmed—but the fish themselves aren't so lucky. They get eye-hooked, they bleed, they suffer trauma and dislocated maxillae and infection. Unavoidably, some die. For them, it is not a game, and certainly not a dance. On some days I feel it's hypocritical to profess love for these creatures while endangering and abusing them so wantonly; better to enjoy the thrill of the sport honestly, kill what I catch, and stop fishing when I've had a surfeit of killing. On other days I do dearly enjoy holding them in the water, gentling them as they regain breath and balance and command of their muscles, then watching them swim away. The dilemma remains unresolved.

'Yet each man kills the thing he loves,' wrote Oscar Wilde, and I keep wondering how a person of Wilde's urban and cerebral predilections knew so goddamn much about trout fishing.

'Why do you live in Montana?' people ask. For the trout, I answer. 'Oh, you're one of those fanatical fishermen types?' No, not so much anymore, I say. It's just a matter of knowing that they're here.

# E R I C
# R O L L S

# My Places

Birds define my places: they sing memories. The falling and rising cadence of Whistling Kites carries more than seventy years from the gentle slopes of Pine Hill near Grenfell in the central west of New South Wales. There is a long whistled glissando, then a climb in seven or eight short notes up the scale again.

For a few years my father leased a farm on the good creek flats at the Eight Mile. Newly married, he was breaking out on his own. As a four-year-old on summer days when distance shimmered, I watched Wedge-tailed Eagles circling silently so high they were almost out of sight, and below them, scarcely moving their wings, half a dozen or so Whistling Kites drifted in interlocking circles and sang their delight in being alive. It was cooler up in the air. Lesser birds sat on shaded branches and panted with open mouths. We knew the kites as Carrion Hawks because they clean up the dead.

After a couple of good harvests and successful deals in a few mobs of sheep, my father had enough money to buy his own farm in the north-west of New South Wales. Our 1929 Essex ran off formed gravel road at Gunnedah and for the last eighty miles (130 kilometres) we threaded our way through trees on bush tracks to Taylors Plains east of Narrabri. Superb Wrens coloured the grey of Old Man Saltbush sprawling along one garden fence. Years of their bulky grass nests with clever side entrances littered the hedge. As they feed in family groups, they trill to one another to keep in touch. The males are aware of their beauty. Now and again one transfixes himself in a shaft of light, and metallic blues and blacks roll round him and through him as though he has turned to opal.

But it is the wailing of the Southern Stone-curlews that has never left me. Each night they called from the high brown grass on a blacksoil plain. The cries seemed to come from underground as though the earth were in pain. My hair bristled as I lay in bed.

One night my father and I sat before a fire—my mother and young sister were away. Bimble Box logs burnt with the two hundred years of colours that grew them: orange, pink, crimson, brown, black, grey, white, blue and an occasional leaf-shaped spurt of green. Curlews called. I drew nearer the fire. A car pulled up at the garden gate. We heard the car door open, the creak of hinges as the gate opened, footsteps down the gravel path, three knocks on our wooden door. 'It's late for someone to be coming,' said my father. 'See who it is!' The door was in a latticed annex we called the breakfast room. I pulled it open. There was no one there, no car at the gate. Whoever it was, whatever it was, I am glad I saw nothing.

———

Keewaydin, my first farm, was chocolate-brown self-mulching soil sloping from the foot of a low hill down to the Namoi River. As a Soldier Settlement block it was a reward for war service to be paid off over many years. Fifty years ago farms were profitable and produce was in demand. It is wondrous to take up a handful of earth, feel its richness, and know that for a time it is yours to be nurtured. As I weighed my first handful I seemed to hold my future.

Summer storms came to us as fluffy grey clouds climbing the hill and drifting towards us with a few rolls of thunder. A sharp clap of thunder in the right place produced echoes, two, three, four, five, bouncing off a ring of hills. Once, seemingly after a few seconds, there were two more faint echoes from the Nandewar Range twenty-five kilometres away.

Almost always four or five Channel-billed Cuckoos preceded the clouds, raucously challenging the thunder. 'Ork! Ork! Ork! Ork!' they chanted with such tremendous volume it did not seem possible for birds to produce it. We knew them as Storm Birds.

In lush years the wheat grew high. Too often late rains and wind beat it flat, leaving twisted stook-shaped cones here and there to demonstrate how high it had been. The paddocks looked like untidy yellow-brown carpets. If the grain were not mature it continued to ripen normally, but harvesting of such a crop was slow work. We fitted triangular wooden crop lifters to the comb of the header (combine). As the machine moved forward, they lifted the heads to the serrated knife sliding backwards and forwards through long steel fingers.

Stubble Quail, somehow aware of sudden plenty, flew in thousands from western grasslands and fed and sheltered under the crop. Unaware of the danger, many did not move away from the machine. When I stopped to clear a build-up of awns on the riddles that separated grain from chaff, my hands encountered warm blood and feathers.

The screams of Sulphur-crested Cockatoos carry from those days. Across the river a clump of old River Red Gums sprawled as they do when they have room to grow and an occasional flood to excite them. At dusk, when crops of grain sorghum were ripening in the first winter frosts, our trees grew white and raucous with a flock of two thousand of the birds resting for the next day's foraging of the precious grain. Although our home was a kilometre off the river, sometimes during the night we would hear screams as a great branch crashed and dislodged its white load. As these birds feed, look-outs with alert raised crests take position on high bare limbs. Heads twist from side to side, bodies circle, black eyes survey paddocks and sky. If a farmer appears with a gun or an eagle appears overhead, loud shrieks warn the flock and all take off to safety. Every half hour or so the look-out is relieved to feed.

----

We sold that river block. After twenty years and many floods, dams and weirs made the river unpredictable. It began to threaten, 'If you stay I'll drown you.' We bought Cumberdeen, sandy plains on the western edge of the great Pilliga forest. As I drove in to inspect the property, I saw a Spotted Harrier patrolling one of the paddocks. The bird stayed with us for years, seemingly adjusting its beat to the boundary fences. In search of game—a quail, a mouse, a leveret—it flew two-metre-high transects from fence to fence, sometimes perching on a strainer post to rest or to wipe its beak clean if it had made a catch and eaten it on the ground.

On frosty mornings Pied Butcherbirds sang the day warm. Known as butcherbirds because they keep larders of small birds and lizards hanging by the neck in forked branches, these birds are great songsters. Their tunes can be written down, at least three run through several bars. One early morning seven males stationed themselves in trees about a hundred metres apart. One began a tune, another took it up, then another with variations, then all joined to finish the song. Usually, before the song finished, one began the next song, always in time, always in harmony. After a couple of bars, all joined. They sang till the frost began to melt.

Cumberdeen's bird song is that of the Grey Shrike-Thrush that spent one winter only with us. Somehow he learnt that if he sang we would give him pieces of steak. He knew where we slept. About sunrise on frosty mornings he hopped to the gauzed verandah door and directed his several harmonies towards our open bedroom door. He always checked that we were there before he began his song: we would see him sitting in a grapevine looking in. These birds sing in chords. If neither of us got up after the first song, the thrush repeated it with a few harsh notes thrown in at the end of each phrase. If the song ever had to be repeated a third time they grew very harsh indeed and usually ended with several piercing alarm calls.

Early in the spring a pair of strange thrushes came to the house. All one day the strange male chased our thrush about the garden and next day he was gone. The strange pair did not stay either. We hoped our thrush would come back the next winter but he did not. But whenever a thrush called we went out to see if he knew us.

———

Twenty-five years after I was in the Markham-Ramu valley of Papua New Guinea signalling for the Air Warning Wireless Company, I wrote *The Green Mosaic*, a collection of poems about that wildly beautiful country, a harmony of thirty-seven tones of green. So much did my imagination carry me back to Papua New Guinea, Cumberdeen rumbled with the surging drone of toucans.

They had a regular beat across our signal station at Dumpu between the Kratke Range on the south of the Ramu and the Finisterre Range on the north. Half a dozen of these birds filled the valley with sound, not from their beaks but from their wings. I wrote a poem about them:

> How can twelve inches of lean black feathers
> Hold up eight inches of horn?
> Perhaps his beak anticipated plastic foam.
> When he flies
> He pushes his beak before him
> Like a surf-board rider in shallow water.

He continually draws attention to his difficulties.
Air-pockets in his wings act as pipes.
They roll like an organ
With too many stops out.

It might be more than complaint.
Being partly hollow
And feeding tamely on fruit
He needs noise to bolster himself into legend:
Of a bird with twenty-foot wings
Carrying off pigs and cassowaries
And occasionally terrifying piccaninnies.

I never saw a Bird of Paradise. They screamed at me as I walked narrow, muddy paths, trying to force their colours through the green canopy. Goura Pigeons thrashed unseen beside me; I still hear them if I listen. Sometimes one flew slowly down the path ahead and perched on a branch above it. Three kilogrammes of pale blue feathers and plump awkward flesh fearlessly let me approach. But no stillness could hold their topknots steady. Fine as cobweb, an exquisite lace of feathers shivered above their heads. *Goura* is pidgin for 'quake'. These seemingly solid birds accentuated our fragility.

———

Red Wattlebirds dominate the Camden Haven, the lively system of estuary and lakes about North Brother Mountain on the mid-north coast of New South Wales where we live now. Savagely territorial, these big honeyeaters with long red earrings loudly resent any intrusion into their domain, which includes our garden. If I am on my knees weeding, a dominant male swoops from grevillea to banksia, slowing and clattering his wings above my head. Then he rests awhile, barking and chuckling coarsely.

Along with their plainer relatives, the Little Wattlebirds, they lived undisturbed in the Coast Banksias and Coastal Tea Trees fringing the former Pilot Station after it was abandoned in the 1950s. Now, due to imaginative instigation by Elaine van Kempen, my wife, the station is being restored as a self-sufficient centre for natural history to demonstrate that people can live in an environment without destroying it. In the extensive grounds, which will grow native plants only, are house, boatshed and the signal shed from which the pilot hoisted balls to tell captains whether the difficult bar at the harbour entrance was negotiable. An upright triangle sandwiched between two balls warned that the entrance was closed.

In May 2000 when Roger Deakin was in Australia to promote his remark-able *Waterlog*, he and I gave a reading at the station. No work had yet been done on it, the audience sheltered under a tarpaulin. In front of us on the sloping ground waves rolled in so closely we heard the pulse of ebb and flow. Behind us wattlebirds voiced loud disapproval. It is a supreme atmosphere for natural history. There will be many great readings there and great writers to live-in and work.

Kookaburras are our wake-up alarm, chortling in chorus at the first streak of light. They are followed by resident Black-backed Magpies warbling flute-like notes accented by sharp calls. Such waking guarantees a good day.

If one wakes during the night a Willy Wagtail, always active, always self-important, is sure to be broadcasting different versions of 'Sweet pretty little creature'. And between September and April a Koel will be calling. The males are long-tailed black birds, the females prettily freckled. They are named for their penetrating call, a whistled 'koo-ell' over and over. No cuckoo ever knows when to stop calling, several species are known as 'brain-fever birds'. Sometimes, especially in the evening, the Koels sing a number of musical notes so different it seems that another species of bird has begun to call.

Four species of lorikeets in bright chattering flocks work the eucalypt blossom and the fruit of huge Port Jackson Figs that are out of their element here but grandly handsome.

Australian Pelicans, much bigger birds than those of the northern hemi-sphere, oversee each boat ramp with its fish cleaning table. They fly up and swim about watching as a boat pulls in. If someone backs a trailer down, hooks on, and gets into the vehicle to drive away, the pelicans take no notice. But, if someone lifts a box out of a boat, the pelicans beat it to the table to wait the cleanings, so often including the heads that we keep to make fish stock. The dominant male, shown by his size and longer beak, takes more than a fair share.

All have to be watched or they will hop onto the table and snatch a fish, even out of the cleaner's hand. Children feeding them have been dismayed when the pelican gulped arm and all. The one who takes the head of the biggest flathead gets least free food. Swallowing such a wide triangle requires a great deal of strutting about while stretching the neck and lowering it. One can watch it moving down millimetres at a time. It would take a ten-metre python to swallow the head of the biggest flathead in Gogleys Lagoon. Sometimes she plays with fishermen, pretending to take a bait and swimming in with it to spit it out a couple of metres from a boat. It looks like the head of a crocodile when she raises it to spit.

White-faced Herons parade shallow water on the sand flats, each watching alertly for fish, worm or prawn. They are aloof birds, seldom acknowledging one another as they feed. Blue-grey with long yellow legs, they were once known as Blue Cranes. Shaw Neilson, the South Australian poet who wrote wonderfully imaginative poetry while he worked as a labourer told of one of these birds in 'The Crane is my Neighbour'. He would have seen the bird as a lone dweller by a farm waterhole, not in the numbers that we see them.

> The bird is my neighbour, a whimsical fellow and dim;
> There is in the lake a nobility falling on him ...
> He bleats no instruction, he is not an arrogant drummer;
> His gown is simplicity—blue as the smoke of summer ...
> The bird is a noble, he turns to the sky for a theme,
> And the ripples are thoughts coming out to the edge of a dream.

Whimbrels with long downward-curving beaks feed in numbers on the sand flats, so do a few big Eastern Curlews with even longer downward-curving beaks, and little greenshanks with upward-curving beaks. Silver Gulls, always hungry, always quarrelling over food no matter how plentiful, watch for fishermen wading out to the flats with yabby pumps. They circle low overhead as he works, diving to snatch a swimming yabby before he can reach it.

A couple of pairs of White-breasted Sea Eagles are permanent residents. When hang gliders take off from the side of North Brother and drift out over the water, the eagles welcome them to their domain and fly with them. Sometimes we see a pair of Brahminy Kites. The males are spectacularly beautiful with a mantle of white head and breast over deep chestnut.

The birds that distinguish the Camden Haven for me are a species I had not seen elsewhere, small grey Mangrove Herons sitting alone, silent and hunched like bitterns on the lower rocks of what are arrogantly called 'the training walls', the long barriers of disciplinary rocks on either side of the estuary designed to make the entrance behave as engineers think it ought to behave. These birds make no sound to live in the memory: the only call that I have heard is a harsh squawk if something surprises them.

*The Slater Field Guide to Australian Birds* says that they 'skulk among mangrove roots and on mud flats'. My birds do not skulk. Seemingly blue-grey, close-up they reveal an exciting gold patterning on the edges of the wing feathers. It lifts them to new dimensions. They spend hours watching the water, a serious study, not a mere lookout for food. They know more about the estuary than I know.

# SCOTT RUSSELL SANDERS

## Buckeye

Years after my father's heart quit, I keep in a wooden box on my desk the two buckeyes that were in his pocket when he died. Once the size of plums, the brown seeds are shriveled now, hollow, hard as pebbles, yet they still gleam from the polish of his hands. He used to reach for them in his overalls or suit pants and click them together, or he would draw them out, cupped in his palm, and twirl them with his blunt carpenter's fingers, all the while humming snatches of old tunes.

'Do you really believe buckeyes keep off arthritis?' I asked him more than once.

He would flex his hands and say, 'I do so far.'

My father never paid much heed to pain. Near the end, when his worn knee often slipped out of joint, he would pound it back in place with a rubber mallet. If a splinter worked into his flesh beyond the reach of tweezers, he would heat the blade of his knife over a cigarette lighter and slice through the skin. He sought to ward off arthritis not because he feared pain but because he lived through his hands, and he dreaded the swelling of knuckles, the stiffening of fingers. What use would he be if he could no longer hold a hammer or guide a plow? When he was a boy he had known farmers not yet forty years old whose hands had curled into claws, men so crippled up they could not tie their own shoes, could not sign their names.

'I mean to tickle my grandchildren when they come along,' he told me, 'and I mean to build doll houses and turn spindles for tiny chairs on my lathe.'

So he fondled those buckeyes as if they were charms, carrying them with him when our family moved from Ohio at the end of my childhood, bearing them to new homes in Louisiana, then Oklahoma, Ontario, and Mississippi, carrying them still on his final day when pain a thousand times fiercer than arthritis gripped his heart.

The box where I keep the buckeyes also comes from Ohio, made by my father from a walnut plank he bought at a farm auction. I remember the auction, remember the sagging face of the widow whose home was being sold, remember my father telling her he would prize that walnut as if he had watched the tree grow from a sapling on his own land. He did not care for pewter or silver or gold, but he cherished wood. On the rare occasions when my mother coaxed him into a museum, he ignored the paintings or porcelain and studied the exhibit cases, the banisters, the moldings, the parquet floors.

I remember him planing that walnut board, sawing it, sanding it, joining piece to piece to make foot stools, picture frames, jewelry boxes. My own box, a bit larger than a soap dish, lined with red corduroy, was meant to hold earrings and pins, not buckeyes. The top is inlaid with pieces fitted so as to bring out the grain, four diagonal joints converging from the corners toward the center. If I stare long enough at those converging lines, they float free of the box and point to a center deeper than wood.

———

I learned to recognize buckeyes and beeches, sugar maples and shagbark hickories, wild cherries, walnuts, and dozens of other trees while tramping through the Ohio woods with my father. To his eyes, their shapes, their leaves, their bark, their winter buds were as distinctive as the set of a friend's shoulders. As with friends, he was partial to some, craving their company, so he would go out of his way to visit particular trees, walking in a circle around the splayed roots of a sycamore, laying his hand against the trunk of a white oak, ruffling the feathery green boughs of a cedar.

'Trees breathe,' he told me. 'Listen.'

I listened, and heard the stir of breath.

He was no botanist; the names and uses he taught me were those he had learned from country folks, not from books. Latin never crossed his lips. Only much later would I discover that the tree he called ironwood, its branches like muscular arms, good for axe handles, is known in the books as hophornbeam; what he called tuliptree or canoewood, ideal for log cabins, is officially the yellow poplar; what he called hoop ash, good for barrels and fence posts, appears in books as hackberry.

When he introduced me to the buckeye, he broke off a chunk of the gray bark and held it to my nose. I gagged.

'That's why the old-timers called it stinking buckeye,' he told me. 'They used it for cradles and feed troughs and peg legs.'

'Why for peg legs?' I asked.

'Because it's light and hard to split, so it won't shatter when you're clumping around.'

He showed me this tree in late summer, when the fruits had fallen and the ground was littered with prickly brown pods. He picked up one, as fat as a lemon, and peeled away the husk to reveal the shiny seed. He laid it in my palm and closed my fist around it so the seed peeped out from the circle formed by my index finger and thumb. 'You see where it got the name?' he asked.

I saw: what gleamed in my hand was the eye of a deer, bright with life. 'It's beautiful,' I said.

'It's beautiful,' my father agreed, 'but also poisonous. Nobody eats buckeyes, except maybe a fool squirrel.'

I knew the gaze of deer from living in the Ravenna Arsenal, in Portage County, up in the northeastern corner of Ohio. After supper we often drove the Arsenal's gravel roads, past the munitions bunkers, past acres of rusting tanks and wrecked bombers, into the far fields where we counted deer. One June evening, while mist rose from the ponds, we counted three hundred and eleven, our family record. We found the deer in herds, in bunches, in amorous pairs. We came upon lone bucks, their antlers lifted against the sky like the bare branches of dogwood. If you were quiet, if your hands were empty, if you moved slowly, you could leave the car and steal to within a few paces of a grazing deer, close enough to see the delicate lips, the twitching nostrils, the glossy, fathomless eyes.

———

The wooden box on my desk holds these grazing deer, as it holds the buckeyes and the walnut plank and the farm auction and the munitions bunkers and the breathing forests and my father's hands. I could lose the box, I could lose the polished seeds, but if I were to lose the memories I would become a bush without roots, and every new breeze would toss me about. All those memories lead back to the northeastern corner of Ohio, the place where I came to consciousness, where I learned to connect feelings with words, where I fell in love with the earth.

It was a troubled love, for much of the land I knew as a child had been ravaged. The ponds in the Arsenal teemed with bluegill and beaver, but they were also laced with TNT from the making of bombs. Because the wolves and coyotes had long since been killed, some of the deer, so plump in the June grass, collapsed on the January snow, whittled by hunger to racks of bones. Outside the Arsenal's high barbed fences, many of the farms had failed, their barns caving in, their topsoil gone. Ravines were choked with swollen couches and junked washing machines and cars. Crossing fields, you had to be careful not to slice your feet on tin cans or shards of glass. Most of the rivers had been dammed, turning fertile valleys into scummy playgrounds for boats.

One free-flowing river, the Mahoning, ran past the small farm near the Arsenal where our family lived during my later years in Ohio. We owned just enough land to pasture three ponies and to grow vegetables for our table, but those few acres opened onto miles of woods and creeks and secret meadows. I walked that land in every season, every weather, following animal trails. But then the Mahoning, too, was doomed by a government decision; we were forced to sell our land, and a dam began to rise across the river.

If enough people had spoken for the river, we might have saved it. If enough people had believed that our scarred country was worth defending, we might have dug in our heels and fought. Our attachments to the land were all private. We had no shared lore, no literature, no art to root us there, to give us courage, to help us stand our ground. The only maps we had were those issued by the state, showing a maze of numbered lines stretched over emptiness. The Ohio landscape never showed up on postcards or posters, never unfurled like tapestry in films, rarely filled even a paragraph in books. There were no mountains in that place, no waterfalls, no rocky gorges, no vistas. It was a country of low hills, cut over woods, scoured fields, villages that had lost their purpose, roads that had lost their way.

'Let us love the country of here below,' Simone Weil urged. 'It is real; it offers resistance to love. It is this country that God has given us to love. He has willed that it should be difficult yet possible to love it.' Which is the deeper truth about buckeyes, their poison or their beauty? I hold with the beauty; or rather, I am held by the beauty, without forgetting the poison. In my corner of Ohio the gullies were choked with trash, yet cedars flickered up like green flames from cracks in stone; in the evening bombs exploded at the ammunition dump, yet from the darkness came the mating cries of owls. I was saved from despair by knowing a few men and women who cared enough about the land to clean up trash, who planted walnuts and oaks that would long outlive them, who imagined a world that would have no call for bombs.

How could our hearts be large enough for heaven if they are not large enough for earth? The only country I am certain of is the one here below. The only paradise I know is the one lit by our everyday sun, this land of difficult love, shot through with shadow. The place where we learn this love, if we learn it at all, shimmers behind every new place we inhabit.

———

A family move carried me away from Ohio thirty years ago; my schooling and marriage and job have kept me away ever since, except for visits in memory and in flesh. I returned to the site of our farm one cold November day, when the trees were skeletons and the ground shone with the yellow of fallen leaves. From a previous trip I knew that our house had been bulldozed, our yard and pasture had grown up in thickets, and the reservoir had flooded the woods. On my earlier visit I had merely gazed from the car, too numb with loss to climb out. But on this November day, I parked the car, drew on my hat and gloves, opened the door, and walked.

I was looking for some sign that we had lived there, some token of our affection for the place. All that I recognized, aside from the contours of the land, were two weeping willows that my father and I had planted near the road. They had been slips the length of my forearm when we set them out, and now their crowns rose higher than the telephone poles. When I touched them last, their trunks had been smooth and supple, as thin as my wrist, and now they were furrowed and stout. I took off my gloves and laid my hands against the rough bark. Immediately I felt the wince of tears. Without knowing why, I said hello to my father, quietly at first, then louder and louder, as if only shouts could reach him through the bark and miles and years.

Surprised by sobs, I turned from the willows and stumbled away toward the drowned woods, calling to my father. I sensed that he was nearby. Even as

I called, I was wary of grief's deceptions. I had never seen his body after he died. By the time I reached the place of his death, a furnace had reduced him to ashes. The need to see him, to let go of him, to let go of this land and time, was powerful enough to summon mirages; I knew that. But I also knew, stumbling toward the woods, that my father was here.

At the bottom of a slope where the creek used to run, I came to an expanse of gray stumps and withered grass. It was a bay of the reservoir from which the water had retreated, the level drawn down by engineers or drought. I stood at the edge of this desolate ground, willing it back to life, trying to recall the woods where my father had taught me the names of trees. No green shoots rose. I walked out among the stumps. The grass crackled under my boots, breath rasped in my throat, but otherwise the world was silent.

Then a cry broke overhead and I looked up to see a red-tailed hawk launching out from the top of an oak. I recognized the bird from its band of dark feathers across the creamy breast and the tail splayed like rosy fingers against the sun. It was a red-tailed hawk for sure; and it was also my father. Not a symbol of my father, not a reminder, not a ghost, but the man himself, right there, circling in the air above me. I knew this as clearly as I knew the sun burned in the sky. A calm poured through me. My chest quit heaving. My eyes dried.

Hawk and father wheeled above me, circle upon circle, wings barely moving, head still. My own head was still, looking up, knowing and being known. Time scattered like fog. At length, father and hawk stroked the air with those powerful wings, three beats, then vanished over a ridge.

The voice of my education told me then and tells me now that I did not meet my father, that I merely projected my longing onto a bird. My education may well be right; yet nothing I heard in school, nothing I've read, no lesson reached by logic has ever convinced me as utterly or stirred me as deeply as did that red-tailed hawk. Nothing in my education prepared me to love a piece of the earth, least of all a humble, battered country like northeastern Ohio; I learned from the land itself.

Before leaving the drowned woods, I looked around at the ashen stumps, the wilted grass, and for the first time since moving from this place I was able to let it go. This ground was lost; the flood would reclaim it. But other ground could be saved, must be saved, in every watershed, every neighborhood. For each home ground we need new maps, living maps, stories and poems, photographs and paintings, essays and songs. We need to know where we are, so that we may dwell in our place with a full heart.

# CAROLYN SERVID

## The Right Place for Love

Earth's the right place for love:
I don't know where it's likely to go better.

ROBERT FROST

Today I watched a varied thrush die. Our porch was alive with birds—juncos, sparrows and thrushes—chittering and skittering around the feeders I had been filling daily during the unusual two-week snow. Dorik and I were sitting at the dining room table, watching with delight. The smaller juncos dominated the feeder perches while the sparrows and thrushes scuffled about below. Suddenly, in a whirring instant of alarm, they all took flight. One thrush tried to veer off into the open stretch alongside the house, but was foiled by the sudden shape glass gives to air. He smashed into the window, hard, two or three feet from where I sat. I gasped and threw my hands up in front of my face as though my own life were in danger. Then there was the silence after and the wrenching moment of uncertainty. Dorik stood up to look.

'Is he down?' I asked.

He nodded, but added, 'He might be all right.'

I hesitated a few seconds and then headed for the door. Outside the bird congregation had already returned. They completely ignored the wounded thrush who lay on his back, mustard-yellow feet clutching the empty air. I approached slowly. Soon I could see that his eyes were still bright, his orange breast pulsing with rapid breaths. He opened and closed his beak haltingly. I spoke softly, apologizing, my uncertain steps all too loud in the crystallizing snow. Crouching down, I reached my hand out carefully, not wanting to startle him, but found that I was the one who flinched, so foreign was that soft form to my touch, so precarious its moment. I stood again, shook my hands in anguish, and almost walked away. With all those signs of life maybe he would be all right. But he lay in cold snow. Surely I should move him from there. I shifted cautiously to a position where I could use both my hands to pick him up. What if I would need to end his life in mercy? My heart turned. But I crouched down again, and at last pushed my trembling hands gently under him through the snow to cup his warmth in my palms. When his head fell limply against my fingers I knew my efforts were in vain. Still, I asked Dorik to bring a box and a couple of towels. I nestled him there to rest. His life filled only a few more minutes. Then his breathing stopped. The brightness in his eyes was gone. When I went out a bit later that morning, I took his still-warm body up the trail and found a hollow under a tree that became his grave.

———

I harbored that thrush's death much of the rest of the day and wondered about my timidness as I tried to help. The tender fear that filled me seemed like another side of love, a connection I couldn't make into anything more than sentimentality until I thought about it in the context of a startling piece of scientific information I'd learned some months earlier. It came from poet and biologist Melinda Mueller in a talk she gave about myth and theory, about creationism and evolution. Her talk incorporated a wonderful review lesson about DNA that I'd been mulling over ever since. Because she is skilled in both poetry and science, she laid out her review in the metaphor of language, and that helped fix it in my mind.

The DNA alphabet, she reminded us, is made up of four letters, one for each of the nucleotides—adenine, guanine, cytosine, and thymine—that pair themselves across the double spiral of the DNA molecule. That alphabet arranges itself along the DNA strand in three-letter sequences or words. With a four letter alphabet, there are sixty-four possible three-letter words. Each DNA cell contains billions of these nucleotide pairs, sequencing themselves in three-letter words that are arranged in any number of ways, creating the possibility of an infinite number of stories. Each of these stories is distinct, and corresponds to a particular species of plant or animal, giving us the biological diversity we know to be the gamut of life on this planet. But the sixty-four words in the DNA cells of all of those species—plant and animal alike—are precisely the same sixty-four words. And in every species, those words mean precisely the same thing. All living things on earth are linked by a common language.

I thought about that thrush against the backdrop of this biological and earthly bond of a common chemical language contained in our separate DNA cells. His story and mine were clearly different, of course. The particular sequence of his sixty-four words laid out the genetic code that made him a bird, that determined his size and the shape of his beak. Its certain order spelled out the details that created the sharp necklace stripe of black feathers around his orange neck. It determined that he would prefer the coniferous forest habitat outside my windows, that he would be attracted to the sunflower seeds I offered. That distinct genetic code gave him the trilling voice of an early singer of spring. My own DNA contained a parallel story that laid out an analogous set of characteristics—human being, female, fair skin, dark eyes, medium build, soft voice, the perceptive faculties to pay attention to birds. But behind all those species-specific details, in the genetic subworld that distinguished us, bird from human, the words that were strung together to create our definitive stories were sixty-four consistent words whose meanings stayed true across the species.

I remember being astonished by this gem of scientific knowledge when Melinda laid it out. I was also embarrassed by my astonishment. Surely such rudimentary information was common knowledge. Why had I missed out? A bit of historical retrospective reminded me that, although the structure of the DNA molecule had been discovered in 1953, the full genetic code and its universal application across all species wasn't understood until the late 1960s—too late to filter into the high school biology class that was the last focused dose of science I'd received. That eased some of my embarrassment, but the astonishment still remained. Why, I wondered, didn't more people pay attention to this bit of biological bedrock? Why hadn't it revolutionized the way we thought of ourselves, the way we lived our lives?

Dorik remembers being in Washington D.C. the day that President Lyndon Johnson held a news conference at the Smithsonian to announce an extraordinary breakthrough with DNA. Though the memory isn't all together clear, Johnson's announcement most likely was about the fact that scientists had cracked the full genetic code. The presidential delivery must have been intended to underscore the importance of this scientific news. But even Dorik, with his curious and attentive mind, when offered the rare opportunity to hear the word first hand, opted to read about it the next day. I probably had the option of watching the news on television, but my high school interests were otherwise. I wonder now if my biology teacher took it in. She, at least, would have understood its significance. My perspective was more likely to be akin to that of many other people—untrained in the complexities, unlikely to be mindful of the shifting parameters of science unless they directly affected my personal life. What I often fail to realize is the extent to which they can and do. And in many respects, the more we know by way of science, the broader the context for our lives and the more uncertain we are of our own importance. It is no wonder many of us, almost by default, leave the world of scientific discovery alone.

But thirty years later, the news about DNA struck home. I was fascinated by the paradox within it—the core that unifies all living species and the simultaneous possibilities for infinite diversity. I imagine that the diversity piece of the paradox was celebrated as the miracle of the discovery. Clearly, the extraordinary DNA structure, its distinctions, species by species, and its replication process, cell by cell, was ingenious almost beyond belief. And that part of the miracle reaffirmed our human uniquenesses, underscoring the way history has helped us come to think of ourselves—as a singular species of distinct individuals, each with our own remarkable selection of traits, set apart and above other animals by our capabilities and certainly from plants by our physical characteristics. But the other piece of the DNA paradox was what astonished me. The miracle was the common language, the steadfast bond, the necessary connection, the irrevocable relationship, the divine intersection, the underlying coherence, the unquestionable consistency.

Perhaps my tenderness toward that thrush was mere sentimentality, but then again, perhaps the emotion was grounded in this scientific and holy truth. And perhaps my timidness and uneasiness as I tried to help that bird lay in the fact that, almost all of my life, I had been unaware of this truth, disconnected from this holiness. What a marvel it was. What a comfort it offered. And what a contrary idea. What a threat to the way we humans are accustomed to living in the world.

Poet and essayist Alison Deming once wrote to me, 'I don't think Americans know how to be reverent. Maybe the idea of revering anything means acknowledging its authority over us—a most undemocratic idea!' Her comment reminded me of William Sloane Coffin's acknowledgment in one of his essays of 'the threat authority always poses to power.' Most of us are willing to acknowledge an authority greater than ourselves—indeed we often seek it out as a guiding principle for our lives. But we are inclined to give that authority a human likeness so that it can sanction our own sense of power. If such authority lies, instead, in the chemical language of a molecular structure that proves we have a fundamental bond to all other life on the planet, our conception of our own power begins to shift, to come into question. Perhaps that is why we, in Western cultures, have lived for centuries as though that bond did not exist. Perhaps that is why even something as compelling as the DNA discovery has not prompted us to give that bond the reverence it is due.

Our discomfort with this notion of a biological authority over our lives seems to be enough to keep us from taking the concept seriously. But what if we approached that essential truth from a different angle? What if we used a different metaphor? As Melinda Mueller was wrapping up her review lesson on DNA, she commented, 'It is not a romantic notion to say that the earth is our home. Biologically, it is literally true.' Home is not a place where we are uncomfortable. Home is a place that nurtures us, a place that reassures us of ourselves, a place to which we feel obligated, a place we are willing to protect, a place where relationships are fast and true. Home is a place where we know we belong. Home is a place infused with love.

In his book, *The Land*, theologian and historian Walter Brueggemann recognizes a human yearning for place—for home—and acknowledges that yearning as a primary human hunger. I think of it as an instinctual desire and need for my own clearly defined habitat, a word primarily used to describe an ecological home range that allows a given species to thrive. We usually don't think of ourselves as the sample species, but I'd like to consider the notion of habitat in a human context for a moment. For those of us who use the English language, it is interesting to note that *habitat* is related to a cluster of other words—*habit, ability, rehabilitate, inhabit,* and *prohibit*. They all come from a common Latin root, *habere*, and spin off a fundamental concept of relationship: 'to hold, hence to occupy or possess, hence to have.' They constitute a family of words that ground us by describing where we live, how we live, what we are able to do, how we heal ourselves, what our connections are to the landscape around us, what the boundaries are for our behavior. Together, they offer a set of parameters that might allow us to thrive in a place we think of as home.

Given the biological evidence that the earth is our home, it's not difficult or even particularly imaginative to assert that we in Western societies have been living for centuries in a perpetual state of homesickness. We have worked hard—somewhat blindly and somewhat successfully—to disconnect ourselves from the source of our being. Our efforts have only partially succeeded because we cannot, in fact, separate ourselves from the fundamental truth of the context for our lives. For all those centuries we were not in a position to see and clearly understand the evidence, but science—one of the very tools that has given us the knowledge and capability of disengaging ourselves—has pointed us right back to where we belong.

One of the ironies of the human endeavor of science is that it rests on a foundation of objectivity and rational thought. It allows no room in its method for the emotions that are so fundamental to the human condition. The scientific evidence offered by the DNA discovery didn't exactly elicit a response of love, and yet it strikes me that such a reaction may be exactly right. Our legacy of homesickness stems in part from our inability to love the biological facts of our lives. The human hunger for place that Brueggemann speaks of might be thought of as a longing to be reconnected to the very source of our being. That longing is also a hunger for love—for the nurturing that a home place provides, for its familiarity, its comfort, its human community, its natural community, its light and landscape. I believe, too, that our hunger for place is a yearning for a sense of the holy, for home ground sacred enough to sustain our faith, sacred enough that we will not violate it , sacred enough that our commitment to its holiness will not falter.

A spirited gospel hymn I learned when I was growing up still rings in my memory. The first verse goes like this:

> This world is not my home, I'm just a-passing through
> My treasures are laid up somewhere beyond the blue
> The angels beckon me from heaven's open door
> And I can't feel at home in this world anymore.

The hymn was part of the indoctrination that had me believing for too many years that it wasn't worth my while to attach myself to any particular place on Earth and that the sacred did not exist here. Only when my heart defied the first notion did the second proved itself untrue. Only when I opened myself, as a Taoist scholar has said, to the scripture of the landscape did the sacredness of Earth's life became apparent. Only when I followed my own calling to a particular place did I begin to ground myself in that larger context—human and other—that contains my life. And it has been here, in the place that is now my home, that I have come to understand the strength of love.

I don't find it difficult to move from my heart's ties to the water-bound forested mountains of Baranof Island to a sense of loyalty to that landscape and place. And it is not much of a stretch for that loyalty to develop into a covenant, an agreement that I live well in this place in exchange for my respect and regard for the natural communities that surround and support me as well as the shared human community. Brueggemann speaks of the yearning for place as a decision to enter history. I opted to join the local Sitka story at a point well along in its evolution. The Tlingit people had inhabited the place for millennia in the company of hemlock and cedar, salmon berry and skunk cabbage, brown bear and black-tailed deer, sea lion and orca, sockeye and halibut, raven and chickadee. My European predecessors, arriving some two hundred years ago, found a landscape largely undisturbed by human occupation. They and the many who have come after did not leave it as they found it. In places the landscape is irrevocably altered. Still, it offers itself as an extraordinary conjunction of forest and mountain and ocean that is home to every species that existed when Westerners first arrived. The Tlingit are still here too.

In its more recent history, Sitka was thought of as a timber town, with fishing and tourist-flooded streets in summer providing secondary sources of revenue. A Japanese-owned pulp mill was the unassailable mainstay of the economy for thirty years, with timber harvesting privileges that were the envy of the industry outside Alaska. The related environmental controversies couldn't have been wished on anybody. They pitted neighbor against neighbor and created a deep festering wound in the community. The day the management broke the news that the mill was going to close its doors, people stood by radio speakers in homes and businesses all over town, listening in stunned silence. Some later celebrated, others grieved. Everyone wondered what would happen next. I had lived for years with the tea-brown water in the bay beyond my windows. I had walked outside into sulfured air on the many days when the wind carried the mill's emissions toward town. I was not going to be sorry to see those things go. But the scale of the change for the community made me uneasy. What, indeed, would happen next? Would people's worst fears come true? Without the mill as its economic backbone, would the community be diminished beyond repair? Would Sitka remain a town where I could live?

In the years since the mill closure, I have threaded my way in and around the social and economic challenges that have faced this small island community. I've listened to voices of fear and anger, satisfaction and hope. I've watched the change: some families have left town, others have moved in; property values and new home construction have climbed; a regional Native hospital has taken the economic lead; new small businesses have both failed and succeeded, several old businesses are thriving. I've listened to people slowly let go of the past and imagine a different future. And I've made it my work to collaborate with others to encourage the community to face some of its hardest questions: How can we delineate those parameters that will allow us to thrive here? How can we reassure ourselves that we will be able to live well on into the future? How can we create a stable economy? How can we make use of the natural resources around us without abusing them? What can we do to keep people—young and old—from being disillusioned about their lives? How can we make sure there is adequate affordable housing for all who live here? What can we do about racism? About equity? How can we improve on the ways we resolve our differences? After years of divisiveness on a variety of public issues, how can we learn to trust one another?

What has become apparent in this period of community transition is that one of the things that binds together people of almost all persuasions is their love of this place. I find it remarkable that we don't use that common ground more often to heal ourselves, for such love of place is as strong a bond as most any that can be found. Essayist Kathleen Dean Moore noted recently how quickly our obligation to a place and its human community follows on the heels of our love for the land and for each other. Our commitment begins with the fact of our love. And the health of a human community—economic, social, spiritual—is sustained first and foremost by the shared commitment and engagement of its citizens. If we expect to live well in this place, expect it to support us, expect it to be the source of what we need for both vocation and avocation, I believe we are obliged to acknowledge not only our responsibilities to each other, but the deeper connection—the holy connection—we share with the rest of life here. If the stands of spruce and hemlock and cedar gracing a secluded mountain-rimmed bay fill us with a quiet joy, if the silver flash of a salmon on the end of our line delights us, if the breach of a humpback whale thrills and silences us, if the first spring thrush song gladdens us, we can do no better than to return the love we've found. We can do no better than to live our lives—individually and in community—as though all those living things mattered.

———

When I returned to the haven of our snowbound house, I listened as I approached and could hear the chirping bird chorus coming from the front porch. I walked quietly along the back side to a corner where I could sneak a look without disturbing them. They were busy. Juncos fluttered at the feeder perches not occupied by pine siskins. Chickadees ducked in and out, grabbing a sunflower seed and flying off with it into the trees. Thrushes hopped along the edge of the porch picking up whatever had fallen. Sparrows scratched methodically at the snow to uncover yesterday's seeds. I smiled. When I moved around the corner, they whirred away to the safety of surrounding bushes and branches. As soon as I got inside and closed the door, they returned. I settled down to watch. The day's light was fading. It had softened the whiteness of the snow. The clouds above the mountains across the bay were tinged a rosy gray. The birds took advantage of every moment of light, scurrying about, fortifying themselves against the coming hours of cold darkness. The water beyond them seemed to move in a steady easy current as a slight breeze riffled its surface. That breath of wind caught the cedar boughs hanging in front of the house and slipped on by. As it did, the corner of my eye caught a motion. A few thrush feathers fluttered where they were stuck on the window. I went out, gathered them up, and brought them inside. They were soft and almost silky, weightless in my hand. At their base they were downy and fluffy and a gentle blue gray. Midway up the shaft they gained a flatter rounded shape and turned burnt orange. And against that orange, the end of each feather was tipped in black. Feather upon feather, they had been layered to create first warmth, then the distinctive contour and color of that thrush's breast, then the dark necklace stripe around his neck. I savored their miracle, their particularity and purpose, and put them in a small birch bark box where I will keep them as reminders of the sacred bond that underlies our lives.

# GARY SNYDER

# Kitkitdizze: A Node in the Net

Jets heading west on the Denver-to-Sacramento run start losing altitude east of Reno, and the engines cool as they cross the snowy Sierra crest. They glide low over the west-tending mountain slopes, passing above the canyon of the north fork of the American River. If you look north out the window you can see the Yuba River country, and if it's really clear you can see the old 'diggings'—large areas of white gravel laid bare by nineteenth-century gold mining. On the edge of one of those is a little hill where my family and I live. It's on a forested stretch between the South Yuba canyon and the two thousand treeless acres of old mining gravel, all on a forty-mile ridge that runs from the High Sierra to the valley floor near Marysville, California. You're looking out over the northern quarter of the greater Sierra ecosystem: a vast summer-dry hardwood-conifer forest, with drought-resistant shrubs and bushes in the canyons, clear-cuts, and burns.

In ten minutes the jet is skimming over the levees of the Sacramento River and wheeling down the strip. It takes two and a half hours to drive out of the valley and up to my place. The last three miles seem to take the longest—we like to joke that it's still the bumpiest road we've found, go where we will.

Back in the mid-sixties I was studying in Japan. Once, while I was on a visit to California, some friends suggested that I join them in buying mountain land. In those days land and gas were both still cheap. We drove into the ridge and canyon country, out to the end of a road. We pushed through manzanita thickets and strolled in open stretches of healthy ponderosa pine. Using a handheld compass, I found a couple of brass caps that mark corners. It was a new part of the Sierra for me. But I knew the assembly of plants—ponderosa pine, black oak, and associates—well enough to know what the rainfall and climate would be, and I knew I liked their company. There was a wild meadow full of native bunchgrass. No regular creek, but a slope with sedges that promised subsurface water. I told my friends to count me in. I put down the money for a twenty-five-acre share of the hundred acres and returned to Japan.

In 1969, back for good in California, we drove out to the land and made a family decision to put our life there. At that time there were virtually no neighbors, and the roads were even worse than they are now. No power lines, no phones, and twenty-five miles—across a canyon—to town. But we had the will and some of the skills as well. I had grown up on a small farm in the Northwest and had spent time in the forests and mountains since childhood. I had worked at carpentry and been a Forest Service seasonal worker, so mountain life (at three thousand feet) seemed doable. We weren't really 'in the wilderness' but rather in a zone of ecological recovery. The Tahoe National Forest stretches for hundreds of square miles in the hills beyond us.

I had also been a logger on an Indian reservation in the ponderosa pine forests of eastern Oregon, where many trees were more than two hundred feet tall and five feet through. That land was drier and a bit higher, so the understory was different, but it grew the same adaptable cinnamon-colored pines. The trees down here topped out at about a hundred feet; they were getting toward being a mature stand, but a long way from old growth. I talked with a ninety-year-old neighbor who had been born in the area. He told me that when he was young he had run cattle over my way and had logged here and there, and that a big fire had gone through about 1920. I trimmed the stump on a black oak that had fallen and counted the rings: more than three hundred years. Lots of standing oaks that big around, so it was clear that the fires had not been total. Besides the pine stands (mixed with incense cedar, madrona, a few Douglas firs), our place was a mosaic of postfire manzanita fields with small pines coming through; stable climax manzanita; an eight-acre stand of pure black oak; and some areas of blue oak, gray pine, and grasses. Also lots of the low ground-cover bush called *kitkitdizze* in the language of the Wintun, a nearby valley people. It was clear from the very old and scattered stumps that this area had been selectively logged once. A neighbor with an increment borer figured that some trees had been cut about 1940. The surrounding lands and the place I was making my home flowed together with unmarked boundaries; to the eye and to the creatures, it was all one.

We had our hands full the first ten years just getting up walls and roofs, bathhouse, small barn, woodshed. A lot of it was done the old way: we dropped all the trees to be used in the frame of the house with a two-man saw, and peeled them with drawknives. Young women and men with long hair joined the work camp for comradeship, food, and spending money. (Two later became licensed architects; many of them stayed and are neighbors today.) Light was from kerosene lamps; we heated with wood and cooked with wood and propane. Wood-burning ranges, wood-burning sauna stoves, treadle-operated sewing machines, and propane-using Servel refrigerators from the fifties were the targets of highly selective shopping runs. Many other young settlers found their place in northern California in the early seventies, so eventually there was a whole reinhabitory culture living this way in what we like to call Shasta Nation.

I set up my library and wrote poems and essays by lantern light, then went out periodically, lecturing and teaching around the country. I thought of my home as a well-concealed base camp from which I raided university treasuries. We named our place Kitkitdizze after the aromatic little shrub.

The scattered neighbors and I started meeting once a month to talk about local affairs. We were all nature lovers, and everyone wanted to cause as little impact as possible. Those with well-watered sites with springs and meadows put in small gardens and planted fruit trees. I tried fruit trees, a chicken flock, a kitchen garden, and beehives. The bees went first. They were totally destroyed in one night by a black bear. The kitchen garden did fairly well until the run of dry winters that started in the eighties and may finally be over. And, of course, no matter how you fence a garden, deer find a way to get in. The chickens were constant targets of northern goshawks, red-tailed hawks, rac-coons, feral dogs, and bobcats. A bobcat once killed twenty-five in one month. The fruit trees are still with us, especially the apples. They, of all the cultivars, have best made themselves at home. (The gosbeaks and finches always seem to beat us to the cherries.) But in my heart I was never into gardening. I couldn't see myself as a logger either, and it wasn't the place to grow Christmas trees. Except for cutting fallen oak and pine for firewood, felling an occasional pole for framing, and frequent clearing of the low limbs and underbrush well back from the homestead to reduce fire hazard, I hadn't done much with the forest. I wanted to go lightly, to get a deep sense of it, and thought it was enough to leave it wild, letting it be the wildlife habitat it is.

Living in a place like this is absolutely delicious. Coyote-howl fugues, owl exchanges in the treetops, the almost daily sighting of deer (and the rattle of antlers at rutting season), the frisson of seeing a poky rattlesnake, tracking critters in the snowfall, seeing cougar twice, running across humongous bear scats, sharing all this with the children are more than worth the inconveniences.

My original land partners were increasingly busy elsewhere. It took a number of years, but we bought our old partners out and ended up with the whole hundred acres. That was sobering. Now Kitkitdizze was entirely in our hands. We were cash poor and land rich, and who needs more second-growth pine and manzanita? We needed to rethink our relation to this place with its busy—almost downtown—rush of plants and creatures. Do we leave it alone? Use it, but how? And what responsibility comes with it all?

Now it is two grown sons, two stepdaughters, three cars, two trucks, four buildings, one pond, two well pumps, close to a hundred chickens, seventeen fruit trees, two cats, about ninety cords of firewood, and three chainsaws later. I've learned a lot, but there still is plenty of dark and unknown territory. (There's one boundary to this land down in the chaparral—it borders the BLM—that I *still* haven't located.) Black bear leave pawprints on woodshed refrigerators, and bobcats, coyotes, and foxes are more in evidence than ever, sometimes strolling in broad daylight. Even the diggings, which were stripped of soil by giant nozzles washing out the scattered gold, are colonized by everhardy manzanita and bonsai-looking pine. The first major environmental conflict in California was between Sacramento Valley farmers and the hydraulic gold miners of the Yuba. Judge Lorenzo Sawyer's decision of 1884 banned absolutely all release of mining debris into the watershed. That was the end of hydraulic mining here. We now know that the amount of material that was washed out of the Sierra into the valley and onto good farmlands was eight times the amount of dirt removed for the Panama Canal.

The kerosene lights have been replaced by a photovoltaic array powering a mixed AC/DC system. The phone company put in an underground line to our whole area at its own expense. My wife Carole and I are now using computers, the writer's equivalent of a nice little chainsaw. (Chainsaws and computers increase both macho productivity and nerdy stress.) My part-time teaching job at the University of California, Davis, gives me an Internet account. We have entered the late twentieth century and are tapping into political and environmental information with a vengeance.

The whole Sierra is a mosaic of ownership—various national forests, Bureau of Land Management, Sierra Pacific Industries, state parks, and private holdings—but to the eye of a hawk it is one great sweep of rocks and woodlands. We, along with most of our neighbors, were involved in the forestry controversies of the last decade, particularly in regard to the long-range plans for the Tahoe National Forest. The county boosters still seem to take more pleasure in the romance of the gold era than in the subsequent processes of restoration. The Sierra foothills are still described as 'Gold Country,' the highway is called '49,' there are businesses called 'Nugget' and 'Bonanza.' I have nothing against gold—I wear it in my teeth and in my ear—but the real wealth here is the great Sierran forest. My neighbors and I have sat in on many hearings and had long and complicated discussions with silviculturalists, district rangers, and other experts from the Forest Service. All these public and private designations seem to come with various 'rights.' With just 'rights' and no land ethic, our summer-dry forests could be irreversibly degraded into chaparral over the coming centuries. We were part of a nationwide campaign to reform forest practices. The upshot was a real and positive upheaval on a national scale in the US Forest Service and the promise of ecosystem management, which if actualized as described would be splendid.

We next turned our focus to the nearby public lands managed by the BLM. It wasn't hard to see that these public lands were a key middle-elevation part of a passageway for deer and other wildlife from the high country to the valleys below. Our own holdings are part of that corridor. Then we were catapulted into a whole new game: the BLM area manager for central California became aware of our interest, drove up and walked the woods with us, talked with us, consulted with the community, and then said, 'Let's cooperate in the long-range planning for these lands. We can share information.' We agreed to work with him and launched a biological inventory, first with older volunteers and then with our own wild teenagers jumping inn. We studied close to three thousand forested acres. We bushwhacked up and down the canyons to find out just what was there, in what combinations, in what quantity, in what diversity.

Some of it was tallied and mapped (my son Kai learned Geographical Information Systems techniques and put the data into a borrowed Sun Sparc workstation), and the rest of our observations were written up and put into bundles of notes on each small section. We had found some very large trees, located a California spotted owl pair, noted a little wetland with carnivorous sticky sundew, described a unique barren dome with serpentine endemics (plants that grow only in this special chemistry), identified large stands of vivid growing forest, and were struck by the tremendous buildup of fuel. The well-intended but ecologically ignorant fire-exclusion policies of the government agencies over the last century have made the forests of California an incredible tinderbox.

The droughty forests of California have been shaped for millennia by fire. A fire used to sweep through any given area, forest historians are now saying, roughly every twenty-five years, and in doing so kept the undergrowth down and left the big trees standing. The native people also deliberately started fires, so that the California forests of two hundred years ago, we are told, were structured of huge trees in parks that were fire-safe. Of course, there were always some manzanita fields and recovering burns, but overall there was far less fuel. To 'leave it be wild' in its present state would be risking a fire that might set the land back to first-phase brush again. The tens of thousands of homes and ranches mixed among the wooded foothills down the whole Sierra front could burn.

The biological inventory resulted in the formation of the Yuba Watershed Institute, a nonprofit organization made up of local people, sponsoring projects and research on forestry, biodiversity, and economic sustainability with an eye to the larger region. One of the conclusions of the joint-management plan, unsurprisingly, was to try to reduce fuel load by every available means. We saw that a certain amount of smart selective logging would not be out of place, could help reduce fuel load, and might pay some of the cost of thinning and prescriptive burning. We named our lands, with the BLM's blessing, the 'Inimim Forest, from the Nisenan word for *pine*, in recognition of the first people here.

The work with fire, wildlife, and people extends through public and (willing) private parcels alike. Realizing that our area plays a critical biological role, we are trying to learn the ground rules by which humans might live together with animals in an 'inhabited wildlife corridor.' A project for netting and banding migrant songbirds during nest season (providing information for a Western Hemisphere database) is located on some Kitkitdizze brushlands, rather than public land, simply because it's an excellent location. It is managed by my wife, Carole, who is deeply touched by the spirit of the vibrant little songbirds she bands. Our cooperative efforts here can be seen as part of the rapidly changing outlook on land management in the West, which is talking public-private partnership in a big way. Joint-management agreements between local communities and other local and committed interests, and their neighboring blocks of lands, are a new and potent possibility in the project of responsibly 'recovering the commons' region by region. The need for ecological literacy, the sense of home watershed, and a better understanding of our stake in public lands are beginning to permeate the consciousness of the larger society.

Lessons learned in the landscape apply to our own lands, too. So this is what my family and I are borrowing from the watershed work as our own Three-Hundred-Year Kitkitdizze Plan: We'll do much more understory thinning and then a series of prescribed burns. Some patches will be left untouched by fire, to provide a control. We'll plant a few sugar pines, and incense cedars where they fit (ponderosa pines will mostly take care of themselves), burn the ground under some of the oaks to see what it does for the acorn crop, burn some bunchgrass patches to see if they produce better basketry materials (an idea from the Native basket-weaving revival in California). We'll leave a percentage of dead oak in the forest rather than take it all for firewood. In the time of our seventh-generation granddaughter there will be a large area of fire-safe pine stands that will provide the possibility of the occasional sale of an incredibly valuable huge, clear, old-growth sawlog.

We assume something of the same will be true on surrounding land. The wildlife will still pass through. And visitors from the highly crowded lowlands will come to walk, study, and reflect. A few people will be resident on this land, getting some of their income from forestry work. The rest may come from the information economy of three centuries hence. There might even be a civilization with a culture of cultivating wildness.

You can say that this is outrageously optimistic. It truly is. But the possibility of saving, restoring, and wisely (yes!) using the bounty of wild nature is still with us in North America. My home base, Kitkitdizze, is but one tiny node in an evolving net of bioregional homesteads and camps.

Beyond all this studying and managing and calculating, there's another level to knowing nature. We can go about learning the names of things and doing inventories of trees, bushes, and flowers, but nature as it flits by is not usually seen in a clear light. Our actual experience of many birds and much wildlife is chancy and quick. Wildlife is often simply a call, a cough in the dark, a shadow in the shrubs. You can watch a cougar on a wildlife documentary for hours but the real cougar shows herself but once or twice in a lifetime. One must be tuned to hints and nuances.

After twenty years of walking right past it on my way to chores in the meadow, I actually paid attention to a certain gnarly canyon oak one day. Or maybe it was ready to show itself to me. I felt its oldness, suchness, inwardness, oakness, as if it were my own. Such intimacy makes you totally at home in life and in yourself. But the years spent working around that oak in that meadow and not really noticing it were not wasted. Knowing names and habits, cutting some brush here, getting firewood there, watching for when the fall mushrooms bulge out are skills that are of themselves delightful and essential. And they also prepare one for suddenly meeting the oak.

# JOHN
# TALLMADGE

## A Matter of Scale

It was not a happy day when I learned that my family and I would be moving to Cincinnati, Ohio. What wilderness lover would ever dream of living deep in the Rust Belt, downstream from places with names like Ironton, Oil City, or Nitro? It was a long drive from our home in Minnesota, every mile falling farther away from the Boundary Waters, where big pines still towered over pristine forests and lakes. At the time, it felt like hurtling into exile. But now, after ten years in the heart of it, I find the city as rich with lessons as any wilderness. Reaching this point has been a long, fantastic voyage, and the best guides have been my children.

Early on, it was hard not to dream of remoteness. Our plain brick house in an aging suburb bore the usual wreath of lawn, shrubbery, and petunias, with only a thin belt of trees to screen us from the neighbors. More enticing were the hundred-meter woods that separated our yard from the city park, with its soccer field. I used to walk there dreaming of mountain heather and Parry primrose, while stumbling amid the jewelweed and mayapples. Out in the park, a west wind teasing the grass always made me think of snowy cirques high in the Rockies or yellow prairies along the hundredth meridian.

And why not? The very idea of wilderness presumes the viewpoint of some- one immersed in civilization, gazing far off. We may encounter wilderness 'out there,' but we normally think about it 'right here'—that is, in the city, where most of us live and work. We habitually think of wilderness as something with big trees, big animals, and big scenery, a place of 'mountains and rivers without end.' This classic view of wilderness seems to pose only hopeless choices: nature or culture, adventure or home, wildness or civilization.

My children solved this conundrum by proving, inadvertently, how much our sense of wildness is really a matter of scale. From our earliest walks they brought attentiveness and wonder to even the most common things. Rosalind discovered feathers—blue jay, cardinal, mourning dove. In her tiny hands they looked as big as fans, beautiful talismans of airy life. Elizabeth loved 'treasure walks,' where we gathered acorns, sweet-gum balls, and dried grass stems as stiff and precise as architecture. Each discarded husk was as precious to her as a golden apple dropped by some passing goddess.

As the girls grew, so did the grass in the park beyond our woods. One year the city failed to mow, and the grass grew heedlessly into a tossing prairie. On a June day when Rosalind was eight and Elizabeth almost six, we went out there to escape the house, threading our way through poison ivy and amur honeysuckle until we were able to stand up straight at the meadow's edge. The sight of all that glowing, rippling grass washed over us like pure delight. Did our ancestors feel like this when they first stepped out of the forest onto African savannas more than a million years ago? The soccer field was calf-deep in blooming timothy, English plantain, and oxeye daisies, and on the far side unmowed grass rose up in a green wave, shoulder high. With a shout the girls plunged in like swimmers breasting the surf, then reappeared leaping and burrowing as I thrashed along behind.

When I caught up with Rosalind she was down on her hands and knees. 'Look!' she cried, 'a slug!' Then, nose to the ground, 'Daddy! Look!' I dropped beside her, staring into a patch of moss that grew on the damp, shad- ed floor of the meadow. Tiny mushrooms had sprouted there, stems thin as horsehair, ribbed caps delicate as Chinese parasols. Over them towered smooth, straight stalks of grass, their ink-black shadows slanting across the moss. A beetle lumbered into view, as big and shiny as a pickup truck. What lives, what emotions, what battles or discoveries were being played out here while I sat indoors dreaming of distant, glamorous wilds? 'It's a grass forest!' I murmured. But Rosalind had already bounded off toward Elizabeth, who was chasing white and orange butterflies. 'Let's be naturalists!' she cried.

It occurred to me then how grown-ups, who have become adept at living, often miss the wildness at the heart of life itself. That's why we hanker after the strong drink of wilderness; we need such tonics to take us out of ourselves. To find the wildness near at hand we need, somehow, to regain that beginner's mind before which the world still appears fresh and luminous and unbounded. But how? On those early walks, my children taught me that wildness is not just a state of nature but a state of mind. Where do you suppose the horizon lies for the small denizens of the grass forest, which grows up today and tomorrow is mown down? We humans bring all things to the text of ourselves. But the world is larger than our conceptions of it.

Gauged by average human dimensions—say, a body five and a half feet tall, weighing 130 pounds and lasting 70 years—the Cincinnati landscape manifests little wildness. Few trees in my neighborhood are more than 50 years old, and the only animal approaching human size might be a stray deer or coyote wandering through. Move down the scale, however, and the living world becomes more prolific and diverse. Although our woods no longer hold black bears, elk, wolves, or buffalo, we do have opossums and raccoons, plus smaller mammals such as squirrels, chipmunks, rabbits, moles, and mice. More than two dozen species of birds have passed within a block of the house, from great blue herons and pileated woodpeckers to juncos, warblers, and house sparrows. Insects abound, especially in summer, when hundreds of fireflies rise into the trees on hot June nights, and crickets rasp outside the windows all through July.

At smaller scales, it becomes even harder to distinguish our woods from wilderness, particularly when you reach the teeming metropolis of the soil. Turn over any rotting log or clump of decaying leaves, and you'll expose a host of wriggling invertebrates, some barely visible without a lens: thrips, centipedes, grubs, springtails, roundworms, annelid worms, nematodes. A microscope would reveal even more: tiny crustaceans, mites and spiders, transparent rotifers bulging frantically into view, plus all kinds of protozoans—ciliates bumping along like barrels, flagellates whipping around—and clots of blue-green algae, delicate meshworks of mycelia destined to fruit eventually as yellow honey mushrooms or red-capped boletes, perhaps even the gloppy plasmodium of a slime mold programmed—who knows how?—to gather one day into a bright, chrome-yellow dollop, soft as mayonnaise, on the surface of some damp, unassuming log. Not to mention, of course, the myriad bacteria, many unknown to science, whose job it is to perforate, ferment, digest, and otherwise transform all the vast residuum and waste of 'higher' life into the nutrients those very forms can use. Without them, the planet would be no more than a gigantic landfill, clogged with junk.

Time offers a similar venue for thought experiments with the sense of scale. The Cincinnati landscape bears dramatic testimony to the Ice Age: moraines, changed drainages, valleys cut by meltwater, even the present course of the Ohio River itself. The ice stopped here before retreating north, and a glance at the weather map shows that Cincinnati still rests on the isotherm between two climate zones: Our winters seesaw between ice and thaw, wreaking havoc on city streets and concrete bridge abutments. Walk outside a few days after a snow, and you'll find water running in the gutters, cutting small canyons in slabs of remnant ice. Up close, the ice resembles that found at the snout of a glacier, congealed to a waxen uniformity by freeze-thaw cycles and studded with relics of the surrounding landscape—in this case, bits of sand and concrete lifted from the pavement, wood chips, bark, seed husks, broken glass, perhaps a bottle cap or twist tie, or even a feather dropped by some passing bird.

All these are first embedded, frozen in, and then released by scouring water, washed downstream, and eventually deposited in the elbow of a curve against the ice, or else in a small delta at the lip of a storm-sewer grate. One can see the same processes at work that created the vaster landscape over tens of thousands of years. All at once, time begins to lengthen out. It becomes harder to distinguish the present and future from the past. The landscape begins to shimmer, seem less permanent; its current 'damaged' and domesticated state appears as little more than an eddy in the larger flow of climate, ecosystems, and advancing or declining species.

But one does not need geological epochs to appreciate how wildness depends on the sense of time. Imagine a smooth granite surface in Yosemite's High Sierra—specifically, the top of Sentinel Dome. A crack has formed, and, over the years, it begins to fill with sand weathered out of the bedrock. Soil forms, and one day a blown seed catches in the crack and sprouts. A tree begins to grow—specifically, a Jeffrey pine. It hangs on for 100 years, buffeted by prevailing winds, until its trunk extends like a twisted arm far out above the bare rock surface, while its twigs and needles bristle upward, stiff as a comb. One day a photographer—Ansel Adams—frames it at high noon against a dark horizon. In the remorseless light the tree looks totally exposed, no cover anywhere between it and the churning clouds. The awed viewer sees it as an icon of rugged individualism and endurance, like a climber achieving some first ascent by 'fair means' alone. Its splendid isolation and tortured form seem an expression of character, as if its entire history were bodied forth. We think, This is what it means to be wild, to be in the wilderness and survive.

Now imagine another smooth rock surface—specifically, a concrete sidewalk in downtown Cincinnati. Soil has accumulated along a joint, and one day a ragweed seed lodges and sprouts. It grows for 100 days, buffeted by wind and sun, gnawed by insects, beaten and bruised by passers-by. It is small, dusty-looking, of no more account to the casual eye than any of hundreds of other vigorous, opportunistic, and street-tough weeds that flourish like some green stain at the edge of the human world. By summer's end it, too, has attained an eloquence of form that testifies to a lifelong spirit of survival. Both plants are dead now, yet who can say that one was more wild than the other? Both lived out their allotted time, accumulating a history expressed in their very shape and so achieving character. The only difference is that the pine lived longer than a human life and grew in a place removed from human work. It therefore acquired an air of sublimity that Adams, with his art, converted into the radiance of an icon.

It is easier, I admit, to dream of remote and glorious places than to exercise the imagination upon the humble and near at hand. An icy gutter or a spoonful of garden soil cannot match the glamour of an Alaskan fjord or a tropical rainforest—unless you are willing to shift your perspective dramatically. For children, this comes naturally. For adults, it takes commitment and concentration, especially in middle age, when there's so much else to attend to. I still need the wild, with its tonics and challenges, as much as I ever did when young; it still refreshes my spirit, startles me, helps me learn and grow. But now, my children teach me how to perceive it close to home. They show me how the wildness of modest, unassuming landscapes, even in the midst of cities, connects with that of remote, untrammeled places. Deliberate imagination can expand the eye to see them all as part of a larger landscape in which people might learn to live sustainably, even for centuries. To connect the places we inhabit with those we admire, the lands of heart's rest with the lands of heart's desire—such is the challenge and hope of an urban practice of the wild.

Now, in midlife, I seek a beginner's mind that floats on history like the water lilies of Quetico. I find its traces in the footsteps of my children, even after they have run far ahead, disappearing into the grass forest. Out there, beyond the trees, it's quiet now. I emerge gingerly, stand for a moment, and bend down. There is a certain slant of light at the base of smooth, translucent stems that stirs both memory and desire. I think of Minnesota prairies tossed by a wind out of the Rockies. I think of the sandy-colored grass that grows in western Kansas and high on the tableland of Mount Katahdin. I wonder what adventures lie in wait for my daughters as they leap toward adolescence. Standing, awash in light, I watch them bound away, cavorting like young lions.

# MARK TREDINNICK

## Falling Water

### I. THE BLUE PLATEAU

Night-time on the blue plateau. Maree falls asleep beneath these hands of mine, which run along ridges, hold for small moments the high ground of a shoulder, then fall and press into the low places of her body. On the metal roof above, on the corrugated iron and its peeling green paint, its carpet of needles, rain falls in a slow, irregular beat. A cypress stands right by the house and reaches its arms over the roof, over us beneath. The tree was planted here, along with the timber cottage, back when the first war had just ended in Europe. And in weather like this, it catches rain and holds it in its fingers, letting water fall now and then in round heavy notes upon the crests and gullies of the pitched tin roof. The rain runs down to gutters that camber the wrong way, aged and uncared for. I think again that I must mend them. These worn channels fill with the moult of the tree and spill their cargo of rainwater hard onto the pavement. This is how the place speaks tonight. I near sleep within the sound of falling water.

———

In November 1911, George Matcham Pitt, a surveyor from North Richmond, down by the Hawkesbury River, became the owner of thirty-seven acres of what was, until then, a wooded heath called Banksia Park. On the map that accompanies the registration of title, the woodland has already become a cleared expanse of neat allotments. One of them, passed through many sets of hands, is now mine: lot 142 in plan 7667. Between 1911 and 1925, the native timber was felled and this house, and one or two of its neighbours, built. Someone—I am not sure who—planted the cypress. It must be nearly as old as the house, and I suspect it was Lily May Palmer, who bought the place in 1925 and became Lily May Butters in 1927 when she married. Since then, other owners have surrounded the cottage in exotics—ivy, cherry laurel, black pines, grey maple, hemlock, alder, cherry and oak among them—and Banksia Park has retreated to a few square acres that shield us from the road that runs along the cliff's edge from Leura to the Three Sisters. If the cottage had been set down within the existing woods, the tree beside the house would be a eucalypt—a scribbly gum or silver top ash—and the water on the roof would be falling from sclerophyll fingers, making a different music. But I can't go back and do it over. I follow them, so I inherit their tree as I inherit their cottage. And I like it well enough. Though it does not share the language of the place, it stands graciously by. Though it speaks more of the men and women who planted it than it does of the ground it grows from—of the long, long history of this place, its rock and its soil and its shaping by weather—still this tree makes for me some of the sounds of home here.

———

Cloud surrounds the house, though I cannot see it in the darkness. We are high, and the sky is low. The main ridge of the plateau rises to 1100 metres here, and we often sit, as we do tonight, inside the cloud base. If the saturated air is gathering and holding anywhere on the ridge, it will be doing it by our house. The water in the air loves the escarpment's edge. Cloud settles here, shifts and plays in winds that draw it down into the valley, or shoot it back up again.

We live within a hundred metres of cliffs that fall into the wide valley cut by the Kedumba. We live within a broken plateau. We perch on one of the ridges where the tableland still holds, where its old roof still runs, within a country of deep valleys. Water laid this sandstone down—that was long ago.

And water—ever since the stone basin dried, hardened and rose to form the plateau—has been wearing it away again, and again, as it does right now, collapsing it into itself, shaping gorges and valleys and carrying the old plateau away east—to river beds, to gullies, to creek bottoms, swamps and beaches, and finally to sea.

———

It has been raining on and off for three weeks. The track along the escarpment ran in some places like a river, when we walked there late in the day, just before dark. Cloud filled the valley, hiding it. Beside the path, on the high side, the cliff-faces shone with water. Some of it comes from inside the rock. Water leaks—more rapidly today than normal—from its veins, having run down into the rock along a fault line in the surface somewhere higher up and found its way, along a stratum of the stone, to the air again where the rock ends here, cut by erosion long ago or more recently by the making of this track. Some of it pours down the face of the stone, faster than it does when the weather is dry, down from swamps hanging below the plateau's lip. The hanging swamps always leak—they bleed the water that makes them what they are down into the streams that make the valley what it is. In this weather they cannot hold all the water the sky has to give; they cannot tend it all so long in fern and sedge, in root and mud and mire before they give it up to the creeks and the valley.

We walked, and the drizzle fell on us, straight out of the low sky, and in heavier drops from branch and leaf of casuarina and eucalypt, banksia and geebung, tea-tree and wattle. I had my hood pulled over my head, but drops formed on its lip and fell, cold, onto my face. When I breathed the air, I tasted rain.

———

You can never walk beside the valley, or down in its deeps, in silence. Always water falls down from the high ground to the low, continuing the work of rending the plateau, of rendering the valleys. And its falling fills the space with sound, it rounds and fathoms the empty realm where all this ground has been lost, where all these days have passed, where all these stories pool. And there are bellbirds and treefrogs singing all across the valley walls and in the tall trees on its floor. They touch the skin of this body of air with their tongues. They bell it, they sing the departed country, they give its absence weight.

Southwest, around the corner where the Three Sisters stand, the Kedumba falls over the edge of the escarpment, down through two hundred million years or so of space, to the slope of fallen rock, and further down to its own bed, on which it moves north. East of it stands Mount Solitary, Korowal, an island of the old plateau, making its own plateau now, a mesa marooned in the heart of the valley. It has its streams and waterfalls too. A creek that cuts through the back of our place and rises fast in heavy rain runs, as now, down to another watercourse that passes under a bridge along the Prince Henry Walk and over the edge in a thin braid. It falls hard, slaps on rocks two hundred metres down. It pulls back to an insistent spray when the rain holds off and, when it storms, becomes a dense rope of water. Northeast of this, several streams meet and flow through the Leura Cascades and over the edge into the Leura Forest. And beyond them there are other falls—Gordon and the Bridal Veil. There are names here that belong to an earlier time, names that make the sound of a more romantic era. But the waters they name still run and sound in this time, as they will continue to run even when we have gone and they are free of the runoff from road and gutter and garden, free of the names we give them.

All of these waters fall into the valley and fill it with sound, a sheet of breath behind the call of the birds. They all join the Kedumba, cutting into the valley floor as they find their way to that river, and shaping small peaks, shallow gullies, within the terrain ringed by these high cliffs; with the Kedumba they round the northeast end of Solitary and turn south along the face of the King's Tableland to meet the Cox and fill Lake Burragorang. Turning east again past the tip of the King's, the water that falls near my home cuts a narrow gorge through the plateau and runs at last into the Nepean and away north to the sea.

———

Water rises and runs and falls in the voices of many of the birds that favour this country. Have you heard the grey shrike-thrush? Once I heard a pair sing in a river of song that ran a good three minutes. That was in a rocky drainage over in another valley and in the heat of summer. There was water though, even then, and it was colder than you might imagine—a creek that runs deep in a gully where the sun hardly comes. And later, after the thrush song, we walked down to that creek, and we walked, two friends and I, in its waters until they picked us up and carried us over a race, and we sank into an icy pool, cold as death, in a canyon like a cathedral. Rising from that water and drawing breath was like being born again. It was like becoming song.

Bowerbirds, when they are not squabbling, have a way of calling, particularly in the rain, in voices that sound like a river, in cascades.

And then there are the lyrebirds, which have a thousand songs. Many of these mimic other birds, and us, and our noises—chainsaw, burglar alarm, laughter. But among these voices is the lyrebird's own. And that voice, more than any other on the plateau, catches the lyric of the country. It is how the waters must sound on the inside: sweet, turning and returning, rising, sinking and running slick; dark with gully-shadow and sedge-tannin; ciphered with rumours from the banks they run between; grounded by the bass-notes of the bed they pass across. And borne along by this music, sustained by its notes, sediments of the sandstone country run like words, like a libretto.

Lyrebirds love rain and stream, and they love the escarpment, as the clouds do. On our rainwalk, Maree and I saw one come to the stream— Banksia Park Streamlet—that passes behind our own house, flows down over red ironstone among the tree ferns and passes under a bridge toward the valley. The bird entered the stream and winged water over its back. It stayed in the water, bathed in song, and paid us no attention where we stood on the bridge.

I met them out on Mount Solitary another rain-filled day. That day, one September, I found a curled black tail-feather that lay on the path. I picked it up and carried it a little way, meaning to keep it on my desk—a string of the lyre of the bird to inspire from me a song of the place. But in the end I left it on the mountain, feeling it wrong to see the feather as a gift, and wrong to take part of the country away; feeling it right to leave it close to where it fell, to possess it only in imagination. That may have been a mistake, an excess of moral discrimination. For the moment I left the feather, my right knee began to give me trouble, and I hobbled home slowly as night came down. And ever since, I have missed the feather. There will, I am sure, be another.

Lyrebirds haunt the contours close to the Three Sisters, the contours of my own home ground. I often see them there, usually in rain or just before a storm. This last January, in weather just like today's, with my friend Richard Nelson, freshly arrived from Alaska, I came hard around a bend on the track and frightened three birds from a ledge at head height, beside the path. They made us jump; they scared us half to death. Three birds. One of them, the male, took off up the slope of a peppermint that leans over the path into the valley and stayed there long enough for Nels to get a photograph. Then they flew and left us with just the thrill of them, and with the quality of silence they shaped with their passage.

A story I have heard—though I have heard it told differently—speaks of how the rocks we call the Three Sisters, where Nels and I were headed just then, came to be. The story, as you'll see, links those slender rocks and those minstrel birds, just as my living here, my walking here, has taught me they are linked. The story belongs to the country's first people, the Gundungurra, and to the place itself. It is not mine. I do not take it. I hope I tell it straight enough to do them all honour.

It goes like this. Three girls, sisters and orphans, were in their grandfather's care. One day he left them high on the escarpment and went down hunting in the valley. He warned them not to throw stones down into the valley, for this might wake the bunyip. Sure enough, as children still do sometimes, they forgot the old man's good advice and, in their impatience for his return, threw rocks to the valley below. I can understand it—throwing sticks and stones here is an almost irresistible urge. The valley calls. We want to plumb its depth. Anyway, that day they woke the bunyip, and he came for them. Grandfather heard the bunyip's roars. He hurried back and climbed out of the valley to where, on the escarpment's edge, he had left the girls—just before the monster got them, up near Echo Point. To save the girls from the bunyip, the old man used a magic bone to turn them to stone. He then turned himself into a lyrebird and the bone fell to the ground, as bones do. All the bunyip found when he got to the place was the smell of naughty little girls, a lyrebird picking among the rocks and fossicking among the roots of plants and fallen leaves—and three standing rocks he had never seen before. And he also found the bone. In his anger, sensing what had happened, he ground the bone and scattered the fragments in the wind.

The lyrebirds still search for the bone—to wake, to quicken, the girls. The feminine is lodged here, certainly, in this piece of country. But now the magic, of which the place is born, is scattered. It has gone to ground, and it may never be all of a piece again. So there is just the singing and the search. The birds and I are looking for the magic of the place and finding it everywhere; trying to waken the ground to us, trying to free its petrified voices. Nothing done can be undone, though. No mystery here may be divined except by coming and staying and practising wonder. And all you may find is the sound that trees make responding to the wind; all you may hear is the birdsong, and the sound of falling water

———

In the old tongue of the Gundungurra people, or at least the corruption that we have of it, the place where I lie tonight is named 'Katoomba.' One of the early settlers transcribed the name as 'Go Doom Bah', which has a powerful, suitably gloomy shape to it. 'Kedumba' too—the name of the river that carries all these creeks away, and all this rain, through a valley of the same name—Kedumba is the same phrase, the same set of syllables, the same lyric gesture, suggested by the place as its name, and carried for perhaps a hundred thousand years in the mouths and bodies of its first people. What these sounds express is falling water. This is the place of falling water: 'Katoomba.'

———

On a map made in 1909, Banksia Park still appears as a reserve. My street and those in the acres reaching up to Lurline Street, do not appear. By 1911, the original grantee of the land, Robert Peel Raymond, has sold the land to a developer. Katoomba has become by then a fashionable retreat for the middle-class folk of Sydney. Its air, mild and sweet, cooler and lighter than Sydney's in summer and cold enough in winter for snow to fall from, draws them up here. They do not come to wander in wooded heathland or wild valleys. They come, most of them, to stay in guesthouses or their own summer houses and take in the grand sights of what they like to call the Mountains. So Peel sells up, and the land is gridded and sold on in parcels. Most of the banksias for which it is named are felled. And by 1911, my portion of this place is on the map.

One day I went to the Land Titles Office to trace the real estate lineage of this place on earth, this block of land where I make my life—or half of it. On the southeastern corner of the original watercoloured map of these allotments, I noticed a scalloped line, made in black ink and cross-hatched on one side—the south side, away from the village of Katoomba. Beside that line ran this legend: 'the Edge of the Cliff.' The map looks accurate enough to me.

That's about where you'd have fallen, and where you'd still fall, if you'd wandered carelessly through the remnant banksias, beyond the surveyed property boundaries, out into the *Eucalyptus oreades*, the *piperata*, the sandstone bluffs and the lyrebirds. And down you'd go, into the wild, with the water. The edge of the cliff is where the country would not surrender to a grid, where it would not be tamed and allotted. 'Beyond lie dragons,' the map may as well have read, or 'terra incognita'.

All of Katoomba, most of the main ridge within this plateau, was settled like this, pushing a suburban notion, the idea of closely packed houses on small blocks of private land, as far as it would go—and clearly way beyond where it belonged, to the very edge of wild country. There is no poetry in it. It is absurd. Though this is a place full of song, the tune was lost on Edwardian ears, I guess, and what spoke was the eternal command to make the largest return possible on marginal land. That number still plays up here, as it plays most places.

This way of seeing and settling the landscape lacked honour and grace, it seems to me now, though I live here; it lacked imagination and modesty. To take this bone of land in the midst of a wildly fractured plateau as a site for tidy suburban plots was to miss the land's own pattern. It was not a way of coming to country, of seeking to belong, that grew from any sympathy with the place—or allowed much love to grow between the place and its tenants. But it was not the time for such imaginings. It never seems to be. The grids are so narrow-minded, so rigid, so pragmatic. Profit ruled them, and mostly rules them still. This is a plateau configured as a suburb. It is an animal cowed and domesticated, but not broken yet, I think. The place still breathes; the rocks are alive; the magic still dwells here.

Anyway, here—close to the edge of the cliff—I live. This timber cottage is set down at the eastern extreme of the network of streets, named mostly for developers and pioneering councillors, that secures our hold on the ridge. The wind, otherwise, might blow us away, the wild air and water might carry us over those cliffs. Here I am, barely hanging on to Katoomba's frayed ends. Here culture meets nature, and the wind moves roughly between them, as though they were one. And, although the neighbours press close on two sides and the rain falls mostly on trees about the house that have no deeper history here than I have, still, the valley is near, singing, and the place is drumming its name on the roof. And the plateau lies blue all about.

## II. THE SPRING OF FRESH WATER

Another day, and later in the year, the pale blue sky stretches across Lavender Bay. And I sit in another place of home, looking down on green gathered water. My life runs between these: between plateau and bay; between a place of falling water and an embayment of the ocean. It flows, my life, from the edge of the trees to the edge of the sea, stays a time in each small hollow of home, and carries from one to the other—it speaks in my body and mind and gesture—the words that each place utters in water.

Lavender Bay is named not for its colour but for one of its early white settlers. George Lavender, tougher than his name implies, commanded, for a while, the convict hulk *The Phoenix*, which moored in this bay after the coming of the second fleet. He married one of the daughters of Billy Blue, around 1800, and moved ashore. This site was known then and for a while after as Hulk Bay.

Billy Blue was a big man, West Indian or African American, sent to Australia in the first fleet for lifting some extra supplies from the docks of London, where he worked. Once he'd served his time, he began to ferry governors, soldiers, ex-convicts and free colonists about the expanding reaches of the settlement, up and down the Parramatta River, out toward South Head, across the heads to Manly, and across the water from Circular Quay to sites opening up on the north shore. Governor Macquarie granted him land right across the water from the city's docks in Walsh Bay. His grant is now Blue's Point, a nature reserve—the southern-most tip of the arm that holds Lavender Bay.

Before this inlet of the harbour was Lavender and Blue, it was named Quibaree by its own people, the Eora. Quibaree means 'spring of fresh water'. Lavender Bay is a crescent with two elegant arms stretching into the harbour. Cliffs of Hawkesbury sandstone crowd around the beach at the bay's farthest inland reach. And these cliffs leak water along many of their joints. Walk around and you'll see it. Springs, now mostly stopped or diverted into stormwater drains, rise in places at the feet of the stone. The water that once flowed freely out of the ground and made the woodland behind the shallow beach a prized camping ground was sweet and clear, filtered by the stone's grains on its fall through the years and years from the surface to the springs below. In George Lavender's days, not only did these springs water him and his family and the swelling north shore community, they also supplied drinking water to the main colony across the harbour at Sydney Town. In drought, when the Tank Stream failed, Quibaree kept the colony alive. Blue and Lavender shipped its sweet water to Walsh Bay, and got well paid for it.

The site of the main spring lies right beside the apartment building in which I sit, in which I stay when I am in the city, in which Maree lives most of the time because her work lies just up the hill. It is a park now, named for a loyal alderman, Charles Watt, who, a sign tells me, worked tirelessly to preserve public space around these foreshores. Well, I thank him. Walk through his park, pass under the railway siding and you come to the beach, to Lavender Bay itself. There, in the water, sit the remains of the old shipyards. The bay is walled now in places, and jetties point down into its green water. The cleared land at the water's edge between the jetty and the old boat yards and bounded behind by the railway line holds a line of tall date palms and a youthful fig; and it has been named Quibaree Park. It is a good name to have kept for this edge of the land, and the land in behind it to the cliffs, for it speaks the nature of the place well. Water runs here, and it is good to keep that in mind.

In the nineteenth century, settlers dug wells where they could, reaching down into rock or soil, to tap and draw off the subterranean water that runs out of the sandstone ridge of the north shore on its way to the great body of the harbour. No town water came to this side until 1885, when they laid a nine-inch pipe on the harbour's floor to bring in water from the new reservoir at Paddington. Among the century-old trees in Watt Park, trees that belonged to the gardens of Georgian and Victorian mansions higher up on the cliffs, one old well remains. You can stand above the well and look down into its dark perpendicular tunnel. You can stand in its opening to the air because the council has left it where it was and stretched a metal grid across its mouth. Beside it they have put a sign that tells, briefly, the water story of the place. It is the spring of fresh water.

A photograph, taken around 1870, and reproduced on the sign beside the well, shows the foreshores and the land above the cliffs still heavily wooded with eucalypt; Port Jackson figs stretch their toes across the ground closer to the water. Around Quibaree a few pines already rise. In Watt Park, beside our apartment, tall trees grow now, remarkable trees and quite old, planted in this place of spring water, putting their roots down, presumably, into the sweet water that used to come up in buckets from the well. Our place is on the top floor of an apartment block built on steps cut in the cliff face in the depression years. So my eyes, as I sit now at a table by the sash window, look out in a line two hundred feet or so above the water. I can see the canopy of these trees. The top of the tallest of them, a Norfolk pine, reaches up above my line of sight, and just beneath its tip spreads the crown of a kauri. This last, close cousin of the ancient, remnant Wollemi pine just found deep in the country near my place on the plateau, belongs in the tropics really. It has leaves not needles. The hoop pines, which I can't see from here, lovely trees with soft bunches of dark green needles on the ends of slender arms, must be over a hundred years old. Their massive and stately trunks reach up, bearing those arms, well above the ridge of our roof. They too come from further north, though not as far away as the kauris. These trees have come to signal home for me in this other place of falling water. You can make out their gaunt and elegant frames tall beside the stucco edifice of this block even as you come by train from the city across the iron bridge. As well as these, there is a massive fig, whose crown I can make out below me, the tallest jacaranda I have ever seen, and, holding the bank at the top of the cliff, at the head of the stairs that come up beside our block under the arms and through the mulch of the hoop pines, another old and storm-battered fig.

The figs are most at home here by the harbour. All the rest, antipodean natives like the pines and sympathetic ring-ins like the jacaranda, come from elsewhere and owe their presence on this ground to a Victorian garden ideal. I have seen parks treed like this in other parts of old inner Sydney, particularly in the suburbs east of the city. They make Quibaree a very different place than the one that it grew into all by itself, and with the subtler assistance of its first gardeners, the Eora. But that is just the way it is. It has become what it has become. It is a storied place, like Katoomba. Some of its stories are told by trees and some by rocks. Some by buildings like this one and by people like me who live in them. But most of the stories of this place are told, most of its songs are sung, by water. And from water it takes its oldest and truest name, Quibaree.

———

The same water that moves through the layers of this rock to fill the old well, that nourishes the trees, that sustained the city in earlier days, flows into the foundations of this building. We have our feet in water. I know, because I am down here in it now. I have my feet in water.

Thirty-five of us live here, spread over five storeys running down the cliff's strata. And down below it's wet. All the apartments in the building, a Spanish Mission-deco affair, came up for sale at once. Few of us, I guess, thought to look into the natural history of Quibaree before we made our bid and put our deposit down. Most of us looked hard at the building, made allowances on account of its age and the great advantage of its position, and went ahead. This is, after all, the Sydney real estate market, and there is not much time to think, much less to investigate the geomorphology. Company title runs here, and we were too worried about the arcane requirements of the building's legal title to look down at its feet. If we had, some of us would have gone elsewhere. We thought, of course, we were just buying a piece of personal space close to the harbour. In fact, we were buying shares in a community to whom fell the responsibility for a whole building. And it was a building, had we looked, that had its feet wet in the natural history of the place. The problems of subterranean water ingress down in units eight and twelve belong, it turns out, to all of us.

Right now, George and I are standing in the dark in the bowels of the building. George owns the apartment below ours. Both of us are on the board, and wishing, about now, that we weren't. George flicks on a torch and shines it about. With us is the building contractor we have signed up for help with our water problems. I am looking with fascination at the wet rock and the small river flowing in an old trench south to north against the foot of one of the steps cut in the cliff, right under Jane's unit, number eight. The brick foundations that hold up Jane's floor rise from the rock, and they are saturated. George thinks there's water pooled behind them. The old bricks are sucking it up into Jane's place, which smells of mould, of not so sweet water. We walk forward, following the flashlight's beam, where the foundation runs back, away from us, into the next shelf cut in the rock. I touch the rock. It is cold, and it is wet.

'I'll tell you something,' says Tom, the builder. I wait. Builders, I have noticed, like dramatic pauses.

'One thing I can't work out. A small miracle.' He is looking up at the exposed wooden rafters and floor boards above. I wait again.

'I can't believe the termites haven't found out about this. They'd love it.'

Well, there is something else to look forward to, I think. And then he tells us how we can deal with this water problem.

The problem on the next step, two floors up, is tougher to get to and harder to mend. Norman's apartment lies under the entrance and right against the cliff wall. His floor sits right on the ground. It was built as a storeroom—no-one was meant to live there. The family who owned the building for seventy-odd years decked it out for habitation in the late fifties. They wanted the place to yield the most rent it could, regardless of the insistent work of the water.

Though the men who put this building up must have known, must have seen, how the water would come down out of the cut strata, they did not have the means or the time or the money to make sure they channelled that water away. This is what we now have to do between us. Short of knocking Norman's wall out and digging him a rubble drain where the cliff meets the line of his floor, it isn't clear how we can help him. Help ourselves, that is. It is all our building, regardless of who lives closest to the water.

'All of us walked past this apartment,' says George, 'and said to ourselves, "What kind of an idiot would buy that?" It was so small and dark. And it turns out we all bought it. At least we all bought into the responsibility to make that little apartment waterproof. So what does that make us?'

That makes us part of a community; that makes us participants in the natural history of this piece of rocky ground by the water. That makes us all fools for this place.

We are never as smart or as separate from each other, we are never as immune from the landscape, as we think we are.

We thought we were buying a piece of property. We thought we were buying a piece of a city. Office towers and the iron arch of the harbour bridge shoulder us here. The ferry takes you to Circular Quay in five minutes. This is the city here. And so, despite the lap of the green water and the companionship of the trees; despite the well; despite the black butterflies and the lorikeets; despite the grey butcherbirds I have surprised down there in the rain; despite the mating currawongs who cry to each other at ungodly hours of the morning from the terracotta ridge caps of the building next door to the point of the Norfolk pine—we forgot this was a place on earth, lodged in landscape and washed by weather. We forgot that this too is a place where nature runs. We forgot this building is rooted to earth. We forgot that water runs through rock looking for lower ground, looking for a spring by the sea.

I live in two places made and bothered, shaped and sustained, by water. Both of the names I have for home come from water, water that falls through, that runs over, that loves, rock. And the rock itself is sandstone—layers of old storeys of older mountains, left behind by even older water.

——

Blue, too, lives in these places' names—the Blue Plateau and Lavender Bay.

Above my head, now, on the white and patterned ceiling of the apartment at Lavender Bay, I see the red stains left when water came in on one day of heavy rain, from the terrace above and its red gravel surface. And when a front moves across from the southwest, over the lower reaches of the Blue Plateau and down into the Sydney Basin, it brings rain up hard against these window panes. And if I leave the windows open, the rain comes right on in, as though that were the most natural thing in the world for rain to do.

On the wall beside me I have the calendar open at April. Our friend Joanna, who lives across the hall, gave it to me for my birthday. Each of its months shows a different face of an architect's masterpiece, a home built somewhere far from here, though not so far from this one in time; a home made of, and set down within, its particular place, where water falls over stone. Its architect, of course, was Frank Lloyd Wright. And he called the place 'Falling Water'.

# TERRY TEMPEST WILLIAMS

## Labor

Life comes, life goes, we make life ...
But we who live in the body see with the body's
imagination things in outline.

VIRGINIA WOOLF, *THE WAVES*

I forget the first time I saw this boulder, maybe thirty years ago as an adolescent traveling through Utah's redrock desert with my family. Or maybe it was twenty-five years ago, as a young bride making a pilgrimage to this part of the world with my new husband, not only in love with him but also with this arid landscape that ignites the imagination.

Today, I return once again to the Birthing Rock.

I return because it is a stone slate of reflection, a place where stories are told and remembered. Call it my private oracle where I hear the truth of my own heart.

Yes, the actions of life are recorded, here, now, through the hands of the Anasazi, the 'ancient ones,' who inhabited the Colorado Plateau from AD 500 to 1200. Their spirits have never left. One feels their intelligence held in the rocks, etched into the rocks. This rock stands in Kane Creek Canyon, the size of a small dwelling, exposed and vulnerable, only a few miles from the town of Moab, Utah.

There she is, as she has been for hundreds of years, the One Who Gives Birth, a woman standing with her arms outstretched, her legs wide open, with a globelike form emerging. Four sets of tiny feet march up the boulder alongside her. There are other figures nearby: a large ceremonial being wearing what appears to be an elaborate headdress and necklace. It feels male but it could be female. Who knows what these Anasazi petroglyphs might mean? What is translated through stone is the power of presence, even centuries old.

Deer. Mountain sheep. Centipedes. A horned figure with a shield. More footprints. And around the corner of the boulder, two triangular figures, broad shoulders with the points down, made stable by feet. From their heads, a spine runs down the center. They are joined together through a shared shoulder line that resembles the arms of a cross. A slight tension is felt between them as each pulls the other, creating the strength of scales balanced. Next to them is another figure, unattached. A long snake with nine bends in its river body is close to making contact. All this on the slate of blue sandstone that has been varnished through time; when carved it bleeds red.

Piñon. Juniper. Saltbush. Rabbitbrush. The plant world bears witness to the human one as they surround the Birthing Rock. They are rooted in pink sands when dry, russet when wet. It is a theater-in-the-round choreographed on Navajo sandstone, reminding us of dunes that once swirled and swayed with the wind in another geologic time.

There is much to absorb and be absorbed by in this sky-biting country. At times, it is disorienting, the Earth split open, rocks standing on their heads, entire valleys appearing as gaping wounds. This is the power and pull of erosion, the detachment and movement of particles of land by wind, water, and ice. A windstorm in the desert is as vicious as any force on Earth, creating sand smoke so thick when swirling it is easy to believe in vanishing worlds. The wind and fury subside. A calm is returned but not without a complete rearrangement of form. Sand travels. Rocks shift. The sculpting of sandstone reveals the character of windgate cliffs, sheered redrock walls polished to a sheen over time.

My husband is climbing the talus slope above me. I hear a rock fall and call to him. His voice returns as an echo.

In repetition, there is comfort and reassurance.

I return to the Birthing Rock, this panel of petroglyphs that binds us to a deep history of habitation in place, this portal of possibilities, a woman giving birth, a symbol of continuity, past generations now viewed by future ones.

As a woman of forty-four years, I will not bear children. My husband and I will not be parents. We have chosen to define family in another way.

I look across the sweep of slickrock stretching in all directions, the rise and fall of such arid terrain. A jackrabbit bolts down the wash. Piñon jays flock and bank behind a cluster of junipers. The tracks of coyote are everywhere.

Would you believe me when I tell you this is family, kinship with the desert, the breadth of my relations coursing through a wider community, the shock of recognition with each scarlet gilia, the smell of rain.

And this is enough for me, more than enough. I trace my genealogy back to the land. Human and wild, I can see myself whole, not isolated but integrated in time and place. Our genetic makeup is not so different from the collared lizard, the canyon wren now calling, or the great horned owl who watches from the cottonwood near the creek. Mountain lion is as mysterious a creature as any soul I know. Is not the tissue of family always a movement between harmony and distance?

Perhaps this is what dwells in the heart of our nation—choice—to choose creation of a different sort, the freedom to choose what we want our lives to be, the freedom to choose what heart line to follow.

My husband and I live in this redrock desert, this 'land of little rain' that Mary Austin described at the beginning of the twentieth century. It is still a dry pocket on the planet one hundred years later. Not much has changed regarding the aridity and austerity of the region.

What has changed is the number of needs and desires that we ask the earth to support. There are places where the desert feels trampled, native vegetation scraped and cut at their roots by blades of bulldozers, aquifers of water receding before the tide of luxury resorts and homes.

And the weight of our species will only continue to tip the scales.

The wide-open vistas that sustain our souls, the depth of silence that pushes us toward sanity, return us to a kind of equilibrium. We stand steady on Earth. The external space I see is the internal space I feel.

But I know this is the exception, even an illusion, in the American West, as I stand in Kane Creek where my eyes can follow the flight of a raven until the horizon curves down. These remnants of the wild, biologically intact, are precious few. We are losing ground. No matter how much we choose to preserve the pristine through our passion, photography, or politics, we cannot forget the simple truth: There are too many of us.

Let me tease another word from the heart of a nation: sacrifice. Not to bear children may be its own form of sacrifice. How do I explain my love of children, yet our decision not to give birth to a child? Perhaps it is about sharing. I recall watching my niece, Diane, nine years old, on her stomach, eye to eye with a lizard; neither moved while contemplating the other. In the sweetness of that moment, I felt the curvature of my heart become the curvature of Earth, the circle of family complete. Diane bears the name of my mother and wears my DNA as closely as my daughter would.

Must the act of birth be seen only as a replacement for ourselves? Can we not also conceive of birth as an act of the imagination, giving body to a new way of seeing? Do children need to be our own to be loved as our own?

———

Perhaps it is time to give birth to a new idea, many new ideas.

Perhaps it is time to give birth to new institutions, to overhaul our religious, political, legal, and educational systems that are no longer working for us.

Perhaps it is time to adopt a much needed code of ethics, one that will exchange the sacred rights of humans for the rights of all beings on the planet.

*We can begin to live differently.*

We have choices before us, conscious choices, choices of conscience and consequence, not in the name of political correctness, but ecological responsibility and opportunity.

*We can give birth to creation.*

To labor in the name of social change. To bear down and push against the constraints of our own self-imposed structures. To sacrifice in the name of an ecological imperative. To be broken open to a new way of being.

———

It begins to rain softly in the desert; the sand is yielding, the road is shining, and I know downriver a flash flood is likely, creating another landscape through erosion, newly shaped, formed, and sculpted.

*I wonder when this catastrophic force will reach me?*

Erosion. Perhaps this is what we need, an erosion of all we have held secure. A rupture of all we believed sacred, sacrosanct. A psychic scouring of our extended ideals such as individual property rights in the name of economic gain at the expense of ecological health.

*I wonder when ...*

The wall of water hits. Waves turn me upside down and sideways as I am carried downriver, tumbling in the current, dizzy in the current, dark underwater, holding my breath, holding my breath. I cannot see but believe I will surface, believe I will surface, holding my breath. The muscle of the river is pushing me down, deeper and deeper, darker and darker. I cannot breathe, I am dying under the pressure, the pressure creates change, a change of heart. The river changes its heart and pushes me upward with the force of a geyser. I surface, I breathe. I am back in the current, moving with the current, floating in the current, face up, on my back. There are others around me, our silt-covered bodies navigating downriver, feet pointing downriver. We are part of the river, in boats of our own skin, finally, now our skin shining, our nerve returning, our will is burning. We are on fire, even in water, after tumbling and mumbling inside a society where wealth determines if we are heard, what options we have, what power we hold.

*How can I get my bearings inside this river?*

Erosion. I look up. Canyon walls crack and break from the mother rock, slide into the river, now red with the desert. I am red with the desert. My body churns in the current, and I pray the log jam ahead will not reduce me to another piece of driftwood caught in the dam of accumulation.

*Who has the strength to see this wave of destruction as a wave of renewal?*

I find myself swimming toward an eddy in the river, slower water, warmer water. We are whirling, twirling in a community of currents. I reach for a willow secure on the shore; it stops me from spinning. My eyes steady. The land is steady. In the pause of this moment, I pull myself out. Collapse. Rise.

Now on shore like a freshly born human, upright, I brush my body dry, and turn to see that I am again standing in front of the Birthing Rock, my Rock of Instruction, that I have sought through my life, defied in my life, even against the will of my own biology.

No, I have never created a child, but I have created a life. I see now, we can give birth to ourselves, not an indulgence but another form of survival.

We can navigate ourselves out of the current.

We can pull ourselves out of the river.

We can witness the power of erosion as a re-creation of the world we live in and stand upright in the truth of our own decisions.

*We can begin to live differently.*

We can give birth to deep change, creating a commitment of compassion toward all living things. Our human-centered point of view can evolve into an Earth-centered one.

Is this too much to dream? Who imposes restraint on our imagination?

———

I look at the rock again, walk around to its other side, the side that is hidden from the road I experienced as a river. The panel has been shot away, nicked by bullets, scraped and chipped to oblivion.

Six small figures have survived the shooting rampage. I bend down and look more closely at the deliberate nature of these petroglyphs.

Someone cared enough to create life on a rock face, to animate an inanimate object. Someone believed she had the power to communicate a larger vision to those who would read these marks on a stone, a vision that would endure through time.

I see a spiral and what appears to be a figure dancing, her arms raised, her back arched, her head held high.

We can dance; even in this erosional landscape, we can dance.

I have come full circle around the boulder.

There she is, the One Who Gives Birth. Something can pass through stone. I place one hand on her belly and the other on mine. Desert Mothers, all of us, pregnant with possibilities, in the service of life, domestic and wild; it is our freedom to choose how we wish to live, labor, and sacrifice in the name of love.

# TIM WINTON

## Landing

I was twenty-one the first time I flew in an aeroplane. On a flight from Perth to Sydney I saw the wheatbelt stretching breadlike into the saltlands and noticed how the two commingled ominously. We tracked over the Bight, crossing near Esperance and staying with the coast the whole distance to the Eyre Peninsula in South Australia. I'd seen these places before but now I struggled to connect them with my earlier view. The endless dreariness of the WA wheat country was changed to a subtle quilt of textures. The colour was mostly uniform blond, but light fell on crops of different height, stirred by wind, and it was beautiful. The Southern Ocean, usually a maelstrom, looked blue as nursery wallpaper. The cliffs of the Bight still had shadow and therefore power, but the whitecaps of the Southern Ocean looked, from 10,000 metres, no more menacing than dandruff. The new perspective was fascinating but it left me with mixed feelings which I've never really resolved. Seeing the land from above offers a fresh outlook, something that can't be had in nature, so it always comes with a thrill and a shock at the very outrageousness of it. In a plane, too, you often see the geological connections between things, see landforms dissolve into one another. You can take it in quickly, comprehend distances (well, versions of distances) relieved for a while of human limitations.

But so many things can be diminished from the air. Trees often seem belittled. So impressive on the ground in their life bearing and shade throwing, from a great altitude they're reduced to mere texture. From far enough up, Uluru can look no more remarkable than a stale school bun. I've flown over country in the north Kimberley that days before on foot I found heartbreakingly rugged. From the air it seemed merely, well, interesting. Jump-ups and breakaways and nests of spinifex that so recently had me in tears of frustration and fright seemed beautiful, harmless. An afternoon's hike gone in moments. So much to envy the birds.

Aborigines sometimes question the 'European' urge to climb high and look out across land from a bluff or peak. I suppose if you know what's there, if you're intimate with it in a bodily, spiritual way, you don't need to look. In colonial days explorers and surveyors climbed points of elevation to see what lay before them. They captured it with their maps, claimed it for their empire simply by being there, looking. Looking with something very specific in mind. These days the urge remains but not every gaze is a colonising of what lies ahead. Some of that staring comes from a slow-waking reverence, a respectful curiosity, a yearning to understand.

Flying very high (if it doesn't terrify you) can induce godlike fantasies. You feel safe from the land and its logic, its necessities of shade and water, food and fuel. Even the Great Sandy Desert can seem cute in a pastel sort of way. But come down a few thousand metres to where the trees are still trees and the ranges riven with shadows and the smoke of bushfires penetrates the cockpit—that can be a different matter. The perspective is more birdlike than godlike. Here it's still possible to feel small. The land is still big but not wallpaper. You're close enough to feel the heat of stones, and the skin of the land looks creaturely, like the hide of a crocodile, the pelt of a kangaroo, the feathers of corellas, the bark of boabs. You see its very bones revealed by wind and water. It's so beaten down it often looks stubborn, threadbare. Most of it is the embodiment of pure necessity, though there are always surprises: patches of rainforest in the driest range country, the livid animation in the seagrass meadows of Shark Bay, the shocking colours of corals, of even spinifex. Or the bewildering tumults of water pouring out of land that defies any sign of rain. The land divides itself up in gullies, craters, rivers, valleys and its shadows retain some secrecy instead of being merely lines. From the air you see the repetition of pattern and shape: the scalloping of beaches in the very pattern of shells that are tossed on their shores, the pointillism of salt lakes repeated in the crowns of trees, the same design you see in the pitted surface of rocks

and wood you later hold in your hands. To see the land from the air is to witness the forces it has endured: ice ages, floods untold, wind, several mining
booms, the feudal grazing industry. And yes, there is an abstract beauty that
has nothing at all to do with what you're looking at. Shape, colour, repetition,
juxtaposition. Even completely manipulated landscapes with their rigid fence
or road lines, their concentric plough patterns, their terrible spiderwebs of
cattle erosion can be beautiful.

Mostly from the air I've felt small rather than godlike. The humbler the
plane and the fewer its engines the smaller I feel. Not to mention queasy. The
perspective is temporary, conditional, but it can be truly revelatory.

From the air I've seen the vandalism of clearfelling in native forests which
would otherwise be hidden from view. I've seen salt creeping up on land
cleared with government backing. Rivers turning colours they were never
meant to be. Those times I've felt tiny and impotent and furious. And yet I've
flown offshore and seen pods of humpback whales coursing up the coast the
way they never were in my youth and felt small in a happier way. I've flown
over kilometres of country burnt out by lightning and looked at the contused
fields of ash shifting in the wind and been forced to see myself connected to
all that carbon, the stuff you and I and all the rest are made of.

Humans have become accustomed to imagining themselves at the centre
of the universe. Galileo never quite shook us out of that. We're used to being
the pinnacle of creation, the final power. Travelling into landscape reminds us
of our true position, as dependants, as fellow travellers. Confronted with our
sudden smallness we may panic, become angry, disoriented, afraid, and scram-
ble back into the shell of our pre-eminence—the airconditioned car, plane,
house, university, shopping mall. But there is something to be gained from
persistence if at first we see wood but no trees. An engagement with landscape
can be profoundly humbling, and revelatory, a scrambling of precious codes.
The land can mystify us in a time when we're resigned to being hypnotised. I
don't mean to make a personal cult of the land. Like it or not, everything I've
learned about nature has been revealed with a gun, a spear or a knife and fork
in my hand. I know the odds of our being able to live without somehow doing
it at nature's expense. But I've longed for some way to be a conscientious
objector in the war against nature. I'm not the romantic young man I was, but
I now have children and I see the results of the way we live with growing
alarm.

At the very least we must resolve to live in some balance with our natural world, to understand that it has a life independent of us. Even this grudging

acknowledgement brings a sacred responsibility. In a nation where nothing is sacred but the race to have all the toys, it might seem bizarre to see the continent as sacred. Only our 'way of life' is seen in sacred terms. I just hope we'll be wise enough one day to sacrifice some luxury, some speed, some chattels in order to preserve the land that gives us such a life. I don't care for New Age notions of the sacred, for something truly sacred will eventually demand something of us, something deeper than the credit card. Learning respect and paying it is sometimes a solemn and painful business. Part of this learning is at the heart of our reconciliation with Aboriginal Australia. It seems to me that non-indigenous Australians may yet be required to modify the way they live— not merely the way they speak—in order to make peace with this place.

Like the kids they once were, Australians bolt for the outdoors the moment the bell goes. They stream out in hordes and stomp across the bits they can't drive over. They try to catch the light on the stones, the lorikeets in trees, with their disposable cameras and fill albums with the results while planning the next excursion. Why? Perhaps because deep down, at some level, they recognise that conquest has brought neither beauty nor satisfaction. The ugliness of urban Australia leaves them hungry. And love it as they do, they are still not intimate with the land of their birth. We're looking for a common language to describe these yearnings, these suspicions even now. Thankfully there are people in our midst who have been where many of us would like to go, who have a language of feeling, a tradition of thought that prevails despite all. Listen to Bill Neidjie's practical mysticism:

> I love it tree because e love me too.
> E watching me same as you
> tree e working with your body, my body,
> e working with us.
> While you sleep e working.
> Daylight, when you walking around, e work too.

> That tree, grass ... that all like our father.
> Dirt, earth, I sleep with this earth.
> Grass ... just like your brother.
> In my blood in my arm this grass.
> This dirt for us because we'll be dead,
> we'll be going this earth.
> This the story now.

What an age to go looking for a sense of scale, something as important as ourselves, some quiet low-tech moment, a bit of humility.

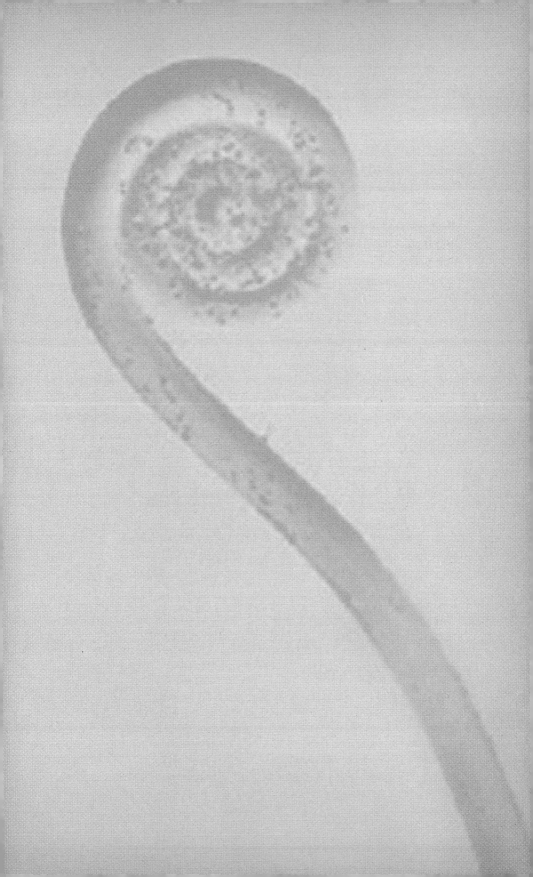

## LOOKING FOR BLACKFELLAS' POINT:
## AN AUSTRALIAN HISTORY OF PLACE

**Mark Mckenna**

*Looking for Blackfellas' Point* is a history that begins by looking across the Towamba River, in south-eastern New South Wales, to the arc of bush know as Blackfellas' Point. From his property, Mark McKenna's gaze pans out from the history of one place he knows intimately, to the history of one region and, ultimately, to the history of Australia's quest for reconciliation between Indigenous and non-Indigenous Australians. It is a history that explores what happened between us, how we learnt to forget and, finally, how we came to confront the truth about our past and build a movement for reconciliation.

**WINNER**
of the
**BOOK OF THE YEAR**
and
**DOUGLAS STEWART PRIZE**
for Non-Fiction
in the 2003
NSW PREMIER'S
LITERARY AWARDS

ISBN 0-86840-644-9

# THE DEFAULT COUNTRY: A LEXICAL CARTOGRAPHY OF TWENTIETH-CENTURY AUSTRALIA

## JM Arthur

In this highly original book, lexicographer JM Arthur explores the relations between language and landscape, investigating typical descriptions of Australia – and their implications. Our common daily language, she argues, directs our thinking about normal features of Australia into exception and anomaly. This language also betrays a persistent colonising relationship to landscape and much more. Thus, 200 years on, we still describe the climate as 'unreliable, unpredictable and unexpected'. We talk of inland regions as 'endless, limitless, featureless'. Are we still in the process of discovering where we are – and where we are not?

ISBN 0-86840-542-6

# WORDS FOR COUNTRY:
## LANDSCAPE AND LANGUAGE
### IN AUSTRALIA

**Tim Bonyhady & Tom Griffiths (eds)**

*Words for Country* explores the inter-relationship between Australia's landscape and language. Historians Tim Bonyhady and Tom Griffiths have brought together an illuminating collection of essays whose subjects range from the Ord River, in the far north-west, to Antarctica in the south, from the centre to the coast, the prehistoric to the present. Their terrain is environmental and cultural, political and poetic, and reveals not just how language grows out of the landscape but also how words and stories shape the places in which we live.

ISBN 0-86840-628-7